Mobilizing Minerva

*American Women in the
First World War*

KIMBERLY JENSEN

University of Illinois Press

URBANA, CHICAGO, AND SPRINGFIELD

Library of Congress Cataloging-in-Publication Data
Jensen, Kimberly, 1958–
Mobilizing minerva : American women in the
First World War / Kimberly Jensen.
p   cm.
Includes bibliographical references and index.
ISBN-13: 978-0-252-03237-0 (cloth : alk. paper)
ISBN-10: 0-252-03237-3 (cloth : alk. paper)
ISBN-13: 978-0-252-07496-7 (paper : alk. paper)
ISBN-10: 0-252-07496-3 (paper : alk. paper)
1. World War, 1914–1918—Women—United States.
2. Women and war—United States.
3. Women—United States—History—20th century.
I. Title.
D639.W7J36   2008
940.3'73082—dc22   2007020857

Contents

Preface

"Mobilizing Woman Power" in the First World War

In 1918 suffrage and labor activist Harriot Stanton Blatch published *Mobilizing Woman-Power*, a compendium of the accomplishments of British, French, and American women in the world war. Blatch joined many contemporary chroniclers in asserting that the increasing and expanding activities of women in wage work, the professions, volunteer associations, politics, and community leadership were key features of the war. But what was woman power? Who was mobilizing women? For what purposes were women being mobilized? And what would be the results? These were questions that consumed people concerned with the status of women in and around the First World War, and they are questions that continue to provide historians with a compelling analytical task in the present.

Some observers and opponents saw "woman power" and women's increased opportunities as a temporary, carnivalesque reversal of traditional gender roles: "woman on top" in the topsy-turvy emergency wartime world.[1] "War," veteran-turned-sociologist Willard Waller wrote, "is a sort of gigantic masquerade. . . . School teachers dress up in brilliant uniforms and become handsome young officers; business men strut and pose awhile as bureaucrats; the harmless postman becomes a hard-boiled sergeant . . . the housewife drives a taxi; everybody pretends, everybody moves out of his customary orbit, in order to win the war."[2] In this view the uniforms of factory, farm, military, and volunteer organizations were merely costumes in a masquerade, donned with corporate and government sponsorship for the transitory purpose of winning the war and to be discarded after the crisis was over.

But supporters saw the wartime mobilization of "woman power" as a culmination of the collective accomplishments of women prior to the war in civic, professional, economic, and social terms. Standing on this foundation, fueled by heightened wartime need and accomplishments, women would go "over the top" to a new level of equality.[3] The strength of women's mobilization and the success of "woman power" would make it impossible, they believed, to slip back into the trenches of inequality after the war was over. The final achievement of the seventy-two-year goal of national woman suffrage was just the first of many important changes that many believed would characterize this new equality for women.

The mobilization of a nation for war can provide the context for women to take advantage of social and economic advances due to direct needs for women's labor in industry, agriculture, and the military. The nation also needs their organizational skills in voluntary organizations and management. And service to the state may be seen as a vital component of citizenship. Yet the linkage of the military to women's lives and fortunes, as political theorist Cynthia Enloe reminds us, comes with a heavy price. Women are particularly vulnerable to the violence of war and militarization.[4] Whereas part of the violence of war is on the battlefield, wartime can also draw upon and deliver violence in the form of rape, sexual exploitation of women, a hostile work environment for women workers, and intimate or domestic violence. Such violence can sweep away other economic or social "gains" that war might bring to women and can threaten civic accomplishments achieved before the war. Wartime also carries with it strongly conservative elements that reimpose traditional gender roles and relationships. And wartime advances are most often cast in terms of special, emergency circumstances that will not last past "the duration."[5]

Although many women viewed the war as an opportunity to mobilize "woman power" and to enter a postwar "Promised Land . . . of equal opportunity," the years surrounding the First World War were also characterized by fears of immigrants, racial and ethnic inequity, attacks on feminism and women's rights, and labor unrest and radicalism.[6] The possibility of the Bolshevik revolution reaching into the hearts and minds of Americans fueled a wartime suppression of civil liberties under the guise of "100% Americanism" and a postwar Red Scare that continued into the 1920s.[7] Those individuals who opposed the war and the Wilson administration's enactment of the draft in May 1917, those who criticized the government, military, or the organizations supporting the war effort, found themselves vulnerable to prosecution under the Espionage Act (1917), Trading with the Enemy Act (1917), Alien Act (1918), and Sedition Act (1918) with the aid of a strengthened government surveillance system and vigilant community members.[8] Professional and political women such as Emma Goldman, Anna Louise Strong, Dr. Marie

Equi, and Kate Richards O'Hare were harassed, tried, and convicted as "disorderly" and "unmotherly" women deemed incapable of true citizenship.[9] In this repressive context, the path "over the top" to the promised land of equality could be a perilous one indeed.

The study that follows analyzes the discourse, strategies, and activism of three groups of women in the United States—physicians, nurses, and women-at-arms—who linked the possibility of achieving professional, personal, civic, and organizational goals with military service during the First World War. At the same time that they sought service with the military as soldiers, as medical officers, and as nurses with officer rank, these women campaigned for the right to define their service to the state and to redefine the military in ways that would protect women from violence. A substantial number of the six thousand women physicians in the United States supported campaigns for officer status in the military medical corps as an expression of more complete citizenship for medical women and equal status with male colleagues. Simultaneously, they identified war and the militaries that fought war as producers of violence against women. To address this position they supported all-female medical units in France to provide direct medical relief to women civilians who suffered rape, dislocation, disease, and poverty in the war's wake. Many nurses campaigned for full officer rank as a way to demonstrate their civic equality and professionalism; many also saw military rank as a way to prevent the gender discrimination nurses had experienced in a hostile military wartime workplace. Women who took up arms to fulfill the traditional citizen's obligation to defend the state claimed fuller female citizenship. They also challenged the traditional gender bargain of men as the Protectors and women as the Protected: women armed to defend the state could defend themselves against the violence of invasion and also domestic violence.[10] These three groups of women, then, offer us a way to consider the intersection of campaigns for civic equality with antiviolence activism. They did not simply wish to enter the military to claim civic rights but acted to change the military and the state that sponsored it in ways that would attend to women's needs.

These case studies enable us to explore major themes relating to women's activism, women's civic and professional roles, and gender and war. First, they underscore that we must consider war, violence, and activism within a specific and developing historical context. Although it is true that "wartime" can draw together assumptions about men as soldiers and women as supporters, the Protectors and the Protected, it is essential to examine the particular ways that the First World War differed from the Civil War, the Spanish-American and Philippine-American wars, the Second World War, and subsequent conflicts. This difference is true for the specific context of women's prewar roles, the organizations and activist projects surrounding the conflict, and the ways that gender worked through each conflict. As Kristin L. Hoganson demonstrates, for many Americans the Spanish-American War maintained the links between male soldiering and civic service forged during the Civil War but enhanced the association of citizenship with manly physical prowess in combat and skilled leadership.[11] As the United States prepared for and entered the First World War, this strengthened "martial ideal" of citizenship competed with the Progressive Era legacy that defined citizenship in wider circles of participatory community action.[12] Women's contributions to the political, organizational, and reform movements of the Progressive Era provided strong credentialing for the participatory thread of citizenship. Many of them argued that their wartime and military service would complete the second strand of civic identity based on soldiering. Their opponents responded by challenging, denigrating, and demonizing the woman warrior.

This contextualization is also important for understanding violence and antiviolence activism, as Shani D'Cruze and other scholars emphasize. D'Cruze notes that particular kinds of violence "are subject to periods when they are not recognized and periods when they undergo moments of rediscovery and redefinition." Thus, the "basic physical realities of violence may be disturbingly repetitive," but the "socio-cultural contexts and meanings, as well as the techniques and technologies of violence, have their historical specificities."[13] In the period of the First World War, for example, many Americans, including the women physicians and women-at-arms in this study, responded to information about the rape and physical assault of women in occupied Belgium and northern France. This response was due in part to the outpouring of media attention to wartime violence and atrocities but also the Progressive Era "white slavery" and other reform campaigns that drew attention to sexual assault and increased media attention to the issue prior to the conflict. In addition, as women participated in the wage workforce and the professions in increasing numbers prior to the war, many experienced or knew of others who experienced gender-based discrimination in a hostile workplace. And women who confronted the wartime claims that men protected women often had experience or knowledge of ways in which women were at risk from men, including those men who were supposed to be their protectors. The women in this study experienced, constructed, and defined violence in new ways based on these prewar and wartime experiences. And their opponents used alternative constructions of violence to challenge these new interpretations.

Second, this study also underscores the importance of these three groups in the history of woman suffrage and citizenship activism and suggests the complexity of these campaigns. Women who took up arms to defend the state, some women physicians, and some women nurses sought service with the military as a way to claim more complete female citizenship and increased postwar equality. For them, "citizenship" comprised the categories that T. H. Marshall defined as encompassing "civic, political, and social" citizenship. It included voting but also professional education and membership and equal participation in careers and professional organizations. Citizenship embraced access to opportunities and the promise of equivalent status in community and society. Citizenship, for some of the women in this study, also comprised what Alice Kessler-Harris refers to as "economic citizenship." For women physicians this economic position included the right to follow a profession and to be placed on equal wage and status footing with male colleagues in the institution of the military and in the postwar professional world. Many of them campaigned for officer status and rank within the military medical corps to achieve their vision of such complete citizenship. Women nurses sought to legitimate the "female profession" of nursing and their right to equal pay and status for equal work. Many women nurses campaigned for military rank as part of full inclusion in the military medical workplace, official status in the institution of the military, and fuller professional recognition in post-war medicine. And women who took up arms for "home defense" claimed the citizen's obligation to defend the state as part of fuller female citizenship. As Linda Kerber illustrates, citizenship has carried "military overtones" from antiquity to the founding of the American Republic through the nineteenth and twentieth centuries to our own day and has been particularly linked to manhood and whiteness. But the "founding generation transmitted to its successors complex and sometimes contradictory understandings of the meaning of citizenship."[14] Women who took up arms followed one strategic line of argument in the arms and citizenship debate by asserting that in armed home defense, and in potential armed military service, women engaged in the citizen's obligation to defend the state and therefore deserved the rights of citizenship in return.[15] The women in each of these case studies claimed a direct relationship between military service and fuller female citizenship at a time when the achievement of suffrage for all women through the Nineteenth Amendment was within reach. This study, therefore, asserts that the years of the First World War and the activism of women physicians, nurses, and women-at-arms are essential to understanding the history of women's definitions of the specifics of complete citizenship, their efforts to achieve it, and the nature of the opposition to their claims.

Third, these case studies reveal that the debates concerning women, war, and violence in the First World War were not simply dialogues between supporters of wartime service and pacifists who opposed the war. Instead, these cases reveal that many women engaged in a complex consideration of war and women's relationships to the military, to citizenship, and to the violence of a militarized state. Members of each group grappled with the question of war and violence against women and took steps to address it within their own arenas of action and influence. Paradoxically, women-at-arms, military nurses, and some women physicians wanted to participate in the military, an institution that produces violence. Yet as they sought a place within the military they also wanted to transform it in ways that would address and end violence. Estelle Freedman suggests that three key elements characterize movements to combat violence against women: naming the violence, providing services for survivors of violence, and fighting back against violence, often by obligating the state to create and enforce antiviolence policies. The strategies and actions of the women in this study were shaped by experience and knowledge of violence against women in the United States before the war and also by information about and experience with violence in wartime. Women physicians who created all-female medical units for service in France hoped to address the core relationship of war and violence against women by providing health care for women and children who had suffered the violent consequences of invasion. Many nurses campaigned for military rank within the Army Nurse Corps (ANC) as a protection against what feminist legal theorist Vicki Schultz terms "hostile work environment harassment" and to create a safe military working environment for women.[16] Women who took up arms called into question the safety of all women in a patriarchal state in wartime but also in peace, and challenged the notion of men as the Protectors and women as the Protected in traditional gender conventions. The actions of each group fall within Freedman's definition of antiviolence activism, yet their differing goals, strategies, and institutional circumstances provide important critical insights into the challenges they faced and the results they achieved while framing campaigns against violence. The ideas and actions of the women in this study are therefore also a significant part of the history of women's antiviolence activism.

Fourth, these cases underscore the necessity of approaching the relationship between women and war by studying their ideas, strategies, and actions prior to the conflict; examining the debates and wartime choices they made during the conflict; and analyzing their claims and actions in the aftermath. The approach of the First World War and the U.S. entry into the conflict raised urgent questions concerning violence against women, the question of military service and support of the war, and the relationship of women to war in a variety of ways. The wartime debates and choices of the women in this study were related directly to their ongoing campaigns for suffrage, professional status, economic equity, more complete female citizenship, and protection against violence. And the postwar demobilization that emphasized women's familial and consumer roles and assaulted women's civic and economic progress impacted women's choices and organizations. It is analytically important, then, not to isolate women's wartime activism but to underscore the relationship between wartime debates and events, issues, and activism before, during, and after the conflict.

And finally, the experiences of these groups emphasize that women and their activism had an impact on how the nation conceived of and waged war. Such an analysis challenges a conventional narrative that frames the story only in terms of the impact of war on women's lives. They were not simply "acted upon" by the forces of war and the state. They themselves acted to make war and the military different because women were there and made a difference in the way leaders made decisions about how the United States would wage war and who would participate and in leaders' arguments and justifications for wartime and demobilization decisions. As Cynthia Enloe's insightful work demonstrates, militaries and states have depended on women's militarization and their support of wartime projects and military objectives.[17] In the First World War, the militarized state needed women's medical services at home and abroad and needed women to support preparedness activities and other wartime organizations and actions. As these three groups of women attempted to enter the military on their own terms, with challenges to the institution and its practices, they required leaders to consider and account for them. Although women nurses received only "relative rank" at the close of their campaign in 1920, their claims about workplace safety resonated with the need to recruit and maintain a nursing force in the present and future. Women-at-arms asked for a response to the question of the "habit of violence" engendered by wartime service and challenged their roles as passive, protected supporters of the militarized state. And women physicians called for equivalent rank and status while also exposing issues of violence against women at the heart of making war. By raising questions of the relationship of women's service to the state and their civic and professional status, by challenging the script of the Protector and the Protected, by seeking to transform the military itself, women challenged policy makers' assumptions and dependence on women's support and the way that they conducted the war.

These themes are significant to our understanding of the First World War, gender and war, and women's civic and antiviolence activism. They provide a context for the war years and analysis of the conflict and its aftermath and offer analytical foundations for contemporary states and movements. An understanding of the evolving paradigms of citizenship and the historical context of violence in which these women operated and an analysis of the ways in which they shaped their activism and sought to transform the military state even as they entered it offer important ways of understanding women's movements within state-building and nationalist struggles, continuing calls for women's rights across nations, and contemporary women's challenges to the structures of militarism.

* * *

In the chapters that follow I will analyze the claims these groups of women made for more complete female citizenship through military service and their campaigns to transform the military and the state to address violence against women. I will also assess the paradigms of citizenship within which they made their claims and the new models of citizenship they developed, the opposition to their activism, and the results. The prelude considers the Washington, D.C., suffrage parade of 1913 that so powerfully mirrored issues of gender, citizenship, militarization, and violence in the approaching world war. Chapter 1 contextualizes the debates concerning models of citizenship and women's citizenship claims prior to and during the war. Chapter 2 provides a context for representations and experiences of violence on the home and war fronts. Chapter 3 analyzes the activities of women who took up arms and their claims for military service on the home front and for "domestic protection" and the presence of the woman-at-arms in the popular culture of the period. Chapter 4 examines the representation and denigration of the woman-at-arms in the popular American interpretation of the female soldiers of the Russian Women's Battalion of Death. Chapter 5 considers the citizenship claims and activities of women physicians and their campaign to receive equivalent officer status with men in the military medical corps. Chapter 6 suggests the importance of women physicians' actions to challenge wartime violence by providing care for women and children who had experienced the violence of the war zone and enemy occupation. Chapter 7 presents the case of military nurses and their struggle for rank in the military, which was in large part an effort to combat hostile work-environment harassment in the military medical workplace and a debate about the best ways to achieve these ends. Chapter 8 analyzes the fears of veteran violence in the demobilization period and the creation of a new civic model in the civilian-consumer and suggests how this new model affected the wartime claims and actions of the three groups studied. The conclusion analyzes the significance of these case studies for our understanding of women's civic and antiviolence activism and evolving models of citizenship.

Acknowledgments

The publication of this book is the culmination of a long journey. So many people have helped me on this path, and I wish to take time to thank them.

Linda Kerber has been a force for clarity and intellectual rigor throughout this project and a generous mentor. She helped me ask questions that led to this work, gave me support and encouragement along the way, and connected me with a wide network of scholars and scholarly ideas. I am forever in her debt. At the University of Iowa, Mary Strottman supported me and my work through countless daily acts for which I will always be grateful. My thanks also to Sara Hanley, the late Kenneth Cmiel, H. Shelton Stromquist, Ellis Hawley, and Dee Morris, and to Malcolm Rohrbough and Richard Kerber for their support and assistance. My colleagues made the adventure all worthwhile. My thanks to the late Andrew Federer, and to Kathy Jellison, Kathy Penningroth, Alison McNeese, Sharon Halevi, Kim Nielsen, Ragna Urberg, and Barbara Handy-Marchello for being friends and colleagues in the most substantial ways. At Western Oregon University my colleagues have taught me the true meaning of collegiality and solidarity. Members of the History Department, the Gender Studies Program, the Social Science Division, students, and others in the campus community have given me the gift of encouraging my scholarly voice and helping to make the work we do rewarding. Thanks, also, to Jeanne Deane for administrative support. Jean Bottcher, Pat Dixon, Debbie Evans, and Cindy Massaro have enriched my life as dear friends and supporters. Karen Jensen knows how and when to give help and laughter. Forrest Jensen and Mary Lindsay Jensen gave me the foundation to pursue my goals. Joshua James lived through much of this project and did so with good humor and support. Todd Jarvis supported this work through crucial stages with generosity, humor, and understanding. To all of them I am most grateful.

I am most fortunate to have worked with the insightful and supportive staff at the University of Illinois Press in the publication of this book. To Joan Catapano I give my deep appreciation for her support and for her discerning facilitation of the entire process. My thanks also goes to Lisa Bayer, Angela Burton, Annette Wenda, and UIP staff members in various departments who contributed to the success of this project. In addition, manuscript readers helped me to strengthen the work and deepen my arguments, and I am most grateful for their suggestions.

I also wish to thank colleagues who commented on various stages of this work at academic conferences, including the American Association for the History of Medicine, American Studies Association, American Historical Association, Western Association of Women Historians, and participants in the "Frontlines: Gender, Identity, and War" conference in Melbourne, Australia. Thanks also to the readers who reviewed and critiqued my articles for the *Bulletin of the History of Medicine, Western Historical Quarterly,* and *Frontiers: Journal of Women Studies,* and to the editors of those journals for help and support in revising and strengthening my arguments. Gayle Gullett provided important perspectives and supported my work on nurses, and Steven Peitzman provided encouragement and support for my work on women physicians. I also wish to thank Judith Walzer Leavitt, who read an early draft of the chapters on women physicians and included "Uncle Sam's Loyal Nieces" in the second edition of her anthology *Women and Health in America;* Roger Cooter for including my work on women physicians in *War, Medicine, and Modernity, 1860–1945;* and John Bodnar for contributing to my evolving thinking on women, citizenship, and patriotism through the "Patriotism and the Family in Modern America" symposium at Indiana University at Bloomington and for including my work in the anthology *Bonds of Affection: Americans Define Their Patriotism.*

I have been very fortunate to receive fellowship and funding support across the years of this project. The Graduate College of the University of Iowa awarded me an Ada Louisa Ballard Fellowship in the Humanities, and the Department of History at the University of Iowa awarded me the Louis Pelzer Fellowship, each for a year of research work. The Archives and Special Collections on Women in Medicine at the Medical College of Pennsylvania awarded me an M. Louise Gloeckner, M.D., summer fellowship. I wish to honor Ada Louise Ballard, Louis Pelzer, and M. Louise Gloeckner, whose exceptional lives inspired these fellowships and continue to inspire research and scholarship in their names. Thanks also to the Western Oregon University Faculty Development Committee and the Social Science Division at Western Oregon for providing support for conference travel.

Archivists and librarians are the guardians and conservators of our historic treasures, and I am grateful to all those who have assisted me with this project. I first began research at the Archives and Special Collections on Women in Medicine at the Medical College of Pennsylvania as a Gloeckner Fellow. Janet Miller, Margaret Jerrido, and Ida Wilson all made my stay successful and opened doors to the treasures of the collection. Joanne Grossman, Karen Ernst, Barbara Williams, and the current staff carry on this fine tradition at what is now the Archives and Special Collections on Women in Medicine and Homeopathy, Drexel University College of Medicine, Philadelphia, Pennsylvania. A research visit to their archives is a delight. My deepest thanks to archivists Sara Piasecki and Karen Peterson, whose knowledge of Esther Pohl Lovejoy and welcoming professionalism make research at the Oregon Health & Science University Historical Collections & Archives in Portland an unforgettable experience. Their support has been extraordinary. At the time I worked with the Julia Stimson Papers at the then New York Hospital–Cornell Medical Center, Adele Lerner was my guide. Cathryn Seelye at the National Archives assisted me with materials on nurses in the military and with Julia Stimson's world war activities. At the University of Iowa the staff of the University of Iowa Main Library, the Microtext Collections, the Interlibrary Loan Department, and the Hardin Library for the Health Sciences all provided invaluable support. And to Gary Jensen, director of library and media services at Western Oregon University's Hamersly Library, and the library staff, including the staff of the Interlibrary Loan Department and Lori Pagel, who knows how to work magic time and again, my profound gratitude for helping me secure books and articles essential to this project.

Prelude

The Washington, D.C.,
Suffrage Parade of 1913

If women fight men, men will certainly come to fight back.
—Everett P. Wheeler, antisuffragist lawyer, 1913

If my wife were where you are I'd break her head.
—Unidentified police officer to suffrage parade
    participant Genevieve Stone, 1913

The *Washington Post*'s front-page headline on Sunday, March 2, 1913, told readers that on the following day supporters of woman suffrage were going to make the city of Washington a "pageant."[1] This was exactly what parade organizers intended. Their goal was to use the capital streets, public monuments, and buildings as an arena to exhibit a suffrage spectacle with floats, banners, costumes, and staged allegorical tableaux to highlight the justice of and the necessity for votes for women. And though the organizers did not intend it, the 1913 suffrage parade became another sort of tableau: a stage upon which participants would test the safety of women in public, expose the limits to the gender conventions of the Protector and the Protected, and claim the civic rights of assembly and political action. Thousands of women activists, workers, professionals, and supporters of women's citizenship rights placed themselves on this public stage and claimed the right to march in safety. Instead, they encountered violence. Soldiers eventually came to the scene to "restore order." Opponents charged that the members of the "suffrage army" were engaged in a gender war and as combatants they got what they deserved.

The suffrage parade of 1913 was not only an important milestone in the quest for female citizenship. It was also an event that caused many women to redefine their understanding of violence against women and to relate this new understanding to their expanding vision of the rights of citizenship. In these significant ways the suffrage parade was a prelude to issues of gender, citizenship, militarization, and violence in the world war that followed.

On January 2, 1913, Alice Paul and Lucy Burns met with members of the Congressional Committee of the National American Woman Suffrage Association (NAWSA) to begin planning a huge woman suffrage parade to coincide with the inauguration of newly elected president Woodrow Wilson that March. Paul and Burns were eager to bring a new militancy and political pressure to the American suffrage movement when they returned from working with British suffragists in England. They were able to obtain their seats at the head of the Congressional Committee of NAWSA with the help of Jane Addams, who interceded with the moderate, cautious NAWSA leadership on their behalf at the fall 1912 convention. Many NAWSA members were concerned that the confrontational politics that the two women had learned from militant suffragists while in Britain would destroy the organization's carefully constructed alliances and respectability.[2] But Paul and Burns moved forward. Three months was a very short time to organize a parade. But they believed that having it at a time when hundreds of thousands of people would be in Washington for the inaugural would send a powerful political message to the new Democratic administration. As historian Christine Lunardini points out, they believed the parade would "put Wilson on notice that they were a group to be reckoned with."[3]

As the committee worked over the next three months to make the parade a reality they took steps to protect the safety of the thousands of anticipated participants. Women would be marching as professional and occupational groups (such as physicians, nurses, factory workers, teachers, and librarians), in state delegations, and as members of other thematic sections including homemakers, college women, club women, international women, and those riding historical floats and in allegorical processions.[4] A group of African American suffragists from Howard University would march, and members of the National Men's League for Woman Suffrage would join the line.[5] The proposed route, west along Pennsylvania Avenue from the Peace Monument (at the west facade of the Capitol) to the Treasury Building and across the Mall, would take them through the heart of the city on the day before Woodrow Wilson took the oath of office. The large number of visitors and residents coming to the historic district for the inaugural events would need to be managed effectively for safety. Members of Congress had already approved a joint resolution on January 29 appropriating twenty-three thousand dollars for the Board of Commissioners of the District of Columbia "to maintain public order and protect life and property in said District from the 28th day of February to the 10th day of March, 1913," the days surrounding the inauguration.[6]

In early February Alice Paul and other committee members met with the superintendent of police for the District of Columbia, Major Richard Sylvester, in their quest to obtain a permit for the parade and to make logistical arrangements. Sylvester told Paul that the "huge inauguration crowds would be too disorderly and that he had too few men at his disposal" to provide proper protection. Paul later recalled that Sylvester claimed "the riff-raff of the South" would be in the city because of the Democratic victory and that the women would be in danger. He told them not to march the day before the inaugural.[7] Committee members believed that Sylvester opposed them and wished to frighten them away from having the parade. When they did receive a permit from the District and Paul reminded Sylvester of his earlier concerns, he would not help her seek additional protection and even acted as if there was no cause for worry. Everything "will be all right," he told her.[8]

Paul and her associates did not believe it. They went over Sylvester's head, writing to the commissioners of the District of Columbia and to Robert Shaw Oliver, assistant secretary of war, and finally meeting with Henry Stimson, the outgoing secretary of war under President William Howard Taft, on the Friday before the Monday parade. They asked for troops, perhaps a cavalry unit from nearby Fort Myer in Virginia, to provide protection for the women marchers. Stimson was sympathetic. His sister-in-law Elizabeth Selden Rogers was part of the parade planning committee, and she intended to march. He was careful to explain the constraints placed on him. He told them that it was up to the police of the District of Columbia to provide protection and that "great care must be taken that the troops are not ordered out unnecessarily." The next day, Saturday, March 1, Stimson discussed the issue with Judge Advocate General Enoch Crowder and wrote a letter to the District board of commissioners incorporating Crowder's legal advice. "It does not appear," he wrote, "that any disturbance of an unusual or formidable character is threatened" that would justify calling troops. He recommended that the commissioners use the money Congress had appropriated for the inaugural to expand the District's own police force to provide protection for the suffrage parade.[9] That same day members of Congress placed additional pressure on chief of police Sylvester. In a joint resolution they instructed him to "stop all ordinary traffic and travel, including the operation of streetrailroads . . . and to prevent any interference with the suffrage procession" on March 3.[10]

The parade organizers were in a classic bureaucratic bind that put women at risk. The superintendent of police would not publicly support the idea that there was any need to have additional security above the protection provided by the police and their reinforcements, even though he had warned Paul and her supporters of just that possibility in private before they had their permit. Without his request the board of commissioners could not ask for troops.

Therefore, the "Secretary of War had absolutely nothing which would justify the use of troops" and could not act officially.[11] Both Stimson and members of Congress put the pressure back on Sylvester, who had demonstrated nothing but opposition to the parade.

Suffrage women continued to take action, and the secretary of war listened even though he was hampered bureaucratically. On Saturday, March 1, Sara T. Moller, a parade organizer from Hartford, Connecticut, requested a meeting with Stimson, and he agreed to see her. Moller wanted him to know that she had new evidence supporting the organizers' concerns about violence against women marchers. Rosalie Jones of New York, dubbed "the General" by the press, had marched with a "suffrage army" from New York to Washington, D.C., "to influence legislators in States through which the army passed and [to] educate the public" in the days prior to the parade.[12] Crowds gathered in cities and towns to see the suffragists on their march to the capital. Although many were supportive, others threw stones and jeered, and "some of the women were knocked down in a scuffle." When Jones and the "suffrage army" arrived outside NAWSA's Washington headquarters on Friday, February 28, a "rough crowd" hemmed in the marchers and gathered in a "demonstration." Concerned NAWSA members called the police. "Even then the crowd was very badly handled [by the police]," Sara Moller later testified. "It was very rough. I stood at the top of some steps and saw a great deal of roughness, and I thought that was rather ominous of what might happen on Monday [at the larger parade]." She shared these concerns with Stimson when she met with him on Saturday.[13]

In addition to contacting the judge advocate general and the District commissioners that Saturday, Stimson went to Fort Myer and asked to drill members of the Fifteenth Cavalry himself. Although he did not mention this fact in his later testimony and the press did not connect his actions with the parade question, it is intriguing to speculate about his motives. Was he, as he told the press, just "anxious to drill a troop of regulars" in his last days as secretary of war? Perhaps he also had the suffrage parade and its protection in mind when he made his journey to Fort Myer. On the morning of Monday, March 3, the day of the parade, Stimson made a series of telephone calls to find out about the situation. He contacted General Leonard Wood, army chief of staff, and "directed him to keep a troop of cavalry in readiness at such place he might see fit in case of call for serious trouble by the authorities of the District."[14] General Wood ordered the Fifteenth Cavalry to bivouac on the western outskirts of Washington, D.C.[15] These members of the Fifteenth Cavalry, whom Stimson had drilled two days before, would eventually come to assist the suffragists and their supporters on Pennsylvania Avenue that afternoon.

As the afternoon of the parade arrived, participants had high hopes for the success of their grand pageant and were delighted that some eight thousand women and men had come to participate. But from almost the first steps, violent crowds and apathetic or hostile police threatened the proceedings. On this day before Wilson's inauguration a half-million spectators lined the avenue to watch the parade. Most of them were men, although there were women in the crowd. Some spectators were supporters, cheering on the floats, marchers, and mounted flag bearers. Some were there because they opposed suffrage, and they passed out antisuffrage literature and hurled insults. Antisuffragists "filled the windows of their headquarters with the coarsest of cartoons" for marchers and spectators to see.[16] Most of the crowd seems to have been there for the spectacle of it all. Many of them had been drinking and continued to drink, and the avenue became a scene of increasing chaos, out of control and dangerous.

After about a half hour, the marchers could, at best, walk a gauntlet one or two abreast, with crowds closing in around those who were walking and those on floats, mounted on horseback, and riding in automobiles. They were pinched, fondled, spat on, insulted, jostled, kicked, pulled, and trampled. Ambulances came with difficulty through the throng to evacuate some marchers. Late in the afternoon officials called in the waiting cavalry from Fort Myer. They helped to restore order, and the parade reached the Treasury Building hours later than planned. The *Washington Post* reported that the emergency hospital was "filled to overflowing" that afternoon and that more than forty marchers were hospitalized overnight.[17]

At a mass meeting that evening, in interviews by the press, and in a congressional investigation convened just days afterward, women and men recounted stories of the violence they had experienced as parade participants. Women reported "ribald insults," "obscene" and "absolutely indecent remarks," at every turn. Men who were marching in support of woman suffrage got "jeers" from men in the crowd who called them "Henpecko" and asked, "Where are Your Skirts?"[18] The crowd surged forward on the marchers "with a great deal of violence." Many participants were trampled or "swept off their feet" by the crowds. One woman was struck in the face, and others were "pinched black and blue."[19] At several points along the way young men in the crowd linked arms to form a chain to prevent the women from passing.[20] Some men took hold of women marchers or those sitting on floats and fondled their arms, legs, and breasts. Others tried to pull them from the procession, tearing clothing in the process. And some threw lighted cigarettes in an attempt to ignite the parade flags and banners as the marchers passed through this human gauntlet.[21]

Mrs. Richard Coke Burleson, grand marshal of the parade, called it a "horrible, howling mob." Sarah Agnes Wallace of Washington, D.C., a young teacher who marched in the college women's section, told the congressional committee about the violence that she experienced as the crowd hemmed in around her. It "made me understand more of what one reads in literature and history of massacres and revolutions and mobs and riots than anything I could have experienced in any other way," she testified. "There was a danger in it that made you hold your breath and look ahead to the Treasury Building, and wonder if you would ever get up there in safety." Helena Hill Weed, a veteran suffragist who marched with the Connecticut delegation that day, wanted to make certain that the committee knew that this violence was more than simply "jests and gibes. Those of us who have taken part in special demonstrations for equal suffrage are accustomed to those. We know what we are going to face when we go into them." But this level of violence and "indecency," she insisted, was altogether different.[22]

Some participants fought back. Section marshals in the parade carried batons, and some used them. Dr. Nellie V. Mark, marshal of Maryland's section of professional women, testified that she used her baton twice. Once was to stop a man who was tearing a young woman's clothing, and the other was to hit a man who had made "a very ugly remark" to the woman in front of her and was about to do the same to the doctor herself. Vernat Hetfield, a seventeen-year-old student, was sitting on a float with her sister in the Pennsylvania delegation. Men were grabbing the young women's feet and arms and trying to pull them off the float. Hetfield kicked one man, who eventually quit his pursuit. Then a "marshal came up and walked along side of me," she recalled, "and she had a little cane in her hand, and she just hit everybody."[23] The women on horseback up and down the parade line did a great deal to move the crowd along from their more mobile and relatively protected positions and protected other marchers.[24] George F. Bowerman, a Washington, D.C., librarian marching with the men's contingent, told the congressional committee, "I fancy that we suffered less than the women, because being men, and most of us armed, as I was, with a good stout cane, the crowd held back somewhat for us, as they probably did not in the case of the women." Most women took the arm of the woman next to them, looked forward, and marched toward their goal as best they could. "Dignity was about the only weapon we had," Mrs. Keppel Hall recalled.[25]

The overwhelming conclusion of the participants, and, eventually, the congressional committee, was that the District of Columbia police had not done what they could or should have done to manage the crowd and to prevent the violence. The testimony of participants and officials focused on police apathy, at best, and police participation in the abuse, at worst. "The attitude of the police was of 'utter indifference,'" Dr. Nellie Mark testified. "I should say jellyfish indifference—as if they did not have much backbone." Participants reported that some police officers folded their arms and did nothing as the crowds pushed beyond the barricades and enveloped the marchers. When the crowds began to harass the women by chucking them on the chin and trying to pull them out of line, Bliss Finley, marshal of the wage earners' section, testified, the uniformed police officer there "simply smiled." Cordelia Powell Odenheimer, a supporter on the sidelines, believed that some police officers left the scene and let the violence happen. Someone in the crowd "tore a woman's suffrage badge from off my coat and nearly knocked me down. When I managed to get up the crowd was very dense," she remembered. "A woman cried out—she was crying—that they had torn two children away from her. . . . When I got to my seat, and this woman was calling . . . I looked around, saw no police, and I braced myself against the crowd and called out, 'Is there not a man here with enough of the spark of manhood in him to at least protect children?' Two men pushed forward, broke the line of the mob, and made a passageway. There were no policemen around whatever."[26]

Some testified that police officers participated in the jeering, name-calling, and physical violence. "It was more than a question of an undermanned police line," Glenna B. Tinnan, one of the directors of the pageant, said. "Those who were assigned to the task not only did little or nothing, but even seemed to encourage the hoodlums in the work of breaking up the parade." Patricia M. Street, another assistant director, was near the Peace Monument, standing on the running board of her car with a megaphone, trying to direct the crowds because the police were not doing so. When a man spit tobacco juice on the face of a marcher, Street asked a police officer to protect the woman. He told her that "there would be nothing like this happen if you would stay at home." When Street hit the man who had spit tobacco juice, the police officer took her by the coat and tore it, and instructed her to go home where she belonged. Genevieve Stone, a suffrage marcher whose husband was a state representative from Illinois, told the *New York Times* that a police officer shouted to her, "If my wife were where you are I'd break her head."[27]

Alice Paul and other organizers pointed out that they had faced opposition from chief of police Sylvester from the beginning and that the District police, augmented by additional staff on the day of the parade, could have stopped the violence "had they really desired as a body to do so." They noted that "a spirit of opposition possessed the men who were on duty." The *Washington Post* reported that an officer "close to the workings of the police department" believed that "if Maj. Sylvester had given the word that not a soul but those having passes should cross Pennsylvania Avenue, not a soul would have crossed and there would have been no trouble."[28] For some, there was ample evidence that the violence was sanctioned at levels above the police department. Alice Paul believed that there was "no question that the police had the tip from some power higher up to let the rough characters in the city through the police lines and try to break up our parade." Others pointed to the double standard of protection. Whereas the crowds were allowed to run rampant in the suffrage parade, police kept order with the inaugural crowds a day later. Chief Sylvester boasted that he wanted to "demonstrate the model way for protecting huge crowds" at the inaugural, and he was successful in his goal.[29] In the end, Major Sylvester lost his post as chief of police.

The committee hearings and press reports also highlighted the actions of those who had helped the marchers. Organizers gave special recognition to the Boy Scouts who protected marchers and controlled the crowd. Many witnesses testified to the support of some individual police officers and those on special detail for the day. The violence on parade day generated support for the suffrage marchers and for the proposed woman suffrage amendment. Press support, increased donations (including one thousand dollars from the editor of the *Washington Post*), and wide visibility for the cause were part of the consequences of the parade and its aftermath. But these gains were set against the destructive context of the violence of the day.[30]

An important consequence of the parade was that suffragists claimed their right to safety in the streets and to participation in political demonstrations as important rights of citizenship. And they insisted that it was the duty of the government to protect them as they exercised these rights. The resolution passed at the mass meeting by supporters the evening after the parade, for example, asserted that the "nation's capital belonged to all citizens, men and women alike." At that same meeting NAWSA president Anna Howard Shaw declared, "I have never seen greater dignity under trying conditions, greater coolness under insult and oppression than was displayed by the marchers for suffrage today. Come what may, nothing shall deter us until we can compel the Congress to protect us as it will protect the men tomorrow [at Wilson's inauguration]." The dignity of the women and men marchers contrasted with the violent crowd and the lack of police protection. Shaw was cheered by the fact that one man who opposed suffrage changed his opinion as a result of the parade. At the beginning of the day he went to the antisuffragists for some literature. When he got it he was so offended by their arguments and their actions at the parade that, Shaw said, he "came and joined us and gave us $20. He said he was not in sympathy with any one who could stoop to things of that kind." Dignified and respectable behavior enhanced suffrage marchers' claims for the right to the streets. For the editors of the *Washington Post,* the "character of the women" who participated in the parade forced "serious recognition of the growing demand for equal rights."[31]

Opponents of woman suffrage lost no time in criticizing the entire enterprise. They focused particularly on what they perceived as the lack of dignity of parade participants and their warlike demeanor. Chief among them was Everett Pepperrell Wheeler, an antisuffragist lawyer in New York. Three days after the suffrage parade he spoke at what was titled "Public Meeting for the Preservation of the Home" sponsored by the New York State Association Opposed to Woman Suffrage. For him, the parade was not a dignified processional march on behalf of a cause. He turned the word *parade* against the suffragists, using it to convey the sense of an ostentatious exhibition with sexual overtones. Women were trying to take the place of men, he told his audience, and he used adjectives of violence to describe the attempt. They were "disputing with the man for public office; contending with the man for mastery; withdrawing from the home, parading in the streets and shouting in the market place." Wheeler saw nothing short of gender war in the campaign for equality, and he named suffragists as combatants. "Let me tell you that the context of politics is what the name campaign implies—a strenuous struggle. The military epithets are not misplaced." He warned that women who advocated for equality would lose the love of men. "The woman that man loves is not the fighting, brawling woman who marches in processions and debates in political conventions." Women had power over men only through influence and propriety, he insisted. "The influence of woman over man is not gained by kicking, scratching and biting and never has been."[32]

Wheeler's anger at suffragists spilled over into a letter to the editor of the *New York Times* printed on March 9, 1913, six days after the parade. After criticizing suffragists for fomenting a "social revolution" and bringing about the downfall of Christian civilization, he blamed the marchers themselves for the violence of the crowd at the suffrage parade. Some of the marchers, he said, were dressed in a sexually provocative way, "exposing themselves to the gaze of the crowd which filled the streets of Washington." Wheeler may have been referring to all of the women marchers or perhaps specifically to the women in the allegorical tableaux and those who rode on the floats representing women of the past, present, and future. They wore gauzy Greek Revival robes, tied at the waist, which exposed some of the arm and leg and were form-fitting. Wheeler proclaimed that the masses of men in the streets could not be controlled when tempted by women dressed in such a manner. "Men with self-restraint in such circumstances would, of course, abstain from violence and keep away. The spectacle to them was disgusting in the main. But all the more the crowd, who had not self restraint, would go and express their disapproval the way that they did." He again underscored that women had only themselves to blame, reiterating his own discussion of violence from his speech several nights before. Suffragists' "attempt to bring women in political warfare with men would break down the protecting barriers which courtesy and chivalry have thrown around women. If women fight men, men will certainly come to fight back and whether they like it or not the suffragists will find that men despise them if, under the pressure of the fight, they whimper and complain."[33]

Wheeler's "explanation" that the marchers were "asking for it" has a familiar ring as a common excuse for violence against women. "If women fight men, men will certainly come to fight back," he insisted. His words illustrate the classic tension between the "right of the streets" and the violence to which "women of the streets," prostitutes, women who are sexually available, "parading" women, were and are subjected.[34] And although Wheeler focused on anonymous "men in the crowd" who would fight back, the words of the police officer to Genevieve Stone also haunted participants and supporters in the aftermath of the parade: "If my wife were where you are I'd break her head," he had said. For Wheeler, for the police officer who spoke to Genevieve Stone, and for other opponents, suffrage marchers had broken gender conventions, taken to the streets, and fomented a "gender war." In so doing they forfeited their right to protection from men. And when women broke these gender conventions, they said, women could expect men to use violence to put them back "in their place."

The tensions around the "political warfare" and the violence of the suffrage parade would surface again several years later for women who sought entrance into the military and for the women-at-arms on the home front. Participants in the 1913 suffrage parade tested women's safety in public, exposed the limits to the gender conventions of the Protector and the Protected, and claimed the civic rights of assembly and political action. The discourse of the participants in the suffrage parade also illustrates a shift in the way that some women were defining violence and the relationship of citizenship to protection against violence. As women took to the streets to claim the rights of citizenship, they saw and experienced violence in new ways. And they increasingly constructed their citizenship claims as including freedom from this new vision of violence. In addition, their opponents were defining the marchers' actions as unsanctioned, violent combat and thereby justified the violent retaliation against them. These new constructions of violence and citizenship would provide a foundation for other redefinitions of violence in the military workplace, at the war front, and on the home front during the war years. In these important ways the suffrage parade was a prelude to issues of gender, citizenship, militarization, and violence in the First World War.

1. Negotiating Gender and Citizenship

Context for the First World War

The old argument that women are not entitled to political rights
because they do not serve their country at times of war seems to be
refuted in every direction by the present conflict.
—*Suffragist,* December 1914

The woman's ballot is a "blank-cartridge" ballot.
—John J. Vertrees, 1916

Like the participants in the Washington, D.C., suffrage parade of 1913,
the women physicians, nurses, and women-at-arms of this study made claims
for women's civic equality, political responsibility, and safety as elements of
female citizenship. They did so in the context of multilayered campaigns for
women's increased participation and civic and professional responsibility in
the American nation. As the First World War approached there were two
major competing arguments for civic identity and authority: the Progressive
Era's emphasis on participatory and community-based citizenship, on the
one hand, and an emphasis on masculine military experience for citizenship
and political authority, on the other. The war ushered in a vigorous debate
concerning these two modes of civic accomplishment and raised the question
of the meaning of women's citizenship in the martial context of wartime. This
chapter will examine this debate as a context for women's civic activism in
the case studies that follow.

Female Citizenship in the Progressive Era

In the era preceding and including the First World War Americans were in
the process of redefining the concept of citizenship to fit the conditions and
concerns of modern life. Yet citizenship was still bounded in powerful ways
by race, class, gender, and the idea of military service and combat. During
the Progressive Era, many native-born residents equated citizenship with

the process of "Americanizing" immigrants as record numbers of people migrated to the United States from different shores. Others saw citizenship as the process of "elevating" the laboring classes to middle-class norms of "good citizenship" through codes of proper behavior. Citizenship was denied to many Americans of color because of violence, intimidation, and legislation. Asian American immigrants continued to be denied citizenship because of race-based naturalization legislation dating from 1790, and in the early decades of the twentieth century western states passed legislation limiting land-ownership to citizens.[1] The Progressive Era's emphasis on urban and political reform, however, demanded civic attentiveness and activism. From 1900 to 1918 the nation's popular magazines published some four hundred articles on citizenship and patriotism, and Yale University sponsored an extensive, widely reprinted lecture series on the meaning of citizenship. This public discourse about citizenship focused on participatory citizenship, emphasizing the duty and privilege of citizens to act in support of the nation.[2]

This examination of citizenship took place in the context of a long history of women's active efforts to redefine citizenship in the United States. Their goals were to include women and their needs in the civic realm and then to shape the construction of state policies accordingly. This was true from the early days of the nation, when women used the concept of Republican Motherhood to build educational institutions for young women so that they could serve their political role as the educators of future citizens. It extended to the movements for the abolition of slavery and the suffrage movement beginning at Seneca Falls in 1848 to citizenship claims in the post–Civil War era and the revitalized suffrage movement of the early twentieth century. Women activists focused their attention on a wide array of the rights and obligations of citizenship. The "Declaration of Sentiments" presented by Elizabeth Cady Stanton to the assembled audience at the Seneca Falls convention called for increased access to education, the professions, and civic and business affairs in addition to the vote. Myra Bradwell's 1870s suit to become a member of the Illinois Bar called for a woman's right to train for and practice a profession as part of citizenship. Women worked for increased rights to property and custody of children within and outside of marriage, and fought to make divorce more equitable and easier to obtain for women. Members of the Woman's Christian Temperance Union (WCTU) called for the vote for women as "home protection" so that they could cast ballots for the prohibition of alcohol to combat domestic violence.[3] Following the Civil War free African American women challenged the state to provide them with the rights of citizenship that would include the right to be treated with respect as women and free workers. Middle-class African American club women and African American women in professions focused on the importance of respectability and community uplift to win full civic status.[4] Other women campaigned for the right to retain their birth citizenship after marriage, to maintain a "nationality of their own."[5] Many women physicians and nurses used their concept of citizenship to utilize the vote and civic leadership to improve public health in the United States through a strong series of programs for maternal and infant care and urban health reform in the Progressive Era.[6] And in this same period women flexed their civic muscles as citizen consumers through the National Consumer's League and support for protective labor legislation, fairer tax policies, and the regulation of monopolies.[7] When the United States entered the world war in April 1917 women in twelve states and territories had achieved full voting rights, and national and state organizations were in the final stages of the campaign for an amendment to the Constitution to enfranchise all women across the nation.

On the eve of the First World War some women in the United States had crossed important boundaries of "economic citizenship" with increasing access to wage work and the professions.[8] By 1910, women made up 20 percent of the paid workforce in the United States, 19 percent of American college professors and instructors were women, and some 6 percent of the nation's physicians and 1 percent of American lawyers were female.[9] As members of organizations such as the National American Woman Suffrage Association, the National Association of Colored Women, the National Women's Trade Union League, the Medical Women's National Association, and a variety of local groups, diverse women worked to bring about social change and to transform women's place in American society. The "New Woman"—sexually free, economically independent, and physically unshackled—was a feature of film and fiction, and some aspects of "new womanhood" were becoming a choice for some real women as well.

The movement for women's empowerment included a variety of perspectives on the manner in which to challenge women's inequalities, among them rights-based liberal feminists who emphasized suffrage, political power, and entrance into male institutions; maternalist feminists who stressed women's difference from men and male institutions and women's collective identity in movements for social justice and peace; and socialist feminists who placed class issues as central to the analysis of women's inequality in American society. The activities of these women, combined with economic and social change, provided for what historian Nancy Cott terms the "grounding of modern feminism" in the decades surrounding the First World War.[10]

The need for labor during the First World War opened new job categories for native-born white women, women of color, and immigrant women, expanding the possibilities for economic and professional citizenship. The number of jobs increased and offered many women the opportunity for upward mobility in the job market and higher wages. This trend was part of an ongoing transformation of women's wage work from domestic service and light manufacturing into the clerical and service sectors. During the war women worked in munitions plants and railroad yards, conducted streetcars, and found employment as telephone operators.[11] More than twelve thousand women worked for the military as yeomen (F) for the U.S. Navy and Marine Corps.[12] At peak strength in November 1918, 21,480 women were serving in the Army Nurse Corps, 10,660 of them with the American Expeditionary Force (AEF).[13] Thousands worked as members of the Signal Corps and were associated with the military as members of voluntary organizations such as the YWCA, Jewish Welfare Board, and Red Cross.[14] In the period of the First World War the U.S. military was becoming a modern, bureaucratized institution. It was the first protracted military campaign in which women's traditional services to armies—nursing and health care, laundering, and cooking—were now part of a vast supply and service bureaucracy. The military also needed the support of an immense clerical staff and employees who could provide support and communication services outside of combat. Voluntary agencies saw urgent needs in supporting soldiers at home and abroad in newer, more professionalized bureaucracies.

Citizenship and the Masculine Martial Ideal

These community-based, participatory Progressive Era definitions of citizenship coexisted uneasily with a set of parallel notions of citizenship and the masculine, martial ideal. The citizenship of masculinity that equated political authority with combat experience and valor countered the participatory Progressive Era vision with exclusion. Both traveled on a competing and conflicting trajectory from the late nineteenth century to the years of the world war.

Kristin Hoganson's consideration of the Spanish-American War and Philippine-American War for Independence suggests the complexities of the impact of these imperialist conflicts on views concerning citizenship and participation in war. During this period, she argues, military service took precedence for many Americans over competing concepts of citizenship, "including natural rights, stake in society, and moral virtue." And whereas the Civil War had emphasized the civic virtues of soldiers, imperialist ventures of the late nineteenth and early twentieth centuries brought military prowess and the "manly" physicality of combat and soldiering, not just participation in the military, to the forefront. Political authority, which according to Hoganson included leadership, office holding, and the vote, was tied by many Americans to this militarized civic role. "By highlighting the idea that military prowess had bearing on governmental capacity, promoters of the political-military nexus suggested that self government was not an inherent right, but rather, one that rested on a specific kind of manly character," she asserts. This type of citizenship was exclusionary rather than inclusive.[15] The rhetoric of exclusionary citizenship included white, native-born men and excluded men of color and all women within the United States, and Cubans and Filipinos outside the nation, as the United States built and strengthened its imperialist identity.[16] Thus, the very concept of "civilization" and political power, as Gail Bederman argues, was composed of notions of privileged masculinities in this nexus of class, race, and gender.[17]

E. Anthony Rotundo locates this new emphasis on military prowess in the broad cultural transformation to "passionate manhood" that peaked in the late nineteenth century. As Rotundo and historian Michael Kimmel demonstrate, this new masculinity was built on foundations of social Darwinism and the anxieties of empire. Both provide extensive evidence that the urgency of this remasculinization movement before the First World War was reflected in the physicality of "muscular Christianity," competitive sports, western dude ranches, bodybuilding, and competition in the workplace and in organizations such as the Boy Scouts and college fraternities. Popular culture presented the manly exploits of Davy Crockett and Tarzan in popular fiction along with Jack London's Northwest heroes. Kimmel and Rotundo both contend that this new masculinity was one of exclusion; to enhance their manhood many white men increasingly separated themselves and emphasized their differences from women, gay men, men of color, and immigrants. Kathleen Dalton joins Rotundo and Kimmel in understanding Theodore Roosevelt, apostle of the "strenuous life," as not only the symbol of this passionate masculinity but also a man profoundly affected by the imperatives of the doctrine that linked physical valor and combat with citizenship and political authority.[18]

Suffragists and supporters of women's rights moved uneasily within these shifting definitions of citizenship. In 1897, a year before the United States entered the war with Spain, suffrage leader Carrie Chapman Catt edited an anthology for the National American Woman Suffrage Association titled *The Ballot and the Bullet.* Catt was responding to the expansionist and imperialist currents active in American culture prior to the U.S. entry into the war that emphasized a militaristic interpretation of citizenship. Her strategy was to embrace the accomplishments of women in wartime, on the one hand, but also to argue that bearing arms to defend the state had no direct ties to voting or was an "outmoded" concept in the progressive, modern world, on the other. "At the close of this century of democracy," Catt wrote in the introduction, "in no period of which has the willingness or ability to bear arms ever been made a qualification for the ballot, an effort is being made to discover in remote customs an origin wherein to establish a military basis for modern American citizenship." Opponents of suffrage were using this "bullets for ballots argument" with "vigor and seriousness," Catt wrote, but their position suffered from three major flaws. First, many of the men who were insisting on the link between armed defense and voting in an effort to deprive women of the vote were themselves incapable of military service. This segment of the population included "ministers and editors, whose occupation exempts them from military duty," and "book worms, lawyers and clerks, whose physical incompetence would dismiss them from the muster." The second flaw was that the antisuffragists ignored the historical evidence of women soldiers such as those who participated in the Civil War. "Women of physical strength and courage, under the influence of ardent devotion to their respective causes," she wrote, "served with honor in the ranks of soldiers, North and South, while it was no uncommon incident for men to hide or even maim themselves in order to protect themselves from the draft." The third flaw in the "bullets for ballots" argument, Catt concluded, was that "the ideal conditions of society demand votes which stand for brains, not muscles for consciences, not bullets; the argument gains ground only with those who sympathize with past conditions and who are blinded by present possibilities."[19]

Yet as the United States entered conflicts with Spain and the Philippines the "political-military nexus" of citizenship gained a more defining hold, and suffragists had to take even greater account of this new cultural imperative equating military service and citizenship. Recognizing the political realities of this definition, some suffrage supporters accepted it and, as Kristin Hoganson finds, "tried to broaden the definition of military service to encompass women." The prosuffrage *Woman's Journal*, local and national organizations, and leaders such as Julia Ward Howe adopted this strategy in arguing for the vote for women based on their considerable efforts to provide food, supplies, and medical care for the troops on the home and battle fronts.[20] Yet these strategies were not successful, particularly because of the enhanced association of military service with male force in combat. Alice Stone Blackwell lamented that as a result of the war there was a "fresh crop of assertions that women ought not to vote, because they cannot render military service."[21] As Hoganson asserts, the gap between 1896 and 1910 during which no state campaigns for woman suffrage were successful, known as the "doldrums" in the history of the suffrage campaign, was due in part to this strengthened association of military combat, white manhood, and citizenship.[22]

Suffragists were divided over the question of support for or opposition to U.S. imperialism and empire, and as a result they articulated different conceptions of citizenship in this period. Many white suffragists, Susan Anthony and Elizabeth Stanton among them, relied on racism and classism to argue that native-born white educated women "deserved" the vote more than "ignorant" immigrant men and men of color and supported the war in the Philippines and empire-building by extension. Hoganson argues persuasively that many white suffragists supported empire as a political strategy "in the belief that allying themselves with their nation's policies would prove their own worthiness as citizens" and encourage support for woman suffrage. Anti-imperialist suffragists, including former abolitionist Mary Livermore, allied themselves with Filipinas and argued for a democratic vision of citizenship that would include the vote for all women. Some women criticized imperialism when the army regulated prostitution for troops in the Philippines. They joined pacifist suffragists in opposition to war and empire and called for women's political empowerment to combat militarism. And suffragists of color and white suffragists opposed to racism joined the anti-imperialist cause, as they understood that "imperialist pursuits were leading to a more exclusionary conception of citizenship." Anna Howard Shaw criticized the "white man's burden" as a militarist system based on fear and force but also as a system based on disregard for self-government at home.[23] Anti-imperialist suffragists defined citizenship as democratic, not militaristic, and used their critique of American empire to call for democratic and inclusive U.S. citizenship.

The First World War provided a new context for debate regarding the relationship of military service to citizenship. As war began in Europe in 1914 many supporters of suffrage for women equated participation in wartime support activities with military service and therefore service that should be rewarded with the vote for women nationwide. Carrie Chapman Catt and members of the mainstream National American Woman Suffrage Association took this stance. And some American women used the existence of women combatants to claim women's rights to full civic participation within this martial mode of citizenship. They argued that women who joined the ranks of combatants represented the female sex as a whole and that their soldierly sacrifices entitled all women to claim complete citizenship. Readers of suffrage journals were familiar with this strategy. For years suffrage journals had been recording the varied accomplishments of individual women around the world and then asserting that these individual achievements represented progress for the cause of all women.[24] As women took up arms to defend the state in the European war, editors of suffrage journals applied this same formula to the woman soldier. The editors of the Congressional Union's *Suffragist,* for example, reported in December 1914 that women were serving in the ranks of the Serbian army. They concluded that "the old argument that women are not entitled to political rights because they do not serve their country at times of war seems to be refuted in every direction by the present conflict." The editors of the National American Woman Suffrage Association's *Woman Citizen* praised the bravery of the Russian women soldiers who "shouldered arms and marched away to war" and saw service on the eastern front. "The doctrine of physical force as the essential for self-government" the editors suggested, was a rather "jaded" idea. But "if one is going to recognize it one must recognize, too, that it is a fact that, like men—rather better than some Russian men, it seems—women can fight and will fight if the call comes." Female soldiers, the editors claimed, had laid another phantom to rest concerning female citizenship.[25]

Such observations about women soldiers were not limited to the pages of suffrage journals. The *Literary Digest* and the National Rifle Association's *Arms and the Man* both quoted from a story in the London *Graphic* in the summer of 1915 that discussed individual women serving with the Russian army, admitting that "the handling of a rifle is not necessarily and exclusively a male accomplishment." Newspapers around the country picked up an International News Service series called "Women in the War" that featured information on individual women soldiers serving with various armies. The *Baltimore Sun* featured a photograph of seventeen-year-old Della Evans, a "female Paul Revere" who "notified ranchers along the Mexican border of [Pancho] Villa's raid" in the spring of 1916. The paper featured a smiling Evans next to her horse, holding her rifle, with a caption indicating that she was an "expert horsewoman as well as a dead shot" who offered her services to accompany U.S. troops as a guide and interpreter. The *Delineator* featured a story in 1916 on Irish women volunteers in the recent Irish rebellion who had been "on the firing line from the first to last day." These Irish women "could throw hand grenades; they understood the use of bombs; in fact, they seemed to understand as much of the business of warfare as their men" and worked "on terms of easy equality" for a national cause that belonged to women as much as it did to men. The *Delineator* placed a Russian woman soldier on its January 1918 cover with the caption "Her All for Russia." The Russian women's regiment known as the "Battalion of Death" represented "the very peak of what has been happening to women during the Great War," wrote Honore Willsie, managing editor of the magazine. "A stock argument against women having the vote always has been that women can not fight for their country. The Battalion of Death has answered that argument."[26]

Another strategy used by suffrage supporters was to turn the fighting-for-voting argument on its head. This tactic was particularly potent after the United States entered the war in April 1917 and policies and social pressures focused on conformity through patriotic support of the war effort. "Slackers" who did not support the United States and the war were suspect. The *Woman Citizen* featured a poem by Alice Foley titled "In the Subway" in November 1917 that made this point clearly:

> Six fat slackers sat so smug,
> Behind their papers slinking,
> While a tired shop-girl "strap-hung" above
> Was thinking, thinking, thinking—
>
> If six fat slackers have the right to vote
> Because they can carry a gun,
> Should the six fat slackers still have the vote
> When they *will not* carry one?[27]

Such arguments floated uneasily among the complex coalition of advocates for women's rights, many of whom were opposed to the war and to militarism in general. Members of the Woman's Peace Party believed that when a state placed military authority above civil rights, women would have no place in it. The preamble to the party's 1915 constitution indicted war because it resulted in "poverty-stricken widows and orphans" and "maimed and invalided men." Jane Addams believed that war reduced women to noncitizens by curtailing civil liberties and through mass violence, including rape, rather than enhancing civic possibilities. Emma Goldman and other pacifists who braved the "legal terror" of wartime home-front restrictions on civil liberties experienced this loss of civic identity. Settlement workers in New York formed the Henry Street Settlement House Anti-Preparedness Committee to publicize their opposition to a militarized state for both men and women as Europe went to war.[28]

State and military policy makers who supported preparedness for and participation in the world war created a differently gendered definition of the "bullets for ballots" argument. Historian Kathleen Kennedy draws on the work of Barbara Steinson and argues that policy makers increasingly identified women's citizenship with "patriotic motherhood" at the same time that they emphasized men's duties as soldiers. In the debates about military preparedness, and especially after the United States enacted the draft in May 1917, "loyal mothers" were those who supported the war and were willing to send their sons to fight. They were not themselves combatants but were citizens by virtue of their role as mothers of soldiers.[29] Theodore Roosevelt, as Kennedy notes, believed that men "who refused military service forfeited their roles as husbands" and therefore Protectors and citizens "because they exposed their families to violence." Roosevelt also vilified women who opposed war, "because their misguided pacifism exposed other women to sexual abuse." Kathleen Dalton notes that Roosevelt characterized them as "women who plead for peace without daring even to protest against the infamous wrongs, the infamies worse than death which their sisters in France and Belgium have suffered."[30] This argument co-opted maternalist feminist discourse about women's suitability for citizenship because of their gender at the same time that it demonized women who continued to claim that mothers stood for peace, not war. With the crackdown on civil liberties during the war, as Kennedy demonstrates, women opposed to war were vulnerable to prosecution as "disloyal mothers and scurrilous citizens."[31]

Antisuffragists also reinforced the links between manly military service and voting in the war years. John J. Vertrees, an antisuffrage lawyer in Tennessee, claimed in a 1916 speech that the onset of the war exploded the Progressive Era hopes for an end to militarism and strongly reestablished the links between military service and voting.[32] "If then the time has not come when swords should be beaten into plowshares, and spears into pruning hooks—and it has not; if government is based on force—and it is; if women cannot 'bear arms'—and they cannot—our *political* institutions should preserve their ancient framework; should continue to recognize the differences and inequalities of *sex*. The woman's ballot," Vertrees concluded, "is a 'blank-cartridge' ballot."[33] Members of the National Association Opposed to Woman Suffrage agreed with Vertrees. In the pages of their journal, the *Woman Patriot*, editors decried the links between women's soldiering and claims for the vote. Victory in war and safety at home depended instead, they believed, on "virility" and "man-power." In a manifesto published in April 1918 the association asserted that members stood for "*balanced* social organization," the "exaltation of womanhood and motherhood against the *imitation-of-man* movement," and "a strong and safe suffrage, based on *man-power*, the deciding factor in the defense of the nation and the enforcement of law."[34]

These debates about the relationship of women to the state and military service and the nature of citizenship were in play and in process as the women of this study made their claims for participation in the military and in service to the state. And as the next chapter illustrates, they would also make their claims within a specific discourse about violence against women on the home front and the war front.

2. Gender and Violence

*Context and Experience
in the Era of the World War*

While much which reaches us cannot be confirmed and certain
horrors may have been exaggerated . . . enough has been confirmed
beyond the shadow of a doubt.
—Jane Addams, May 1916

Women nurses, physicians, and women-at-arms claimed a place within the U.S. military during the First World War as part of their definitions of full female citizenship. They also sought to transform the military and the state in ways that would address violence against women. They did so at a time of particular concerns about violence against women and also in a continuing cultural climate that assigned blame to women themselves for the violence they faced or protested. Many women had experienced or knew someone who had experienced violence at home or gendered discrimination in a hostile workplace environment. Information coming from the war front, a field of violence itself, also included specific information about violence against women, with accounts of rape by invading and occupying forces and workplace harassment of workers in wartime service. This information and these realities had a profound effect on the way that the women of this study shaped their strategies for entering and transforming the military. This chapter will examine the context of violence on the home front and the war front as an additional framework for the case studies of women-at-arms, women physicians, and women military nurses that follow.

The Context of Violence on the Home Front

Violence against women in the form of sexual assault, rape, murder, domestic violence, violence in the streets, and a hostile workplace environment has been a means that some men have used to control women's economic, social, and civic equality and indeed their very lives. In the period before and during the First World War women encountered violence on the home front through direct experience, the experience of family and friends, and information publicized by some reform organizations. Violence against women was also a part of the daily press and popular culture of the era. Although class, race, age, and occupation made a significant difference, most women faced violence or potential violence in a variety of ways on a daily basis or knew of those who faced it.

In the years before the First World War, campaigns opposed to violence against women were part of many organized movements: the social purity campaign to end "white slavery" and to raise the age of consent for young women, the antilynching campaign, the temperance crusade that focused on alcohol as a cause of wife beating, and strikes by women workers such as members of the International Ladies' Garment Workers' Union and the Women's Trade Union League. In most of these campaigns women targeted men, such as factory floor managers, who were outside of their own families as the perpetrators of violence. But there were exceptions. For example, Leslie K. Dunlap demonstrates that southern labor and African American activists worked with white women who were members of the Woman's Christian Temperance Union to reform rape laws in age-of-consent campaigns from 1885 to 1910. WCTU members focused on the sexual behavior of "respectable" native-born white men and boys. Yet Elizabeth Pleck and Linda Gordon emphasize that women who worked to challenge domestic and family violence were often considered suspect and their own respectability questioned. As Cynthia Enloe points out, this "undermining the credibility of the messenger" trivialized violence against women and discouraged antiviolence activism.[1]

In addition, public discussion often stigmatized the women who had experienced violence, as Karen Dubinsky's study of rape in Ontario, Canada, from the 1880s through the 1920s demonstrates. In the United States, as Mary Odem illustrates, the sexuality of young women was increasingly policed by the state as the First World War approached, and young women were blamed for sexual violence. Rape law in the United States reflected these cultural practices and assumptions, holding a woman's behavior as the standard in defining whether rape occurred.[2]

Although race and class have both been key determinants of the experience of violence, all women faced harm most often from "boyfriends, neighbors, fathers, and male relatives," not the mysterious stranger, white slaver, or black rapist that were the icons of popular representations of rape. And contrary to the dominant cultural script of rape that placed white women in danger from men of color, women of color faced sexual harm from white men in community, workplace, and home and from men of color as well.[3]

Murder was on the increase in the years before the United States entered the First World War in 1917, part of an extended rise that alarmed many sorts of observers. The homicide rate for 1911–16 was 8.6 persons per 100,000, a level almost double that of twenty years earlier. A detailed study of the period 1914–16 by statistical consultant Frederick Hoffman showed that women were 20.1 percent of murder victims. Like male victims, women were at greatest risk when they were ages twenty-five to thirty-four.[4] Members of the press placed this "homicide problem" before the American public in a variety of ways, from dry but powerful statistical presentations by experts like Hoffman to lurid coverage of the details of murders and extensive reporting on murder trials. Anecdotal evidence suggests that newspaper editors may have highlighted violence against women by reporting on a higher percentage of women murder victims than the average. From July 1914 until March 1917, for example, roughly the period of the European war before the U.S. entry, the *New York Times* covered 428 murders around the United States and in the state of New York.[5] Of these murders, 139 (32.4 percent) were reports of the murder of women. Whereas women made up one-fifth of the homicides nationally, they were almost one-third of the reported murder victims in the *Times*.

Two legendary murderers of women, Bluebeard and Jack the Ripper, resurfaced during this period in popular representations of real-life crimes. The Bluebeard of European folk legend killed a succession of wives and left their bodies in a forbidden room in his castle. In May 1916 Hungarian police discovered the "work of a modern Bluebeard" in the home of a soldier who had died while serving at the Serbian front. Bela Kiss, a tinsmith before he went to war, told the owner of the house he rented that "machinery that could not be replaced" was stored in his rooms, and "under no conditions was he to enter."[6] But the owner, Martin Greschinsky, eventually decided to check on the rooms. When he saw "seven, 5-foot tin covered, sealed cases," he decided to open them, thinking they might contain precious gasoline. But as Greschinsky opened one of the containers, he smelled "the corpse odor" and called police. They discovered the body of a woman with the "cord by which she had been choked to death" still around her neck.[7] Police eventually opened all seven containers and found a woman's body in each one. Investigators believed that Kiss had decoyed scores of women "by marriage advertisements" after which he took their money "on marriage promises" and then killed them. Police discovered "packages of love letters from all parts of the world, including the United States," and were working on leads from the files of scores of women who had been missing, some for more than ten years. The Hungarian Bluebeard's plan had apparently worked very well. Although rarely employed, "he spent money so generously that he was known generally as 'The American Uncle.'"[8]

Half a world away a murderer dubbed the "New Jack the Ripper" was killing on the streets of New York City. Although this "Jack" did not restrict himself to murdering prostitutes as did the Whitechapel legend of London's East End some thirty years earlier, the public and the press used the name "Jack the Ripper" to evoke the popular images of the serial rapist and killer of women. Two children, Lenora Cohn and Charles Murray, were both killed by someone who slashed their bodies with a knife in the hallway of their tenement homes in the spring of 1915. These attacks inspired a series of reports about the "Ripper" and even copycat crimes. The stories expanded from the slashing deaths of children to include sexual danger and violence against women. Seven young women accused two men of chasing them through the streets with knives.[9] Beatrice Hunter was "dragged into a hallway" of her apartment house by a man thought to be the Ripper but was saved by her mother.[10] A crowd in New York City beat Charles Keyer on the street because they suspected him of being "Jack the Ripper."[11] And there were two copycat Ripper scares in White Plains, New York, and in New Jersey. Police arrested two young women for "sending threatening letters to scare neighbors" that were supposedly from the "Ripper."[12] At least ten suspects were arrested for crimes that spring, but none were prosecuted. "Jack the Ripper" was an available stereotype that mirrored and expressed fears of sexual danger and death for women.[13] Even when officials tried to separate the use of the Ripper legend from the New York murders, popular insistence on the myth surged around the reports. Statistician Frederick Hoffman was still trying to demystify the cases in his national *Homicide Record for 1915* published in December 1916, more than a year and a half after the murders.[14]

Representations of rape, murder, and violence against women in popular culture were not limited to the resurrection of Bluebeard and Jack the Ripper stories. Elizabeth Cerabino-Hess has found that feature films from 1911 to 1920 contained "ten times the occurrence of rape and attempted rape scenes" than films of the 1920s. Her analysis of the *American Film Institute Catalog* provides a listing of 70 rapes and 191 attempted rapes in silent feature films for the decade. Some of the violence against women on stage and screen was politicized, part of the representation of rape in the Progressive Era by reformers and also by apologists for lynching. Productions such as George Scarborough's film *The Lure* (1914) presented the audience with scenes from "white slavery" and contained a message supporting the antiprostitution social purity movement. The incredibly popular 1914 stage and screen productions based on Reginald Wright Kauffman's *House of Bondage* (1910) also followed the white-slavery theme. And stage and screen productions of Thomas Dixon's novel *The Clansmen* (1906) that later became D. W. Griffith's *Birth of a Nation*

(1915) reinforced the southern construction of white womanhood vulnerable to black male lust and the necessity for vigilante "justice."[15] The numerous stage and screen adaptations of Robert Louis Stevenson's *Strange Case of Dr. Jekyll and Mr. Hyde* (1886) explored notions of violence against women with an ever expanding story line, presenting sexual violence and, ultimately, rape, all of which were absent in explicit terms from the original Stevenson novella.

Sexual assault, lynching, and mob violence were part of a system of terror and violence targeting African American communities in the years before and during the world war. Fearful whites justified this trilogy of violence by defining African American men as rapists and African American women as sexualized Jezebels who were "asking for" sex and sexual assault, unworthy of respect or justice.[16] Rape and lynching "merged with their ideological justifications of the rapist and the prostitute," Patricia Hill Collins notes, as fearful whites used these methods of violence to maintain power and control. Glenda Gilmore asserts that in the code of the turn of the early twentieth century South, all black women "stood accused of gross immorality." And African American women also faced domestic and intimate violence from within their families and communities. They fought back in a variety of ways. Some left the South to escape what Darlene Clark Hine identifies as "sexual exploitation from inside and outside of their families and from rape and threat of rape by white as well as Black males." African American club women engaged in what Evelyn Brooks Higginbotham terms the "politics of respectability" with specific campaigns against lynching and for religious, educational, and professional goals to counter negative sexual stereotypes and the violence that resulted.[17]

Ida B. Wells and other activists exposed the lies at the center of the rape and lynching myth. They identified economic and social success, not rape, as the real reasons for the lynching of African American men, and as Rosalyn Terborg-Penn notes, they also publicized the fact that African American women were being murdered.[18] There were 17 recorded cases of lynching of African American women from 1909 to 1918 and 573 cases of men during this same period.[19] The National Association of Colored Women and the Federation of Negro Women's Clubs publicized the 1918 case of the murder of Mary Turner. Turner, who was pregnant, protested the lynching of her husband. The lynch mob tortured her and cut the fetus from her body before burning her alive.[20] And in some cases "it was not the rape of a white woman, but the sexual assault of a black woman," that was the catalyst for the lynching of African American men. Male relatives' and community members' quest for vengeance for the rape of daughters, sisters, and neighbors often ended in their own lynching.[21]

Some women experienced the violence of unwanted sexual advances and a hostile environment from male coworkers and supervisors on factory floors, in office corridors, in domestic service in private homes, and at the hospital bedside.[22] A 1910 congressional investigation of conditions for working women concluded that women in the service industries including factory and restaurant work, domestic service, and home nursing were most vulnerable to gender-based discrimination and a hostile workplace.[23] Susan Reverby finds that professional advice manuals for this period urged nurses in private service to avoid taking positions caring for men in hotels and to reject "the advances of a patient's unscrupulous husband" at all costs. The relationship between nurses and male patients has always been "charged with sexual associations," as Barbara Melosh has noted, and has engendered a "long tradition of jokes, popular fiction, and pornography" as well as nurses' vulnerability to harassment at the workplace.[24] The goal of a 1912 International Ladies' Garment Workers' Union strike at the Kalamazoo, Michigan, corset company was the dismissal of supervisors for creating a hostile and sexualized workplace.[25] In a letter to Rose Schneiderman about the strike, activist Pauline Newman wrote that "you know as well as I that there is not a factory today where the same immoral condition does not exist! . . . [E]very one of the men will talk to the girls, take advantage of them if the girls will let them. The foreman and superintendent will flirt with the girls. . . . It is nothing new for those who know it exists everywhere." The Women's Trade Union League's Rose Pastor Stokes asserted that "there are foremen who insult and abuse girls beyond endurance." And historian Dolores Janiewski has discovered that in southern factories in the years before the war manufacturers made attempts to guard the moral purity of white women workers, but African American women tobacco workers had no protection from workplace harassment. There were some foremen, Janiewski finds, who "sought sexual favors from black women as the price of keeping their jobs."[26]

Professional women also faced gender-based "denigration" of their "competence, authority, or entitlement to the job" as they struggled to cross barriers to occupational advancement.[27] Dr. Emily Dunning Barringer, who would become a leader in American women physicians' struggle for access to military service in the world war, experienced hostilities and gender discrimination at almost every turn as a postgraduate intern at Gouverneur Hospital, the downtown New York branch of the Bellevue and Allied Hospitals, in 1903.[28] From her first assignment of catheterizing the patients on the male surgical ward (the other interns hoped for an "erotic reaction" on the part of the patients that would mean certain scandal from the waiting reporters and certain dismissal for Barringer) to the grueling sixty-hour "first call" jobs on the ambulance run and the false alarms and false rumors, Barringer held her own. Each day she battled fatigue, stress, and loss of appetite from her colleagues' active attempts to "break" her, including their scheduled barrages at her door at night. But with the support of ambulance drivers, nurses, and community members, she overcame the interns' attempts to get her to leave in disgrace, took her turn in leadership positions, and completed her internship with distinction.

Like the marchers in the Washington, D.C., suffrage parade of 1913, many women's occupations took them "into the streets," where they faced danger going to and from work at various hours of the day and night. Chicago physician Anna Blount told her audience at the 1910 National American Woman Suffrage Association annual convention in Washington, D.C., that medical women wanted the vote for protection against the violence of the streets. "We need police protection," she said, "and a city that is well lighted and safe for women." A few years earlier when the "hunters of women became unusually active and several respectable women were in the early hours of the evening hunted to their death and murdered," the police commissioner told the women of Chicago to be inside after eight o'clock or to have a male escort. For Blount and her colleagues, this advice was no solution. "Imagine when the telephone rings for a woman doctor to attend some critical case that she shall be required either to get a male escort or remain at home!" Blount believed that a far better solution was to make the city safe, to take back the streets, and, as activists sixty years later would phrase it, to take back the night. Blount pointed out that this issue was a problem not just for women physicians but also for "nurses and many others." A woman who clerked in a Los Angeles department store wrote to *Harper's Bazaar* in 1908 about her own experiences with the dangers of the streets. "I don't think there was one evening during that time when I worked in that store that I went home unmolested," she wrote. "I have walked block after block through the business part of the city with a man at my side questioning me as to where I lived, and if I would not like to go to dinner, how I was going to spend the evening, etc."[29] One study reported that an African American woman in the South in the decade of the First World War "found herself in danger of being attacked whenever she walked down a country road" and that the "poorest type of white man feels at liberty to accost her and follow her and force her."[30]

Women workers on strike who took to the streets to protest difficult working conditions and poor wages also found themselves targets of violence and vulnerable to charges that they were "women of the streets," or prostitutes, a label they shared with participants in the suffrage parade of 1913. When women in the textile "white trades" struck New York's Triangle Shirtwaist Company in 1909, managers of the company hired prostitutes to "infiltrate the picket lines in an attempt to sully the strikers' reputations by association." Many women strikers in the 1910s were beaten and struck by police officers and the company guards, or "detectives," hired to break strikes with billy clubs, iron bars, and fists. One strategy to combat this violence against working women was for wealthy women (called the "mink brigades") and college women to patrol the strike areas and monitor abuse, hoping that their social prominence and the power of their families would protect them as they tried to deter violence against striking women.[31]

Policy makers debated the question of the use of "legitimate" violence during the years surrounding the war. The military, National Guard, and local police forces all had their jurisdictions. But in battles against workers, corporate security forces, hired strikebreakers, and "detectives" like the Pinkertons were all part of the arsenal used by corporations to quell labor activism and strikes.[32] Workers and political activists faced violence from local and federal law enforcement and from strikebreaking teams. And the extralegal violence of rape and lynching was a constant threat for African Americans. As the United States embraced imperialism and colonialism after the Spanish-American War, Americans debated how and when force and martial law were justified. And as the United States observed the war in Europe, advocates of "preparedness" wanted all young American men to be trained in the use of firearms and military drill as citizen soldiers. As Christopher Capozzola demonstrates, national leaders were negotiating questions of the use of political and physical force in a number of ways, including the separation of "vigilance and vigilantism." They defined vigilance (including "citizen policing, antilabor vigilance, moral vigilance, and racial vigilance") as positive and patriotic, and denounced vigilantism as lawless and illegitimate.[33]

This policy debate often focused on who could use guns in a legitimate way and included the categories of race, gender, and relationship to the military. Congress reacted to the expanding Mexican Revolution in 1912 by giving President Taft executive power to "forbid American firms from exporting arms to countries where he found they promoted violence." Taft used this power to ban the export of firearms to Mexico.[34] Yet the United States had an expanding military presence in Latin America and the Pacific and would soon be involved in the world war. In 1917 military leaders instructed American troops occupying the Philippines to enforce new regulations that prevented Filipinos from possessing any firearms. American citizens in the area were under no such restrictions.[35]

Federal and state troops also used force against American citizens inside the country. The Colorado mine fields were the site of "domestic violence and disturbance" throughout 1913–14 when the Colorado Fuel and Iron Company brought in strikebreaking "detectives" from the Baldwin-Felts Agency and equipped them with more than nine thousand firearms to try to break the United Mine Workers union.[36] Colorado governor Elisha Ammons called in the Colorado National Guard in October 1913,[37] and "armed clashes" between workers, strikebreakers, and soldiers became "routine." After the bloody Ludlow massacre in which company forces killed thirteen women and children and executed three strikers, the UMW, Colorado Federation of Labor, and Western Federation of Miners "jointly and formally called their members to arms."[38] Woodrow Wilson sent in troops in response to Governor Ammons's request. The secretary of war issued instructions to commanding officers in Colorado to disarm strikers, proclaiming that "under existing circumstances the possession of arms and ammunition by persons not in the military service of the United States tends to provoke disorder and to incite domestic violence and hinders the restoration of normal conditions of peace and good order."[39] Yet just three years later when Congress passed the National Defense Act in 1916, as we will see, members made provision for funding and arming male citizen soldiers. Could women be a part of this citizen army and take up the civic obligation to bear arms? Or would their actions be seen as illegitimate, extramilitary, and extralegal examples of nonsanctioned and dangerous use of force?

The Context of Violence on the War Front

The war in Europe presented additional information and evidence to Americans about violence, some of which was directed specifically against women. In the summer of 1914 Americans associated the rumblings of war in Europe with political intrigue and complicated diplomatic arrangements. But by the early fall the full-fledged European war also became a military conflict that involved civilians with the German invasion of neutral Belgium in August and the German army's subsequent control of northern France. Vivid reports from Belgium and France in the U.S. press and in popular English translations of French and Belgian documents highlighted the atrocities of the invaders and featured powerful accounts of physical and sexual violence against women. The *New York Times* and other newspapers and magazines across the country reported accusations that German soldiers had mutilated, raped, and killed Belgian and French civilians. Press accounts also revealed that some civilians had been taken into Germany as forced laborers for the fall harvest, whole villages had been destroyed, and thousands of refugees were in need of support after having experienced the devastation of invasion.[40] A popular summary of a special Belgian investigation published as *The Case of Belgium in the Present War* by the Macmillan Company went through three printings in September and October 1914, and an English translation of a French investigation titled *Germany's Violations of the Laws of War* soon followed.[41]

The press and public began to use the phrase "the rape of Belgium" to describe the German army's invasion, and it was much more than a metaphor. The Belgian and the later French experience drew attention to the violent impact of the war on women. Editors of the *Suffragist,* for example, reported numerous acts of rape from passages in *The Case of Belgium.*[42] One of the most familiar U.S. posters of the war linked the vulnerability of women to rape and sexual violence during the German invasion. Government officials produced "Remember Belgium" to motivate Americans to purchase bonds for the fourth Liberty Loan drive in 1918. The poster shows a brutish, armed German soldier and a young Belgian girl silhouetted against her burning and ruined village. The viewer can almost feel the cruel grip of the soldier's hand as he pulls her along. They are alone in the night, and rape seems imminent. The poster demonstrates that leaders drew on the American public's knowledge of and assumptions about the use of rape in the German invasion of Belgium.

During and after the First World War there was an active debate about the veracity of these wartime-atrocity accounts. Scholars emphasized that Allied governments used anti-German propaganda to make the enemy into a barbaric, inhuman "other" who deserved punishment and death. In this and other conflicts, they argued, soldiers and civilians alike must distance themselves from the enemy, see the enemy as less than human, in order to sanction and participate in war.[43] And, certainly, the reaction to the German invasion of Belgium became an important motivation for the United States to enter the conflict. Although much of the subsequent analysis of the German invasion downplayed the information about rape, and though it is essential to see the complexities and functions of propaganda in this context, from our vantage point at the beginning of the twenty-first century it is difficult to discount the information that women in the path of invading armies suffered sexual assault. The experiences of women in Okinawa, Korea, Pakistan, Vietnam, Bangladesh, Bosnia, Rwanda, Iraq, Sudan, and other locations of invasion and occupation attest to the prevalence of rape as an act of power and conquest by military units.[44] Not all soldiers and not all armies commit rape. The specific historical context, the cultural issues, and the nature of

Ellsworth Young, "Remember Belgium" (1918). (National
Archives, Washington, D.C.)

the conflict all have an influence on whether soldiers rape women in the
path of their invasions or occupations. As Catharine A. MacKinnon observes, wartime rapes are enacted "by *some* men against *certain* women for
specific reasons."[45] For this study it is important that the women physicians
who prepared to provide medical services for women in the wake of war's
violence and the women-at-arms who sought to protect themselves on the
home front did so in the context of a great deal of information and discus-

sion about wartime rape, information that they considered legitimate and worthy of responsive action.

Several historians have recently reexamined and reinstated the accounts of the rape of Belgian and French women in the First World War into the historical record.[46] After a century of additional evidence, we can see that many of the characteristics that scholars and policy makers identify as being conducive to wartime rape apply to the conditions and beliefs of European and Western society at the time of the First World War. Wartime rape may be used as a tool to "terrorize civilian populations and to induce civilians to flee their homes and villages."[47] Wartime rape may often occur when women and their sexual behavior are the symbols of men's honor, when women are considered the "vessels of community honor" and the men of their families and communities are assigned by gender conventions to be their protectors.[48] This was certainly the case in the years before and during the First World War. Interestingly, the body of international agreements concerning wartime conduct in place at the time of the war, The Hague Convention Regulations of 1907, did not use the term *rape* specifically, but affirmed the necessity for respecting family *honor* along with life and property. They reflected this vision of women's sexuality as related to family and community reputation.[49]

War heightens ideas about community and national honor. The "conquest" of women by enemy soldiers who rape them can be a way of humiliating the men of their communities and nation, preventing them from fulfilling their role as protectors. Rape then bolsters the masculinity of the victors and solidifies their conquest and domination while emasculating the men of the defeated nation.[50] Margaret H. Darrow observes that the "gendered terms in which war was imagined" in First World War France included both victory and defeat. "In victory," she writes, "the men were to march home and the women were to cheer. In defeat, the men were killed and the women were raped."[51]

Some American women also found evidence of the rape of women civilians by invading and occupying soldiers in the birth of "war babies" or "*Boche* babies" in 1915 and beyond. Information about these pregnancies and births circulated in print and in private and was part of the national and international debate about the consequences of the invasion. "War babies" were featured in the French and British press in early 1915,[52] and the American press soon followed.[53] Readers in the United States encountered press coverage of the situation of women in France and Belgium and on the Russian front who had been raped and impregnated by invading soldiers. When presenting these women's plight the editors of the *New York Times*, for example, emphasized that wartime rape victimized guiltless women and that the state should be responsible for supporting them and their children.

"War is also the father of many babies," the *Times* editors wrote in April 1915, but nations have "hitherto encouraged the cause" and "left the consequences to women."[54]

The "war babies" debate and the other accounts of invasion alerted and sensitized American women to the question of sexual danger and violence against women in wartime. In May 1915, for example, Jane Addams asserted that American women knew what was happening to women in the war zone and were acting on that knowledge. Addams was on her way to Europe for a meeting of the International Congress of Women to represent the newly formed Woman's Peace Party. After discussing the reports of German soldiers raping women in occupied territories and the "war baby" situation, Addams insisted that wartime made armies and the nation a danger to women, not their protectors. "So long as a State, through the exigencies of war, is obliged to place military authority above all civil rights, women can have within it no worthy place." She believed that all of the Progressive Era's gains in women's health and women's rights had been swept away by the invading armies. Yet the wider technology of communication and women's own networks were spreading the word and educating women about the situation so they could work together to change it. "All the censorship which the ingenious minds of military commanders have been able to evolve have [*sic*] not kept from women a very good idea of the actual state of things. While much which reaches us cannot be confirmed and certain horrors may have been exaggerated . . . ," she insisted, "enough has been confirmed beyond the shadow of a doubt." For Addams, the result was clear. "Women are availing themselves of the wider public knowledge concerning the reaction of war upon women and children," she maintained, "in order to make a clear indictment against war as such." The answer for Addams was a concerted international effort on the part of women to end militarism and to restore and improve women's rights from these devastating losses. Women involved in international suffrage and peace networks before and during the war, as Leila J. Rupp's work indicates, engaged in a discussion about wartime rape that had the potential for unifying women against war.[55]

Other information from the war front suggested that women workers faced violence in the form of a hostile wartime workplace. In 1916, a year before the United States entered the war, Ellen Newbold La Motte published a stark and critical memoir of her experiences as a Red Cross nurse in a French military hospital in Belgium close to the fighting front. Her account of wartime nursing, *The Backwash of War: The Human Wreckage of the Battlefield as Witnessed by an American Hospital Nurse*, emphasized the brutality of war that turned men into machines at the command of states that did not value their lives. She also described the many repugnant characters in the hospital ward in which she worked and her view of the nature of men at war. "Much ugliness is churned up in the wake of mighty, moving forces," she wrote in the introduction. "War . . . stirs up the slime in the shallows, and this is the Backwash of War. It is very ugly." Popular demand for the book resulted in several editions in 1916. But La Motte's forthright observations were too much for British authorities. They banned the book as detrimental to the war effort soon after.[56]

Two of La Motte's chapters stood out as warning beacons for women, illuminating her view of men's attitudes about and treatment of women in wartime. The first was the chapter titled "La patrie reconnaissante" (The Grateful Nation) written in December 1915. Here La Motte cut through the sentimental picture of the long-suffering and gallant wounded soldier and told the story of an offensive, brutish French *poilu* (infantryman) named Marius who was dying in her hospital. He was foul, disrespectful, and lewd and insulted patients and staff alike. When a nurse (presumably La Motte) came to cover him with a blanket, the dying soldier "attempted to clutch her hand, to encircle her with his weak, delirious, amorous arms. She dodged swiftly, and directed an orderly to cover him with the fallen blankets." With that the soldier "laughed in glee, a fiendish, feeble, shrieking laugh. 'Have nothing to do with a woman who is diseased!' he shouted. 'Never! Never! Never!'"[57] Some soldier-patients such as Marius, she was telling readers, attempted sexual advances and, when spurned, challenged the character of the woman in question with the timeworn accusation of sexual promiscuity. For many women readers, it was a familiar plot indeed.

In "Women and Wives," written in May 1916, La Motte used bold sarcasm to illustrate the objectification of women and the sexual danger and blame they faced during the war from the men of both sides of the conflict. In the hospital ward one day the recuperating soldiers brought out photographs of their wives: "from weather beaten sacks, from shabby boxes, from under pillows, and the nurse must see them all," the "working-class wives of working-class men—the soldiers of the trenches." For these men, La Motte wrote, their wives signified everything associated with home and were more important to them than the supposed heroism of the front. They were the "connecting link between the soldier and his life at home." That is why, she said, the military did not allow a wife to come to the front with talk of home-front problems that might pull a soldier away from the military. "She herself must be censored, not permitted to come." But then La Motte noted an important distinction. *Women* may come to the front, but not *wives*. "There is a difference. In war, it is very great. . . . [T]here are plenty of women, first and last, Better ones for the officers, naturally, just as the officers' mess is of better quality than that of the common soldiers. But always there are plenty of women," she wrote. "Never wives, who mean responsibility, but just women, who only mean distraction and amusements, just as food and wine." Whereas wives were forbidden, "women are winked at, because they cheer and refresh the troops."[58]

The male surgeons and hospital staff, La Motte noted, all visited Belgian women for sex at night after displaying photographs of their wives by day. The Belgian women were "decent girls at the beginning of the war," La Motte reported, her words dripping with sarcasm. "But you know women, how they run after men, especially when the men wear uniforms. . . . It's not the men's fault that most of the women in the War Zone are ruined," she continued. The women brought it all on themselves. Compare this situation, she asked the reader, with the fate of women in the path of invading German armies. "The conquering armies just ruined all the women they could get hold of. Any one will tell you that. *Ces sales Bosches* [Those dirty Germans]." The difference was that "over there, in the invaded districts, the Germans forced those girls. Here on this side, the girls cajoled the men until they gave in."[59] La Motte's indictment of the hostile wartime workplace was also a critique of the blaming of women for the hostility and sexualized violence against them.

* * *

Representations of violence on the home front and the war front emphasized the vulnerability and danger women faced in both locations. If women were to participate in war, could they also confront the specific violence that war brought to women? By doing so, women activists would confront powerful notions about masculinity and the military and would call into question the gendered convention of the male Protector. And as women challenging violence against women, they would be vulnerable to charges that they were "public women" who had invited and caused the violence against them, women who "deserved it." As the following case studies will demonstrate, women-at-arms, women nurses, and women physicians called for expansive female citizenship that would include military service and also safety as a civic right.

3. "Whether We Vote or Not— We Are Going to Shoot"

Women and Armed Defense on the Home Front

If American women are ever called upon to defend their homes, their children, and themselves, they will not be helpless as were the Belgian women.

—Lurana Sheldon Ferris of the Women's Defense Club, 1916

[Women] are in the munitions shops, in the mines, in the field, and in various branches of manual and military service. Why not the battlefield?

—June Haughton, markswoman, 1916

As Europe became embroiled in the horrors of occupation and trench warfare after the autumn of 1914, Americans watched and debated the question of their own military readiness. This debate about preparedness included much more than a discussion of armaments and "manpower." Within the preparedness rhetoric was a stark discussion of some of the core issues of gender relationships and the gender conventions of the Protector and the Protected. From this perspective, some Americans believed that the "failure" of Belgian men and men in northern France to repel invading German armies led directly to rape and violence against women in these regions. And as the conflict progressed, there were increasing reports of soldiers who reacted to the horrors of the trenches with the "effeminate" male hysteria of "soldier's heart" or "shell shock." These men had also "failed" as Protectors. Would this happen in the United States, or were American men "man enough" to fulfill their roles as Protectors and male citizens? On the home front, some women claimed the citizen's obligation to defend the state as part of the fulfillment of complete citizenship, and some sought to bear arms to do so. What would happen if they became the Protectors rather than the Protected? Others wondered if the wartime conditioning of soldiers to use "violent solutions" would mean increased violence on the home front as a result. Could the women who had taken on the role of Protectors wield the weapons of war in peacetime to defend themselves against violent behavior that men had learned in soldiering? This chapter will examine some women's claims to armed military service and also self-defense as part of more complete female citizenship and a new construction of violence against women on the war front and home front. It will also consider the gendered categories of Protector and Protected that they disrupted.

Masculinity and Military Preparedness

In her study of the impact of the German invasion and occupation of Belgium and northern France in 1914 and after, Ruth Harris demonstrates that one effect of the rape of Belgian and French women by enemy soldiers was the humiliation of the men of their communities. By "failing" in their role as protectors of women, the men of these regions became "impotent victims rather than . . . heroes defending hearth and home." Racialized discussions of the invasion "voiced the fear of French male impotence" and the ultimate conquest of France by virile Germans.[1] Harris reads in these representations a perceived contrast between Germany as a masculine nation of aggressive power and Belgium and France as passive, feminized states.

For many, the news of Allied soldiers suffering from "shell shock" or "soldier's heart" underscored the supposed failure of masculinity in the wartime generation. Soon after the war began, British medical officers began to report that men in the trenches were suffering from "mental breakdown" and symptoms of hysteria such as numbness, amnesia, the inability to speak, uncontrollable nightmares, crying, and shaking. By 1915 this "war neurosis" created a medical emergency due to shortages of facilities and staff for treating soldiers suffering from its effects. The next year medical officers estimated that cases of shell shock accounted for 40 percent of casualties at the front. As Elaine Showalter illustrates, many believed that shell shock was nothing short of a failure of men to be manly, to "bear up" under the conditions of war. The threat of "wholesale mental breakdown among men," she writes, was a "shocking contrast to the heroic visions" of soldierly masculinity. Military and medical personnel struggled to understand "soldier's heart" in the context of psychology but were influenced by ideas of masculinity and gender roles. Many associated male war neurosis with weakness, effeminacy, or homosexuality—everything that was not "masculine" in soldiers or their behavior. When research could not demonstrate an organic cause, Showalter writes, "many military authorities refused to treat victims as disabled and maintained that they should not be given pensions or honorable discharges." Some suggested that shell-shock sufferers should be shot for cowardice.[2]

This fear of demasculinization was particularly acute because "hysteria" had been a "woman's disease" in the generations before the First World War in Britain and the United States. When men exhibited symptoms of "nervousness," Michael Kimmel notes, medical and social commentators agreed that it was a sign of effeminacy to be cured by bracing visits to the western frontier or other masculine endeavors.[3] If the "Great War" gave men the chance to be manly heroes, it also raised the stakes for proving masculinity.[4] And if that masculinity was vulnerable, as Kimmel suggests, having to be proved over and over again with prescribed behavior, the "failure" of men in Belgium and northern France to repel invasion and "soldier's heart" suggested massive, visible failures on the part of the male citizen Protectors. That sense of failure, as Sandra M. Gilbert has demonstrated in her analysis of literary responses to the war, lasted well beyond the Armistice at the conclusion of the conflict.[5]

In the United States some who observed these "failures" of European masculinity worked to make certain that America would have a record of virility, not impotence. They linked masculinity, military training and service, and active citizenship in the "preparedness" movement. The most prominent supporters of this movement were Theodore Roosevelt and the army's General Leonard Wood. In their view, the primary purpose for military training and preparedness in the United States was the reinvigoration of manhood in the nation. This drive was part of a decades-long preoccupation with proving and shoring up masculinity in crisis. In this context, the fear of masculine failure at the beginning of the European war took on a heightened urgency, and those who offered the solution of military training for manliness became a vocal part of the debate. Roosevelt linked masculinity to citizenship and military service in his call for the training of citizen soldiers and increased military preparedness in the United States as Europe went to war. In his book *America and the World War* (1915), Roosevelt advocated the strengthening of the army and navy and also military training for every young man in the country. "No man is really fit to be the free citizen of a free republic unless he is able to bear arms and at need to serve with efficiency in the efficient army of the republic," he wrote. America's future depended on the citizen soldier who would not shrink from his manly duty.[6]

General Leonard Wood formulated concrete plans for training these citizen soldiers as chief of staff of the army from 1910 to 1914 and commander of the Army Department of the East from Governors Island, New York, from 1914 to 1917. Wood began his military career as a contract surgeon on the western frontier, was a Rough Rider with Roosevelt in the Spanish-American War, and then served as governor-general of Cuba and as military governor in the Philippines.[7] Wood took one side in the debate about military preparedness and the role of the citizen soldier that had been of concern to military planners since the American Revolution. Rather than favoring a large, professional standing army, Wood had faith in the male citizen soldier. He urged that a large-scale program of rifle practice be implemented throughout the country and advocated such instruction in arms as part of the public school education of young men.[8] He believed that young men should then undertake a two-year term of military service after which they would become part of a large national military reserve, making the army a "great mill through which the population is passed and trained to bear arms."[9] Wood spearheaded a program that created summer military training camps for college-age men in 1913, 1914, and 1915. The popularity of the camps led to a greatly expanded program that enrolled other men wishing to prepare themselves in the use of arms and the military life. The core camp was located in Plattsburg, New York, and expanded to camps throughout the country from 1915 to 1917. This Plattsburg Movement, as the training camps came to be called, was an important expression of the remasculinization deemed so necessary by many leaders and reflected in the popular culture of the period.

This aspect of the preparedness movement often focused on rifle and pistol training for citizen soldiers who would then have the power and skills to defend the nation and their communities. Gun practice, its advocates proclaimed, was "a man-maker" and would help to convert the present generation of "effeminates" who would "surprise and shock" America's military fathers, George Washington and Ulysses S. Grant, if they could see them in their current weak condition.[10] In this view, expertise in marksmanship would enable men to recommit to their role as Protectors. And it would save the United States from the embarrassing "failures" of Belgian and French men should the war expand across the Atlantic or should America enter the European conflict.

Women, Military Preparedness, and Self-Defense

Erman J. Ridgway, editor of the *Delineator,* one of the most popular mainstream women's magazines of the period, introduced the "woman question" in military preparedness in the magazine's February 1915 issue. Ridgway believed that the United States needed to strengthen its military and train a citizen army to avoid Belgium's fate. The "rape of Belgium" was indeed on his mind when, in addition to his call for military instruction for boys and young men in the public schools, he cautiously introduced a proposal for training young women as well. "Why is it necessary to leave our homes defenseless?" he wrote. "Why can not women be taught to take care of themselves just as men are?" Hoping that his readers would not consider him "a wholly uncivilized brute," he continued, "I know some very wonderful women who tramp and fish and hunt as well as any man. What's the harm? What do you think of the whole idea?" Invoking the "frontier heritage" of America ("pioneer women all knew how to defend themselves") and lauding the physical benefits of marching, drilling, and shooting for women's health, Ridgway called for readers' opinions on the proposal.[11] The essay was illustrated at the left margin with an endless column of schoolgirls in military formation shouldering guns, complemented on the right margin by a column of schoolboys in the same attitude.

Ridgway, writing six months after the start of the war in Europe, based his article on the assertion that women should be taught "to take care of themselves" and set the discussion in the context of the invasion of Belgium. Armed women would be empowered to resist physical and sexual assault. Although Ridgway did not specifically state it, this proposal could be read as an implicit acknowledgement that American men might not be able to fulfill their roles as Protectors. By the June issue of the *Delineator*, 204 readers had responded. According to Ridgway's summary, their responses were split almost evenly, with 97 readers in favor of his proposition and 107 opposed. Those who wrote in favor of his proposal for military training for young women and men favored the implications for equal training while expressing the hope that militarism and war could be avoided. Most of the women who wrote letters against the proposition opposed it regardless of the gender of those to be trained. Many of those in opposition made it clear that they supported the proposal of equal physical training and opportunity for women and men but resisted the militarism embodied in the use of guns.[12]

The *Delineator* article was only one expression of the debate concerning women's self-defense in the context of national defense and preparedness in this period. At rifle ranges and armories around the country in the war years women joined existing rifle clubs and formed their own rifle and gun organizations in what contemporaries considered dramatic numbers. Thousands joined women's paramilitary organizations designed to promote women's defense and military skills. Many of these women were motivated by a belief in the importance of women's equal rights and the need for equal opportunities with men. Their activities were part of the negotiation for women's full citizenship rights in the context of the suffrage campaign. They hoped to become an official part of the citizens' preparedness army or the

Illustration for Erman J. Ridgway, "Militant Pacifism" (1915).

military itself and in so doing would perform the citizen's obligation to defend the state. For some women, claiming the right of preparedness was also an assertion of their right to defend themselves against male violence, whether in the context of war or in a broader definition of "home defense" against domestic violence or other assault.

In February 1916, the *New York Times* reported that a group of prominent suffragists in Old Orchard, Maine had formed the Women's Defense Club to teach American women "to shoot, and shoot straight." The club was formed, according to the *Times* report, to provide expert instruction in the use of firearms "so that if American women are ever called upon to defend their homes, their children, and themselves, they will not be helpless as were the

Belgian women." The concept of "a woman using a gun in defense of her home, her child, or herself is new to many," wrote club organizer Lurana Sheldon Ferris, "but American women do not intend history to repeat itself—where they are concerned." Rather than wait to be raped or killed by "madmen," Ferris explained, women will be "prepared to kill" if "necessity" requires. "Our men, with all their bravery, cannot protect us all." In letters to the editor of the *New York Times* in 1916 and 1917, Ferris also emphasized the link between the activities of the club and women's responsibilities as citizens. "We are teaching patriotism and courage," she wrote. "Certainly patriotism, with efficiency in shooting, or even the ability to load a gun, is a combination that makes either a man or a woman a national asset in time of trouble." As a suffrage activist, Ferris made it clear that armed patriotism was part of the fabric of female citizenship: "Whether we vote or not—we are going to shoot." Due to expressions of interest from women from all parts of the country, Ferris and her colleagues made the organization open to any woman who signed a pledge to "improve every opportunity for learning how to use firearms as weapons of defense." In the summer of 1917 Ferris personally taught "scores" of women how to handle firearms, and thousands of other members throughout the country received instruction from qualified teachers. Ferris believed that "if every State would aid this equipment of its women we might eventually have a citizen soldiery worth while."[13]

In New York City markswoman June Haughton supervised the formation of several women's rifle clubs that practiced on the rooftops of the Hotel Vanderbilt and the Hotel Majestic and in her own indoor studio rifle range. Here she installed the latest equipment, including new "moving picture" technology that simulated various targets in motion. Haughton specifically linked women's use of firearms to military service and expanded the concept of female citizen soldiery for defense to also include women's presence on the battlefield. Three months before the United States entered the war, she told the *New York Times* that she was organizing women and training them to shoot because women's proficiency on the rifle range might prove to be "the foundation of a great woman's army." For Haughton, the war in Europe was proof that such an army could be organized and would be needed. Women, she said, "are in the munitions shops, in the mines, in the field, and in various branches of manual and military service. Why not the battlefield?"[14]

The American Women's League for Self-Defense (AWLSD) organized a more extensive program of women's rifle-drill and military preparedness. Based in New York City, the group launched a campaign in March 1916 "for women to arm and drill in the use of firearms" in the same spirit as the Women's Defense Club and June Haughton's American Defense Rifle Club.

The *New York Times* reported that the women were "stirred by atrocity tales" from Belgium and other areas of the German occupation. Executive officer Mrs. Leo Boardman emphasized that the league was organizing women all across the country to perform military drills to strengthen their bodies and to handle a gun for defense.[15] In a month the AWLSD had more than three hundred women recruits in New York City alone, including "dentists, lawyers, surgeons, heads of departments, teachers, private secretaries, and stenographers," as well as society women, horsewomen, and "two women with aero pilot licenses." Some members of the league conducted infantry drills at the Ninth Regiment Armory in New York, and others were part of a cavalry corps that drilled in the streets adjacent to the First Field Artillery at Sixty-seventh and Broadway.[16] The league sponsored a variety of other activities to promote women's military skills and the defense of American homes. In May 1916 AWLSD members made an expedition to the shoreline of the New York Palisades and conducted "exercises in map drawing of the terrain, with a view to its possibilities for attacking troops," so they could anticipate enemy invasion strategies for the New York coastline.[17] During the summer of 1916 members sponsored a number of camps for women's

"American Women Ready to Fight alongside of Russia's Brave Legion of Death. Members of the American Women's League for Self-Defense" (1917). (Photo no. 165-WW-600-B-2, National Archives, Washington, D.C.)

"Cavalry Corps of the American Women's League for Self-Defense" (1918). (Photo no. 165-WW-143-B-4, National Archives, Washington, D.C.)

military preparedness on the Plattsburg model, and uniformed members conducted outdoor drills near the military installations on Governors Island, New York, in the spring of 1917.

The American Women's League for Self-Defense also made efforts to extend its programs nationwide. The *Delineator* began a monthly "Women's Preparedness Bureau" in July 1917, and featured the AWLSD prominently in this series. Editors featured the Cavalry Corps of the AWLSD in "Going in for Military Training and How to Set Up a Camp," in the Preparedness Bureau's section in the August 1917 issue. In later issues editors encouraged readers to write to the AWLSD in New York for more information on women's military camps.[18] Individuals formed local camps for women's rifle-drill and military preparedness following the example of the AWLSD. Candace Hewitt organized a summer camp in New Jersey for "fifty young women, daughters of well-to-do New York families." The camp included "shooting, care of weapons, swimming, first aid to the injured, rowing, canoeing, riding, cavalry drill and regular military drills."[19]

Following the U.S. entry into the war, groups of American women followed the example of Russian women who formed a regiment known as the Russian Women's Battalion of Death to fight in the world war and defend the Kerensky government in the Russian Revolution. The *Woman Citizen* reported in October 1917 that women from Oklahoma and Texas, "wives of soldiers in the Regular National Army and National Guard," were organizing their own Battalion of Death "to serve in any way the War Department asks—in trenches if necessary." The *Suffragist* reported in that same month that women's regiments were being formed in Texas, Indiana, and Florida.[20]

Arms and the Woman

These rifle and defense groups and the women's regiments are only the most visible examples of a grassroots movement of American women to promote the female use of guns during the First World War. A close reading of the journal of the National Rifle Association, *Arms and the Man,* from 1914 to 1919 reveals that thousands of women nationwide joined rifle and revolver clubs at indoor and outdoor ranges and for trapshooting (firing at clay targets). The editors of the journal and various contributors linked these activities with the war and preparedness activities and with women's self-defense. For example, in 1915 more than five hundred women participated in special "Beginners' Day Shoots" around the country, and by 1916 there were 193 separate Beginners' Day competitions in various parts of the country specifically for women.[21] These reports emphasized that women's shooting "on a big scale" was a recent development, that women demonstrated an "unusual amount of enthusiasm in learning to use firearms" and were becoming "more and more identified with the sport," and listed women's accomplishments at various tournaments with praise. "Several years ago there wasn't a handful of women trap shots," remarked the writer of a special article, "Feminine Trap Shots," in October 1916. "Now we have thousands of them."[22]

By the time of America's involvement in the war in 1917 and 1918, *Arms and the Man* provided solid documentation of women's participation in gun practice and competitive shooting and linked these activities to the war. "Not many years ago women were conspicuous by their absence in trapshooting matters," one editorialist commented, "but such is not the case today." Many "fair Dianas" were out on the practice ranges and would be competing in tournaments. "Trapshooting Attracts Both Sexes," another editorialist affirmed. In "About Women Shots" another asserted that there were thousands of women who "frequent the traps and shoot regularly," and women were part of the large contingent of newcomers to trapshooting whose interest seemed to be "stimulated by the U.S. entrance into the war."[23] The journal featured articles by two women championship shots in July and October 1917. Elizabeth (Mrs. Adolph) Topperwein of San Antonio, Texas, "the peer of all woman shooters and as good as the male experts with the shotgun," invited all women to join the "standing army of over 500 women" who competed at official trapshooting events. Many of these women, she contended, "hold their own with the best shooters of the sterner sex."[24] Harriet D. Hammond, the Delaware women's champion, "strongly recommended" trapshooting to all women: it helped to develop self-reliance and made women "better able to cope with the affairs of life." After telling of a woman who used a shotgun to protect herself and her home, Hammond concluded, "It makes me wonder why more women have not learned to shoot."[25]

Advertisers were quick to notice the trend. The production of weapons for the army enriched American arms manufacturers during the war years,[26] and the popularity of shooting provided a potential audience of civilian men and women. Women-at-arms were a potential gold mine for gun manufacturers, who catered to this expanding new audience. In some advertisements manufacturers used the tried-and-true method of linking women's sexuality with their product. The Marlin Company, for example, praised the "beauty of build and balance" of the Marlin Repeating Shotgun in an ad featured in *Arms and the Man* in 1915. Potential owners could "double the charm and pleasure in shooting" with "exactly the right gun." A smiling, shapely woman seems to have great pleasure in holding the weapon. Here the woman's sexuality is part of the sale, targeting men as much as women consumers. The advertisers assured women and men consumers of guns that female shots would not lose their femininity and sexual appeal if they took up a rifle; indeed, they might even enhance it.

But gun manufacturers also highlighted gun use for women and featured guns in women's hands that made them their own Protectors. In an ad featured in 1916 we see a woman who is obviously a skilled shot, wearing a field hat and belt, sighting with her Ross rifle. This is a woman who knows her business and wants to have the best equipment to "paralyze with a single shot." No man would wish to be at the other end of her barrel.

The Colt Firearms Manufacturing Company ran an ad featuring a woman shooter in various issues of *Arms and the Man* in 1916 and 1917. A woman with a pistol is shooting at a target in a small indoor cellar range, getting advice from a man over her shoulder. The ad copy for the Colt Target Revolver reads: "Its *small caliber* makes it the ideal revolver for home practice—the ammunition is inexpensive and gives but little noise or recoil." Colt encouraged women to form "cellar clubs" for shooting practice at home. To support this message, *Arms and the Man* printed an article in its January 1917 issue with specific information on "how to construct an indoor or cellar range."[27]

The Colt Company went as far as any manufacturer to encourage women

Marlin Firearms Company advertisement, *Arms and the Man* (July 29, 1915): 357.

"Paralyzes with a Single Shot," Ross Rifle Company advertisement, *Arms and the Man* (July 27, 1916): 360.

"A Unique Field: Form a Cellar Club—Buy a Colt and Learn to Shoot," Colt Firearms Manufacturing Company advertisement, *Arms and the Man* (September 7, 1916): 480.

to use pistols to protect themselves from violence in its ad campaign for 1917, the year that the United States entered the war in Europe. Here the Colt pistol becomes the "Home Protection Colt." Illustrated testimonials from "Colt protected" women who were saved from rape by their use of the pistol emphasize that women and the home are under siege, that women should be their own Protectors, and that self-defense is part of national preparedness.

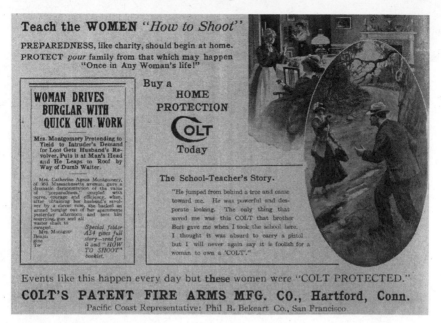

"Teach the Women 'How to Shoot,'" Colt Firearms Manufacturing Company
advertisement, *Arms and the Man* (January 4, 1917): 300.

Violence against women "happen[s] every day," the ad copy suggests, and
"preparedness, like charity, should begin at home."

Much of the rhetoric concerning women shooters in the editorials and
reports in *Arms and the Man* is complimentary, even respectful, of their enthusiasm and expertise. Men of arms were associating with and reading about
women who were proving their own in the shooting world. "The idea of leads,
angles and distances" held "no mysteries" for Chicago women, claimed one
report. The women of the Livermore Falls Rifle Club of Maine were meeting
every Thursday evening at the Armory Hall as they had done since 1914 under
the direction of "crack shot" Lieutenant Roys of the National Guard. They had
become so expert with the rifle that they challenged any team in Maine or the
New England states to a competition.[28] Women seemed to be welcome at many
ranges. "There isn't any suffrage question at the traps," said one reporter, and
the editors of *Arms and the Man* contended, "Today women shoot and vote
under the same conditions as their husbands, brothers and sweethearts."[29]

Another indication that women shots were taken seriously is that *Arms
and the Man* offered specific advice for women that would help them improve
their performance. A question-and-answer column contained information

on the best choices of pistols and small firearms for women shooting on an indoor or basement range.[30] In her 1917 article, Mrs. Topperwein included specific information about common problems for women shots, especially finding a gun with a proper fit. "The borrowed gun is almost certain to be too long in the stock and as a rule too heavy; the result is that it is held in an awkward manner, the recoil received from the shot frightens the shooter and she loses all of her enthusiasm then and there." Have "someone who knows 'fit' you with a proper gun," she advised women readers.[31] In an article titled "Guns for Sportswomen," Henry Sharp advised women readers that they should not be content with firing light guns if they were ready for more powerful weapons. He believed that "women's physical powers have been much undervalued," and that the war work of women—"the remarkable way in which farming implements and other tools have been handled during this war time"—proved that women were ready for heavier guns. Sharp offered specific recommendations for women shots and was enthusiastic about their prospects in the "art of shooting."[32]

We must temper this picture of support for women shots, however, by placing it in the context of the separate sphere for women that existed ideologically and institutionally in the shooting world. Some organizations and many regulations barred female participants from official benefits and many opportunities for competition and recognition. As part of the military-preparedness campaign in the summer of 1914, Congress authorized the U.S. chief of ordnance to issue free of charge to each qualifying member of a registered rifle club one Krag rifle and 120 cartridges of ammunition that were then in government storage. In 1915 Congress authorized civilian use of military ranges and the construction of new ranges.[33] Section 113 of the Defense Act of June 3, 1916, strengthened these provisions and provided for initial and annual issues of targets, target materials, and accessories, as well as rifles and ammunition to rifle groups and free instruction for qualifying individuals at rifle ranges.[34] Congress enacted these measures to foster what President Woodrow Wilson called a "citizenry trained in the use of arms" as part of the program of military preparedness and the training of male citizen soldiers advocated by Leonard Wood, Theodore Roosevelt, and their supporters, including the National Rifle Association (NRA).[35] Although there were some restrictions during 1917 and 1918 on the availability of rifles due to war demand, the government continued to subsidize rifle practice in the United States over the entire course of the war.

Such measures, obviously a boon to rifle clubs and the NRA, were designed in part to eliminate the category of class from a "citizenry trained in the use of arms" through free instruction and the free issue of arms and ammunition.

The category of gender, however, was emphatically written into the rules, because the "citizenry" to be trained was male. The use of rifle facilities was for the use of "all able-bodied male citizens of the United States capable of bearing arms," and in another provision for targets and practice, "only physically fit males between the ages of 16 and 45, who are citizens of the United States," were eligible.[36] The National Rifle Association ruled that women could be only honorary, auxiliary, or associate members of rifle clubs under its jurisdiction, in part because of these government eligibility requirements. If women associated with clubs and qualified in competition for the NRA grades of marksman, sharpshooter, or expert, they were not entitled to the official title or decoration awarded in recognition of these achievements.[37] Because they were ineligible for free government issue, women had to pay for all of their own equipment and ammunition, a situation that reintroduced class into the equation for women shots, as only those who could finance their practice could participate. In addition, these institutional barriers for women shooters came alongside the strong association of the preparedness movement with remasculinization of American men and boys.

Some women found ways to subvert these ideological and institutional constraints that defined citizen soldiers as male. At some military rifle ranges available for the use of the "citizen army," women simply presented themselves for instruction and practice. Men in the U.S. Navy and Marine Corps received instruction in firearms at the Wakefield Rifle Range in Massachusetts on weekdays, and on weekends the range was available for civilian use. Individuals could come with their own ammunition or purchase it at the canteen at the range, and the facilities and targets were available free of charge. On Saturdays military instructors offered free assistance to civilian patrons.[38] Some revealing photographs from the collection at the National Archives demonstrate that women came to the Wakefield range in 1918 and that despite the rules they were allowed to do so and received instruction. The photographs preserve a visit made to Wakefield by a group of Boston women in June 1918 collectively identified by the captions on file as the "wives and mothers of men at the front." The photographer for the series was Richard W. Sears of Boston, the husband of one of the women shooters.

The first photograph is a group portrait of these women as they begin their instruction from Major Portal and other U.S. Marine Corps personnel on duty at the range. Most members of the group seem unaccustomed to the rifle and uncertain, especially the woman turning to see how the others are holding their weapons. The scene is framed by a serene backdrop of trees and an expanse of grass, but the viewer's eye is drawn to the cluttered and chaotic array of hats, arms, hands, rifles, and skirts as the women try to make sense of the directions spoken by the instructors and offered by their guiding hands. There are more male instructors than women shooters. The staff has placed tarps on the ground to protect the women's genteel civilian clothing from the grass and dirt of the range.

By contrast, a second photograph shows these same women after they have gained more proficiency with guns. They point their rifles purposefully at the target; even their bodies form a unified, projectile-like triangle, and their faces show confidence and determination. Now only one male instructor stands behind them, and they no longer appear to need his guidance. They are skilled and efficient shots after one day at the range.[39]

Some women collected the necessary funds and formed rifle and gun clubs as auxiliaries to the male clubs sanctioned by the National Rifle Association. Others formed independent clubs, including groups such as the American Women's League for Self-Defense and the Women's Defense Club. A reading of *Arms and the Man*, the *New York Times*, and *Stars and Stripes*—the newspaper of the American Expeditionary Force in France—provides evidence for the existence of thirty-nine such groups. Some of these groups, including the Women's Auxiliary of the La Creole Rifle Club of Dallas, Oregon, were able

"Wives and Mothers of Men at the Front Being Instructed in Shooting at the Wakefield Rifle Range, Wakefield, Mass., by Major Portal and U.S. Marines, 1918." (Photo no. 165-WW-143-B-1, National Archives, Washington, D.C.)

"Teaching Women to Shoot at the Wakefield, Mass., Rifle Range. The Women Are Learning the Art under the Direction of a Sergeant of Marines." (Photo no. 165-WW-143-B-6, National Archives, Washington, D.C.)

to gain special permission to use the National Guard rifle range in Oregon for their practice.[40]

At least two clubs were formed by groups of women working in factories during the war. Women employees at the Shepard Norwell Company of Boston formed the Shepard Women's Rifle Club. They organized the club according to military discipline, and members earned military titles. In May 1918 the editors of the *Stars and Stripes* in France received a letter from Sergeant Grace M. Brown, an officer of the club and a Shepard worker. Brown wished that she could personally be in France and expressed the solidarity that she and the other women workers at Shepard felt with the soldiers. "We are straight United States through and through," she wrote. *Arms and the Man* reported in March 1917 that nearly two hundred women employees of "a Boston commercial house" were organizing a women's rifle club. It is possible that this was the Shepard Club of which Brown was an officer, or it could have been a separate club formed by another group of working women. The journal reported that this group would probably become an auxiliary of the club organized by the male employees so that the women might benefit from the "free distribution of targets" and other materials the men received. In another case, the "insistent demand" among the women workers at the

Akron Gun Club (Akron)

American Defense Rifle Club (New York City)

American Women's League for Self-Defense (New York City)

Atlantic City Trapshooting School (Atlantic City)

Birmingham Rifle and Revolver Club (Birmingham)

Boston Customhouse Women Yeoman's Rifle Team (Boston)

Bridgeport Remington UMC Women Employees Rifle Club (Bridgeport, Connecticut)

Carondelet Rifle Club (St. Louis)

Centennial Rifle Club (Chicago)

Charleston Women's Rifle Team (Charleston, South Carolina)

Cumberland Women's Rifle Club (Cumberland, Maryland)

Danbury Women's Rifle Club (Danbury, Connecticut)

Engineer's Rifle and Revolver Club (Cleveland)

Gordon–Van Time Rifle Club (Davenport, Iowa)

Iowa State University Women's Rifle Club (Des Moines)

La Creole Rifle Club (Dallas, Oregon)

Laurel House Gun Club (Lakewood, Ohio)

Liberty Rifle and Pistol Club (San Antonio)

Lincoln Park Gun Club (Chicago)

Livermore Falls Women's Rifle Team (Livermore Falls, Maine)

Middletown Women's Rifle Club (Middletown, New York)

Montclair Women's Rifle Club (Montclair, New Jersey)

Mount Pleasant Women's Rifle Team (Mount Pleasant, South Carolina)

Nemours Ladies Trapshooting Club (Wilmington, Delaware)

New York Rifle Club (New York City)

Pahquioque Rod and Gun Club (Danbury, Connecticut)

Parkland Gun Club (Parkland, Maryland)

Portland Gun Club (Portland, Oregon)

Rochester Women's Pistol Club (Rochester, New York)

Salt Lake City Rifle Club (Salt Lake City)

Santa Fe Rifle Club Women's Auxiliary (Santa Fe)

Shepard Women's Rifle Club (Boston)

Soo Gun Club (Sioux City)

South Bend Rifle and Revolver Club (South Bend, Washington)

Warsaw Gun Club (Warsaw, Indiana)

Washington State College Women's Rifle Corps (Pullman)

Women's Defense Club (National, headquarters in Old Orchard, Maine)

Women's Military Reserve of the United States (New York City)

Women's Revolver League (Bayonne, New Jersey)

Remington UMC ammunition factory at Bridgeport, Connecticut, for the organization of a rifle club resulted in weekly meetings at the Park Rifle Club range beginning in April 1917. Male members of the Park team offered their services as instructors and allowed the women to use the club's "regulation NRA rifles" for their practice at the range.[41] These references emphasize that working women were taking the initiative to form rifle groups and also that they were able to further subvert the regulations against women in the citizen army by gaining the cooperation of some of their male colleagues who had official access to equipment.

Some experienced women shots used their skills to teach other women how to shoot and to emphasize women's capabilities with firearms. As we have seen, June Haughton led the movement to form rifle clubs for women in New York City. Mrs. B. G. Earle of New York, a champion woman shot, was employed by the Laurel House Gun Club in Lakewood, Ohio, in 1917 to teach the growing numbers of "Fair Dianas" who were eager to learn to shoot a rifle with precision. At Iowa State University, thirty-five women students practiced rifle shooting for an hour each day under the direction of Mrs. Jacob Maier. Maier was the wife of a sergeant on the military instructional staff at the university. She had learned to be "a crack shot with the pistol and rifle when her husband was stationed in the Philippine Islands and it was necessary for her to carry a gun at all times for safety." Mrs. Jackson Morris provided instruction in shooting to male soldiers "on the range as an instructor and under orders from Uncle Sam" at Camp Shelby, Mississippi. Morris was "the first woman to qualify as a sharpshooter in the American Army" and was living at the camp as the wife of a major stationed there.[42]

Annie Oakley, the woman most associated in the American popular imagination with the female use of guns, became a shooting instructor for women and made an instructional tour of military camps during the war years. By the First World War Oakley was no longer dazzling audiences in Buffalo Bill's Wild West Show, but her place in popular culture as an expert markswoman remained strong. With her husband and partner, Frank Butler, Oakley came to live permanently in North Carolina in 1915 and became a member of the staff of the Carolina Hotel at the famous Pinehurst resort, giving exhibitions and shooting lessons.[43] The local Pinehurst *Outlook* reported that Oakley had "lost none of her magic with firearms" and that there was great enthusiasm among her women students at Pinehurst for learning the art of shooting.[44] In the summer of 1918 Oakley toured military training camps across the country at her own expense, "spending a day or two in each cantonment shooting the rifle, revolver and shotgun for the benefit of the soldiers, and then giving instruction to any or all who desire same."

One report estimated that she visited more than a half-million soldiers on this tour.[45]

Some women who entered the "armed forces" during the First World War joined the women on the periphery of military service in their claims to the female right to bear arms. They had an important incentive to do so, because qualifying "marksmen" received additional pay. Legislation for the U.S. Navy and Marine Corps specified that those who qualified as marksmen received an extra two dollars per month, sharpshooters received three dollars, and expert riflemen received an extra five dollars per month. When monthly paychecks for privates were seventeen dollars per month, the extra money could represent quite a difference in salary.[46] Iona E. C. Myrick, the chief woman yeoman of the U.S. Marine Corps unit at the Boston Customhouse, organized the First Women Yeoman's Rifle Team with fifteen members late in 1917. The women had "a view to qualifying according to the rules and regulations" that governed the men of the navy in their requirements for marksmanship qualification. Captain J. L. Bastey, an official rifle instructor for the War Department, supervised the weekly meetings of the club at a "shooting gallery."[47] It is not clear whether officials allowed the group to qualify under navy regulations and receive additional wages.

Elizabeth Bertram also challenged the issue of firearms qualification for women in the marines. Bertram was working as a legal secretary in Denver when she enlisted as a private to help with U.S. Marine Corps recruiting.[48] She had learned to use a rifle as a young girl, and because she had done "a great deal of target practice" she considered herself "a better than average shot." When she learned that "qualifying on the rifle range added dollars to pay checks" in the marines, she recalled in a later interview, she "asked for permission for a tryout."[49] Bertram's commanding officer refused to send her to the official rifle range located "on the western slope of the Rocky Mountains more than a hundred miles away." He "certainly would not send a female on such a jaunt simply on her say so that she knew how to handle a gun." The major did agree to let her try her skill at the Denver police practice range just outside the city, and he made arrangements for a "one person regulation full course tryout." Bertram recalled that the day of the tryout was cold and windy, "with squalls of icy rain." A corporal from the recruiting office escorted her to the police range, where a number of Denver police officers were waiting under the range shelter to watch what would happen as this woman marine came to shoot. The Enfield rifle provided for Bertram's use was too long in the stock. "I did fairly well on kneeling and sitting, and managed a few good shots prone," she recalled, "but every time I tried rapid fire the result was disaster." She was determined, however, and "stuck it out for the full course."

At the end of the day, because of the poor fit of her borrowed rifle, Bertram's shoulder was "pounded almost to jelly," and she was soaked with rain and mud. When she arrived back at the recruiting office, the major sent her home without comment.

The next day the major called her into his office, where her "target sheets were spread over the desk with every bullet hole carefully evaluated." The major told her that she had "qualified unofficially," and she now had permission to be part of the next group going to the official firing range, where, presumably, she could qualify for extra pay as a marine marksman. Then, as she recalled, the major came around the desk to where she was standing, "pinned his own engraved marksman medal on my blouse," and said, "'in the meantime, you may wear this.'" Bertram was grateful but unable to properly salute, she recalled, because of her sore right arm. Before the next group of marines went to the Colorado firing range, however, the Armistice was signed to end the war. All of the marine reservists (F) were transferred to inactive duty. Bertram never received the extra pay of a marksman. The record does not show whether the major let her keep her borrowed medal.

The relationship between women and guns during the First World War became a part of the fabric of popular culture. The first installment of the *Delineator*'s "Women's Preparedness Bureau" featured a picture of a woman with a rifle as a part of a photographic series on women's preparedness, and the caption told readers that "managing a modern rifle" was one aspect of women's service.[50] A U.S. poster from 1918 titled "Feminine Patriotism" represents three avenues of women's wartime service. Against a sky-blue background, one woman, dressed in a uniform and apron, represents "domestic economy"; another, wearing the uniform of a nurse, represents "aid to the suffering." And in the center, backed by the U.S. flag, is a woman dressed in khaki uniform shouldering a gun, who represents "home defense."

In the suffrage journal the *Woman Citizen*, associate editor Betty Graeme reported in the summer of 1917 that "with everybody going in" for "gun practice or manuals of arms," sewing seemed "relegated to the limbo of forgotten arts." Still, a sewing machine was a "good thing to have in the family during war-time," she said with tongue in cheek, "to place alongside of great-grandmamma's spinning wheel and beneath Aunt Jemima's sampler. Just to show that you came from the right sort of stock, you know." *Arms and the Man* reported in 1916 that the "mammoth electric sign" over the Million Dollar Pier at Atlantic City had been changed "to show a man and a woman shooting alternately" and that it was now attracting "more attention than ever."[51]

* * *

"Feminine Patriotism" (1918). (National Archives, Washington, D.C., Poster no. 6005)

As these examples demonstrate, some American women made their own claims on the preparedness movement, linking self-defense to national defense and to a full expression of the obligations and rights of citizenship. However, as they called for participation in the citizen's army, and some for a place in the military itself, these women defined violence against women on the war front and the home front and exposed the limits of men's power to protect them. Women joined gun clubs and defense groups so that they would not be in the same situation as the women in Belgium and northern

France, unprotected and vulnerable to rape and assault. Once opened, this door also led to a critique of the gender convention of men as Protectors and women as the Protected. It also highlighted the stark reality that some men abused the women they were supposed to protect. Groups of women who gained proficiency in the use of guns were a potential threat to the domestic order in more ways than one. Against the backdrop of the urgent call for remasculinizing men through military training to enhance their role as Protectors, these women's claims engendered strong opposition and backlash. As the next chapter will illustrate, the cultural and social debate about the woman soldier that followed was also a debate about these women's redefinition of violence and self-defense.

4. "The Fighting, Biting, and Scratching Kind"

Good Girls, Bad Girls, and Women's Soldiering

> What manner of women are these? Are they . . . women of the fighting, biting, and scratching kind, women of the kind we associate in this country with night police courts?
> —"Those Russian Women," *Literary Digest,* September 1917

Women-at-arms who claimed the civic obligation to defend the state presented themselves as a potential "great woman's army" for armed defense at the same time that they challenged men's role as Protectors of women. They also subverted "patriotic motherhood" by aiming to defend themselves and to become soldiers. Many American policy makers and authorities in the military and the medical profession, antisuffragists, and other opponents sought to define the female soldier in terms that would discredit her legitimacy, sexuality, and "reputation" in patterns familiar to other "public women." Supporters used the woman soldier to bolster claims for women's enhanced civic roles. The debate about the female soldier was concentrated and contextualized in the popular debate about Russian women soldiers, members of the Russian Women's Battalion of Death. As such it was a metaphor for the fate of American women-at-arms. This chapter will examine the debate about the female soldier in popular culture and its consequences.

For eight months in 1917–18 the *San Francisco Bulletin* sent American journalist Bessie Beatty to Russia to cover the events of the Russian Revolution. Her reports for the *Bulletin,* carried by other newspapers across the country, and her book *The Red Heart of Russia* (1918), featured material gathered from her weeklong stay with the Russian women's regiment known as the Battalion of Death. Beatty believed that "the most amazing single phenomenon of the war" was the woman soldier. "Not the isolated individual woman who has buckled on a sword and shouldered a gun throughout the pages of history," she wrote, "but the woman soldier banded and fighting en masse—machine gun companies of her, battalions of her, scouting parties of her, whole regiments of her."[1]

Many women participated as active combatants in conflicts before the world war, including those who took on a male identity and cross-dressed for employment or to define their own sexual and social identities.[2] T. Hall was an intersexual who fought in the British army in France in the 1620s, and Deborah Sampson served with the Fourth Massachusetts Regiment as Robert Shurtleff in the American Revolution.[3] Mary Edwards Walker challenged gender conventions by cross-dressing and practicing medicine in the Civil War years and after. Many women, intersexuals, and transgender individuals took on male identities in the Civil War, including Rosetta Wakeman–Lyons Wakeman and Sara Emma Edmonds–Frank Thompson. Some of these soldiers, like Edmonds, had a male identity and employment prior to their military service. Many were outed in hospitals when they became sick or were injured.[4]

Following the war, Magnus Hirschfeld suggested that many women soldiers, both historically and in the world war, were, in his terms, "cases of erroneous sex determination" individuals who were intersexuals or transgendered. Because the First World War was more bureaucratized than previous conflicts, bodies and identities were scrutinized more extensively, and individuals had to contend with this increasing level of surveillance. Some welcomed it. Hirschfeld recounted the story of Erna B., of Berlin, who kept trying to enlist in the German army and asserted that "ever since her childhood she had always felt and acted like a boy, and that she had always been interested in masculine activities and professions." Hirschfeld was called in to examine Erna and found "the masculine male sex characters being so predominant that she would be regarded as belonging to the male sex." Erna changed her legal identity to Ernest and requested an expedited enlistment. Others, like John Bauer, tried to escape the increased scrutiny. John had passed as a man for eight years and worked in California's Imperial Valley. John feared the consequences of reporting for the physical examination that was part of the compulsory military draft and also feared that he would be arrested for draft evasion if he did not report. So he fled to Death Valley and "lived in a cave" for a year. When captured, John was "found to be a woman . . . when she refused to submit to the ministrations of a male nurse at the State Hospital."[5]

As the United States entered the world war, many observers discussed the solitary woman/man at arms, but groups of women in defense and rifle clubs and battalions of women soldiers claimed the most serious attention. Organized women soldiers, as women acting together, disordered the gender conventions of the Protector and the Protected openly and could not be as easily explained as anomalies. Bessie Beatty believed that the members of the Russian Women's Battalion of Death were the ones who most powerfully disrupted "the tidy pigeonholes in which we keep our firm convictions."[6]

The battalion was formed in May 1917 in Petrograd a month after the United States entered the war. Its commander, Maria Botchkareva, had been fighting as a regular soldier in an all-male regiment since 1915. When the chaotic politics of the Russian Revolution reached the army, she conceived of a plan of raising an all-female battalion to reinvigorate male soldiers' desire to fight for Russia. With the permission of the beleaguered provisional government under the leadership of Aleksandr Kerensky, Botchkareva made a call for female volunteers and was soon overwhelmed with two thousand applicants. By midsummer 1917 she had a group of three hundred women trained in the use of the rifle and bayonet, and the battalion was placed as a unit in a regular corps along the eastern front. The female soldiers engaged in combat as a battalion and sustained casualties through deaths and injuries. The unit was disbanded at the end of the summer because of chaotic conditions at the front and the unfolding politics of the revolution. Botchkareva's Battalion of Death from Petrograd was only the most famous of several female regiments raised in 1917 from cities such as Moscow, Odessa, Kiev, and Perm. Other women fought in male regiments disguised as men, or dressed in male uniforms with an acknowledged female identity, as did Botchkareva in her early military service. By the fall of 1917, Bessie Beatty reported, there were nearly five thousand women soldiers in Russia. The last public act of the all-female regiments was on October 25, 1917, when a detachment of female soldiers defended the provisional government as the Bolshevik forces took control of the Winter Palace.[7]

The Battalion of Death in American Popular Culture

Americans were fascinated by the Battalion of Death and by Russian women soldiers. Articles about them appeared in major newspapers and journals such as the *New York Times* and the *Literary Digest,* in suffrage and antisuffrage journals, and in major women's magazines such as the *Delineator, Good Housekeeping,* and the *Ladies' Home Journal.* Journalists, statesmen, medical authorities, and leaders of women's organizations all clamored to represent, and therefore to interpret, the Russian woman soldier for an American audience. Defining the members of the Russian Women's Battalion of Death became a way of defining the debate about female citizenship and women's claims for self-defense within the United States. If these women soldiers were legitimate, then women-at-arms in America could also lay claim to the militarized citizenship of combat. And women-at-arms who claimed the right of self-defense against invasion also claimed their right to defend themselves against domestic violence. They joined members of the Russian battalion in a critique of men who failed to protect women at home. Opponents of female soldiers and their challenge to men's roles as Protectors used a proven formula to contest their claims: they questioned and denigrated the sexuality and sexual behavior of women-at-arms to discredit their cause.

The patriotism of members of the Battalion of Death was a key feature in many of the articles. *Good Housekeeping,* for instance, reported that many of the battalion members "were inspired with a feeling that the men had done more than their share in the war and the women had not only a right but a solemn duty to offer their lives next." Caroline Kettle wrote a poem about the battalion for the *Woman Citizen* titled "The Legion of Death." The call *pro patria* meant "more than life could mean" to battalion members, she asserted, and those who had given their lives now stood in the heroic warrior's Valhalla, "holy and white and clean." In her memoirs Maria Botchkareva, who formed and led the battalion, wrote that she started the unit because Russian men were deserting the military in the face of the Russian Revolution. She believed that men needed some powerful reminder of the importance of fighting for the fatherland against Germany. The patriotic service of battalion members, then, would be a way to inspire patriotism in Russian men.[8]

Yet this view of Russian women's patriotism could also underscore the "failure" of Russian men to uphold their part of the gender convention of the Protector and the Protected. Like Belgian men who had "failed" to stem the German invasion, and British soldiers paralyzed with "soldier's heart," from this perspective Russian men had failed to protect their nation and its women. Members of the battalion took up soldiering to shame men to return to their role as Protectors. In an article for the *Delineator* in March 1918, William G. Shepherd reported that he had talked with "scores of women soldiers" during his visit to Russia about this point. "I speak only the bare truth when I say that nine hundred and ninety nine out of every thousand of these women soldiers went into this war for the main purpose of criticizing by their action the laggard portion of the Russian army and spurring it on—yes, even insulting it on—to fight for the Fatherland." The *New York Times* reported on its front page for June 25, 1917, that Botchkareva and her battalion were preparing to go to the front "as an object lesson to the malingerers and peace mongerers." The paper featured an account of the battalion's public appearance before leaving for the front, a scene that Bessie Beatty highlighted in *The Red Heart of Russia* and that the editors of *Good Housekeeping* also included in their lengthy article on the battalion. "Know you that the last hopes are fainting in our hearts and that we weak women will turn like tigresses in defense of our homes and children and Russian liberty?" battalion members asked Russian men. "The time will soon be at hand when it would be better for you to face ten German bayonets than one tigress mother of Russia," they warned. "We, your mothers, wives and sisters, know one party only—the liberty and glory of great Russia. We know only one platform—our country and our homes and the future of our children." The address concluded with an appeal to the women of the Allied nations for patience, "for if Russian men betray the common cause the women of Russia will save it." When Elihu Root returned from Russia after viewing the battalion as a member of the diplomatic American delegation to Russia, he told the nation, "'Russian women are doing a wonderful work in shaming the men into fighting, and when necessary I hope American women will follow their example.'"[9]

The shaming of inadequate men carried with it an implicit promise of sexual reward for men who did their duty. The *New York Times* reported in another front-page story on July 6, 1917, that members of the Women's Battalion of Death paraded through the streets of Petrograd carrying banners with the inscription "Women, do not give your hands to traitors." It was therefore a patriotic act to give one's hand—and by implication one's body—to a soldier. This was the same message of war posters in America such as Howard Chandler Christy's 1917 recruiting poster, "I Want You for the Navy," featuring a sexualized woman in soldier's dress whose desire seems much more erotic than civic. Martha Banta demonstrates that such posters drew upon the sexualized militarism of images of "pert and sexy girls of the theater world" in military uniforms for burlesque shows, posters, and cigar advertising before and during the war.[10]

Authors and editors, therefore, walked a fine line between the representation of battalion members as chaste mothers, wives, and sisters guided by patriotism, on the one hand, and the association of female soldiers with sexually promiscuous "camp followers" who were "asking for it," on the other. Sexual reputation mattered here, just as it did in attitudes about women and violence at home. The *Literary Digest,* quoting a story from the *St. Louis Post Dispatch,* discussed the "type of women" who were battalion members. "What manner of women are these?" the editors asked rhetorically. "Are they female giants from the fields, stupid of mind and strong of arm, women of the fighting, biting, and scratching kind, women of the kind we associate

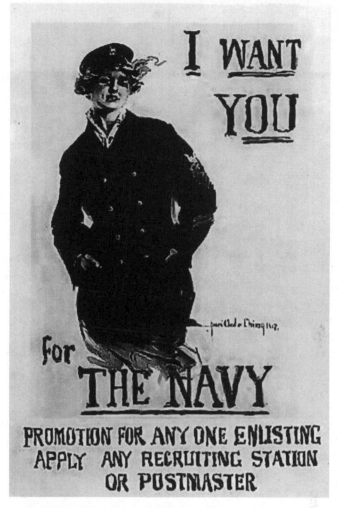

Howard Chandler Christy, "I Want You for the Navy" (1917).
(Library of Congress, Washington, D.C.)

in this country with night police courts? Far from it. The Russian Women's Regiment is made up of some of the best blood in Russia—daughters of noble families, university and high-school graduates, society women, writers and others of the highest type." And most of them, the report concluded, had "a good physique" and were "pretty and refined in appearance." The *Delineator* was most explicit about the relationship of female chastity and soldiering: "In the girl Legions of Russia, good girls make good soldiers and bad girls make poor ones."[11] Social class, reputation, and physical appearance, all elements in women's defense against violence at home, were key elements in the "positive" representation of the members of the Women's Battalion of Death. The *Delineator* featured an idealized portrait of a battalion member on the cover of its January 1918 issue with the caption, "Her All for Russia." This ideal woman stands guard over all of Russia—from the church and village behind her to the life-giving fields at her side.

Fears about women's sexuality and "honor" and also about rape as an act of conquest entered the news stories about the battalion. Several sources emphasized that each woman soldier carried a cyanide capsule so that she could end her life rather than be raped on the battlefield.[12] The cyanide capsule represented, simultaneously, the sexual danger for women at the front and the traditional "rule" that a woman should choose death rather than the "dishonor" of rape that would affect the honor of her community. Thus, women soldiers were to sacrifice their bodies for the state rather than "allow" themselves to be raped and therefore to symbolize the dishonoring of a conquered nation and its men. They could be part of a battalion of women designed to shame revolutionaries into fighting and supporting the state, but they could not "participate" in the dishonoring of the nation through rape by opponents.

The portrayal of Russian women soldiers frequently resulted in comparisons with Joan of Arc. The photograph of one woman appeared in the *Literary Digest* in 1915 with the caption: "The Muscovite Militant: A Russian Joan of Arc." In August 1917 the same journal printed the comments of one of the battalion's male drill instructors concerning their soldierly desires: "The overmastering motive," he said, "is the patriotic desire to save Russia from ruin. Many of them display a zeal and ardor worthy of Joan of Arc." *Good Housekeeping* characterized all of the Russian women soldiers as resembling the French heroine.[13] Joan of Arc was a readily available figure in the war years. In December 1915 an equestrian statue of Joan sculpted by American artist Anna Vaughn Hyatt was erected on Riverside Drive in New York City. The statue was commissioned to commemorate the five hundredth anniversary of Joan's birth in 1412 and coincided with her beatification by the Roman Catholic Church in 1909.[14] Her visual celebration was accompanied by numerous literary and journalistic texts, including C. M. Stevens's *The Wonderful Story of Joan of Arc and the Meaning of Her Life for Americans* (1918). These sources emphasized the saintly, spiritual, sexually innocent Joan, not the female soldier who donned men's clothing, took command, and was burned at the stake as a result. According to Stevens, Joan represented the "lovely soul of womanhood" and the "divine reality of faith that makes possible the process of social civilization." As New Yorkers unveiled the equestrian statue of Joan, a reporter for the *New York Evening Post* wrote, "Anne [*sic*] Vaughn Hyatt, its sculptor, sees only the spiritual in Joan." And the *Delineator* reported: "In spite of the martial air of the armor, and of the magnificent proportions of the horse, by some magic of the sculptor's genius the figure of Joan is infinitely girlish." Her spirituality "becomes a symbol of all that womankind is striving toward."[15]

This spiritual, sexually chaste Joan represented the justice of the French and the Allied cause. When the French ambassador to the United States addressed the crowd at the dedication of the New York statue, he assured them that Joan "personified the spirit of self-sacrifice—the soul of France to-day." According to the *Outlook,* the statue symbolized "the triumph of faith and patriotism over persecution and suffering." In February 1917 G. A. Conkling published a poem in the *Bookman* titled "The Return of Jeanne D'Arc" in which the men of France call to the angelic Joan and ask Christ's mother, Mary, to "lend her out of heaven" to go before their armies. Joan leads France and the Allies to victory in the popular lyrics of "Joan of Arc They Are Calling You," a song that Thomas Walsh claimed had been on the lips of American soldiers since they "marched away to their great adventure overseas."[16] Following the war the *Stars and Stripes* claimed an ethereal, angelic Joan as guardian of American graves in France. Her reverent figure hovering over the markers is nonsexual and suffused with heavenly benediction.

The Joan of Arc that became the symbol for the Allied cause and the symbol of the "right kind" of woman soldier was exceptional at the same time that she symbolized "all that womankind is striving toward." She was called by God, cut her hair, and wore trousers to disguise and minimize her woman-hood and sexuality yet was still a "real woman." She was sexually pure and devoted to France. She did not compete with men. And, as antisuffragist Everett Wheeler insisted, "she never asked the women of France to follow her standard. She knew perfectly well that, for them as a sex, and for France as a country, it was far better that the mothers should stay at home and bring up their children in the love of God and of their country and in devotion to duty, than that they should carry the sword and shield and march to fight the English."[17]

Supporters of the Battalion of Death and of the woman soldier made favorable comparisons between members of the battalion and Joan of Arc. One of the central messages of the Joan of Arc story was that she did not choose to be a soldier but was called to be one, and once called she took a vow of celibacy. Like Joan, supportive sources portrayed Maria Botchkareva as a simple peasant woman who joined the army for the love of her country. Just as Joan reinvigorated French troops and instilled confidence in the impotent Charles VII during the Hundred Years' War, Botchkareva hoped to rally Russian soldiers and reinvigorate the army in the face of Bolshevik pressure to agree to the terms of peace with Germany. Bessie Beatty wrote that Botchkareva was chosen by "Destiny" for her part in the war. According to popular reports she had been married young, and she and her husband were "very fond of each other and were very happy." When he died she went to war to take the place of her beloved husband in the ranks, inspired by patriotic fervor. Presumably, her devotion to her deceased husband prevented her from active sexuality on the battle line.[18] In the print sources journalists often referred to the women of the battalion as girls, and emphasized their youth with accounts of lighthearted frolics, giggling, and off-duty romps. With hair cut short or shaved and dressed in trousers, they were guileless tomboys, as was Joan of Arc.[19]

But there were cracks in these representations of the woman soldier that antisuffragists and opponents of women-at-arms exploited to their advantage. According to her own autobiographical account, Botchkareva's apparently blissful and socially acceptable marriage was a convenient fable. She had been involved in two partnerships with alcoholic men who physically and sexually abused her. She hated and feared them both. In Botchkareva's own account her decision to join the war was a desperate escape to save herself from the violent threats of her estranged husband.[20] The glowing published representations of her personal life and motives for soldiering could not contain these disruptive counterreports. Botchkareva did not garner sympathy or support for her experience with domestic violence. Rather, there were extensive accounts of her stern discipline and conflicts with battalion members. Newspapers featured reports of battalion members quarreling with her and subjecting her to "rough handling," and finally attacking and mobbing her because of her stern discipline or "some acts . . . not clearly defined."[21] Perhaps, these sources suggested, female soldiers really were the fighting, biting, and scratching kind after all.

The *Delineator*'s extensive article on Botchkareva and the Battalion of Death in the March 1918 issue capitalized on and developed this ambivalence. Journalist William G. Shepherd told readers that he visited Botchkareva in her hospital room in Petrograd for an interview. It was necessary for him to secure the permission of her physician, and she lay in her bed "fallen from leadership," her nerves "aquiver with the shock of a shell which had fallen into the very midst of her German-capturing group of girls." Like the shell-shock patients in England and France, Botchkareva had "failed" as a soldier. As she lay in her sickbed, "conquered," Shepherd wanted to know if she did not feel a "heavy responsibility" in taking "potential mothers" out of their homes and "leading them to the firing line." But, according to Shepherd, "her peasant's mind did not encompass" the question. Botchkareva saw these women only as "pairs of legs that can march" or "pairs of arms that can carry rifles" or "index fingers that can pull rifle triggers." In the time of Joan of Arc, Shepherd wrote, when "fighting was hand to hand, and the strongest man won, Botchkareva herself, with her strong peasant's frame and muscle, might have been a good soldier, but she could never have raised a girls' battalion." But now, in the "day of machine warfare," it was possible for her to raise such a battalion and to think of its female members as persons capable of fighting without considering their "essential womanhood." Twentieth-century technology thwarted traditional restrictions against women warriors based on physical size and strength and threatened to erase gender boundaries in general. Instead of a Joan of Arc every hundred years, the modern age could produce entire armies of female soldiers. Yet, Shepherd asserted, Botchkareva's androgynous vision contained "one great mistake." When she organized the Battalion of Death, she "took all comers." "To be healthy and strong was all she asked of a girl," he said. Yet she failed to ascertain whether recruits were "good girls in the moral sense," and this, he believed, was her undoing. Many "bad girls" came into the battalion, and they subverted the whole purpose of the enterprise. After talking with women soldiers, Shepherd concluded, "Girl soldiers should have no sex. Those who can not lose their sense of sex can not be good soldiers."[22]

By casting Botchkareva as a coarse peasant, Shepherd brought readers' notions of class, womanhood, and proper behavior into play, in effect arguing that it was impossible for Botchkareva and her female soldiers to control their sexuality because of their lowly status. He blamed them for their "failure" because they were "sexy." Shepherd brought home his point by contrasting Botchkareva's battalion with a newly formed "girls' battalion" in Petrograd. "Botchkareva had been informed by these girls that they would not accept her for a commander," he wrote, and the new leader was "a quiet, gentle little Russian woman who had taken charge." He visited the soldiers in their barracks, and they were "romping girlishly" just as "one might have expected in the hallways of an exclusive boarding school." He asked the new commander if it was right for women to go to war. "'No! No!' she exclaimed. 'None of us thinks it is right. But we had to begin fighting when the men showed signs of wanting to stop. Women are not made for battle. They are not strong enough physically and their nerves are too weak to stand the terrible strain. It is wrong for women to go to war, but,' she added, 'we Russian women had to do it.'"[23] For readers, the message was clear: women did not belong in war, but if extraordinary circumstances forced their participation, it was essential that they maintain middle-class respectability and norms of heterosexual behavior.

The lesson that woman soldiers should "have no sex" bore a double meaning. They should not engage in sexual intercourse, and they should not manifest a sexual nature. In Shepherd's words they should not be "sexy." This active sexuality was true of heterosexuality and was also embodied in the threat of the female soldier as a lesbian. "'The only girl I'll trust myself to fight beside in a battle,'" a battalion member insisted, "'is a girl who is on the square and doesn't care for men.'" Shepherd told his readers that "in the minds of all the girl soldiers I found a fine scorn [of male soldiers] mixed with a mischievous enjoyment."[24] The extensive use of photographs of battalion members underscored the threat of active lesbian sexuality among the ranks. The photograph captioned "Botchkareva, Commander of the 'Battalion of Death,'" for example, appeared at the beginning of the *Delineator* article of March 1918. A photograph from *Good Housekeeping* showed the officers of the battalion, and the *Delineator* said of another photograph of battalion members: "Would you guess that they were women—these stalwart soldiers with their determined mouths and resolute chins?"

Before the 1920s most mainstream notions of homosexuality focused on a binary-gender analysis, the same sort of thinking that maintained the idea of the gender conventions for heterosexual men and women. In this official, often medical, view, gay men and lesbians were complete sexual "inverts." As neurologist George Beard phrased it, "Men become women and women men, in their tastes, conduct, character, feelings and behavior." The Battalion of Death members posed this threat of sexual inversion, of turning the world upside down in sexual, military, and social terms. If women soldiers were "safe" only when sexless, then active heterosexuality and active homosexuality made them dangerous. Some observers linked various sorts of "mannishness" in women to an all-encompassing social danger. Dr. William Lee Howard represented this view. "The female possessed of masculine ideas and independence," he wrote, "the viragint who would sit in the public highways and lift up her pseudo-virile voice, proclaiming her sole right to decide questions of war or religion . . . and that disgusting anti-social being, the female sexual pervert [by which he meant lesbian], are simply different degrees of the same class—degenerates." As new theories of Freud and other "sexologists" stigmatized lesbianism as "deviant" and "perverse," the "mannish lesbian" came to embody sexual and social disorder.[25] The woman soldier as mannish lesbian expressed social and sexual disorder in the strongest possible terms.

The work of scholars Lynda Hart and Lisa Duggan, who both link cultural representations of lesbians with violence, underscores these definitions of the mannish woman soldier. Hart suggests that popular culture has presented the lesbian as "historically inscribed both as 'not woman' and as violent" in literature, theater, and film. The result has been a "historical displacement of violence onto lesbians," as those responsible for violence against themselves and others. Lisa Duggan's examination of the representation of the lesbian love murder in the popular press from the 1890s through the 1920s suggests that the most hegemonic narratives equated lesbian identity with violence, danger, and the demise of the traditional heterosexual home. The predatory, "dangerous masculine woman," Duggan shows, and her "female violence" had to be "contained by vigilant male and female authority in defense of the home."[26]

"Botchkareva, Commander of the Battalion of Death," *Delineator* 92 (March 1918): 5.

"Officers of the Battalion of Death," *Good Housekeeping* 65 (October 1917): 23.

"Would You Guess That They Were Women?" *Delineator* 92 (March 1918): 7.

The mannish female soldier could imply the possibility that women might not need men at all. If women soldiers loved other women, protected one another, and took on the work and pleasures of the world without men, then what was to become of men, to say nothing of gendered agreements about life? Would men, could men, become obsolete? Charlotte Perkins Gilman posed just such a question in her fictional *Herland* (serialized in her journal the *Forerunner* in 1915). In a lovely valley away from other human contact a race of women evolved through parthenogenesis—spontaneous fertilization without any need for male sperm. They created a tranquil utopia free from violence in which each citizen developed her own talents and skills. Gilman's ideal *Herland* is shattered when male explorers bring not only heterosexuality but also ideas of male authority and superiority as well as violence against women in the form of rape. The rape sequence in the novel highlights the power and control of sexual assault, the attempt to conquer independent women. In *Herland* and its sequels, Gilman pondered the question of the gender conventions of the Protector and the Protected and violence.

The Russian women of the Battalion of Death functioned in the realm of myth in the United States during the world war in much the same way that the myth of the Amazons functioned in classical Athenian society. William Blake Tyrrell has shown that the Amazons were the outsiders who existed in the liminal, frontier regions of Athenian concepts of geography—"out there" somewhere. They took on the social roles of men in their community and existed without men in their midst (like the fictional residents of *Herland*). Yet Athenian myths purposely controlled these disorderly women. The stories that evolved about the Amazons placed them under the final authority of men through conquest. They were either killed, conquered in war, raped, married, or sometimes a combination of these outcomes. Tyrrell suggests that the myths of the conquered Amazons reassured Athenian men of the power of patriarchy and explained "why it [was] necessary for the daughter to marry by creating a scenario of the dangers inherent in her not marrying." The myth of the Amazons instructed Athenians concerning the requisite gender roles in a patriarchal culture. And, as Tyrrell observes, "the message of the myth had to be repeated again and again because the problems of women and marriage could never be solved once and for all."[27]

Like the Amazons, members of the Battalion of Death came from a liminal frontier, from "the depths of dark Russia," far away and little understood by Americans. By 1918 their leader, Maria Botchkareva, lay in a hospital, stripped of her command, shell-shocked and trembling. Reports circulated that she had given up and did not believe that most women could fight. She had been conquered. And final, emphatic "proof" of the ultimate conquest of the members of the Battalion of Death came with reports of their rape; in Lynda Hart's terms it was the displacement of violence onto the women soldiers themselves. Some among them were reportedly raped at the battle front. These were the "bad girls," the "sexy girls," and the "mannish girls" among the battalion. All lost their "honor" and the "honor" of Russia in the violent rapes alluded to in a variety of reports. The mannish soldiers were "resexualized" into heterosexuality by male soldiers acting through rape to reassert their power over all women. And even the "good girls" among battalion members were also "punished" by rape after their defense of the Winter Palace.[28] The ultimate fate of members of the Russian Women's Battalion of Death, then, was rape, dishonor, and reconquest. Representations of their "womanliness" and patriotic service as successful soldiers fell to this more powerful interpretation. Like the stories of the Amazons and lesbians in popular murder accounts, theirs was a cautionary tale for the instruction of "disorderly" women-at-arms. Their challenge to Russian men's failure to protect them and their nation had been politically useful for a time, but ultimately their claim to the role of Protector could not withstand the need to put them "in their place." They were labeled as "sexy" or sexually active women whether heterosexual or lesbian, when the only safety for a woman soldier was to "have no sex." Their sexuality was the mark of ineligibility for full civic responsibility and protection from violence.

The deviance of the woman soldier from proper female behavior was a key element of antisuffragist rhetoric. In his 1916 Tennessee speech, antisuffragist John J. Vertrees acknowledged that "some women, barren, masculine individuals, can bear arms just as there are some men who cannot." They were the exceptions, unsexed, unable to have children, or masculine, mannish lesbians, and therefore not "real women," at all. A woman soldier as a citizen would be ineffectual, impotent, "shooting blanks" with a "blank-cartridge ballot." Vertrees also worried that women empowered with the vote would interfere with military policy relating to male sexuality. Australian women (who had won the right to vote in 1902) objected to the draft of Australian men and helped to defeat national conscription for the world war at the polls. One argument they raised was that war and the military life destroyed the morals of young men because soldiers had brought venereal disease home from the fighting front while stationed in Egypt. Vertrees insisted that this argument was a "whimsical reason" for opposition to conscription and ridiculed what the women thought of as a "higher viewpoint." He then turned the tables and labeled these same women as sexually promiscuous in a stinging example of the way that violence was turned back on women who opposed it. "We can understand how it was those idle, lusty youngsters got into trouble in Egypt," he commiserated. "But if it is true that woman suffrage 'purifies' politics and the woman of Australia, voting all these years, have such 'far-seeing vision' and '*higher* viewpoints' that they are stirred as never before, how was it possible for this Egyptian 'plague' to be spread" throughout Australia? In other words, women were the ones responsible for the epidemic of venereal disease by engaging in sex with the soldiers, and they "masked their sexual wantonness with a veil of purity."[29]

Vertrees shared this vision of women-at-arms with those like Everett Wheeler who blamed the violence at the 1913 suffrage parade on women's sexually provocative dress. For Wheeler, as for others, "the influence of woman over man is not gained by kicking, scratching and biting and never has been. . . . [W]e want no fighting women. . . . [T]he fighting woman is odious to man. It is not by fighting, but by sweetness and light that woman's advancement has been gained." Neurologist Graeme H. Hammond went further, characterizing all women as the kicking, scratching, and biting kind. Journalist George McAdam consulted Hammond, a noted specialist in "nervous disorders," when the "dispatches from Petrograd seemed to give verification to the remarkable tale" of the Russian Women's Battalion of Death. In "When Women Fight," featured in the *New York Times Magazine* in September 1917, Hammond responded to the news of Russian women soldiers and also to reports of American women's interest in "gunnery." "Women make good soldiers?" he asked. "Why not? Women are a great deal more combative than men. If you don't believe me, ask any married man." When McAdam asked Hammond if he believed women were capable of wielding the weapons of war, he replied that they were, because "all women in their hearts have struck men with bayonets." Hammond proposed that allowing women to be soldiers would be a benefit to society: the physically defective women would perish, and the fit would survive to create a better white race.[30]

* * *

This violent backlash was the lesson for all female soldiers, for women who sought to take on the role of the Protector and to shame the men displaced in the process. Popular representations of the members of the Battalion of Death emphasized their deviant, active sexuality. The same cultural script for women who had been raped and otherwise targeted for violence and for women identified as lesbians meant that they were deemed responsible for the violence against them and deserved to be managed and controlled with violence to return them to their place. They were antithetical to the "patriotic mother." Maria Botchkareva could be cast as a heroine when her motives appeared to be to shame Russian men by joining the army and by forming an all-female regiment. But as a woman fleeing domestic violence, she was cast as a course, brutal peasant with aberrant and dangerous sexuality. This process was designed to challenge the definition of violence made by women-at-arms and their claims to the rights of self-defense. As such, it was used to discredit the female soldier and the claims women-at-arms made to a civic identity and to their right to safety in a patriarchal state in war or at peace.

5. Uncle Sam's Loyal Nieces

Women Physicians, Citizenship, and Wartime Military Service

In the sad times coming before the war is over, our Uncle Sam will no doubt ask gladly for his loyal nieces, and grant them a place in his household equally honorable to that occupied by his nephews.

—*Bulletin of the Woman's Medical College of Pennsylvania,*
December 1917

As a woman and as a physician and as a surgeon, I think our days for crawling are over. I cannot see why women should demonstrate their patriotism in any different way from men.

—Caroline Purnell, M.D., 1917

Like women-at-arms, women physicians made claims for military service as part of their understanding of fuller female citizenship. And like women-at-arms, they envisioned solutions to the problems of violence against women in wartime as part of that service. Yet there were important differences between the two groups. Women-at-arms were not part of a single professional group or unified in their skills and preparations for military service. Their claim to soldiering disrupted powerful cultural boundaries between women and combat and the construction of men as Protectors. Women physicians possessed skills that the military needed and had influential supporters and donors. And although women physicians sought officer status in the military medical corps, they were not seeking combat status or to significantly question the role of men as Protectors. Yet they faced strong cultural, professional, and bureaucratic obstacles in their quest for officer status in the military. This chapter will examine women physicians' claims for more complete female citizenship in their campaign for officer status in the military medical corps. The following chapter will analyze their response to violence against women civilians in the wake of the European war through the formation of all-female medical units.

Although many women physicians in the United States viewed the war in Europe as a regrettable global event, they considered the possibility of military medical service as a personal and professional opportunity. Such service would demonstrate their civic contributions and professional skills and would contribute to their fuller definition as women citizens and medical women on equal footing with male colleagues. American women physicians made their wartime claims for equal opportunity in the context of a broader history of struggle for access to educational, professional, and organizational opportunity in the field of medicine and the struggle for women's rights.[1] In addition to the barriers they faced from within their profession, medical women confronted the boundaries between women and military service with which other women interested in such service were grappling. And during the world war, they constructed their case for a place within the military medical corps as officers at the same time that male colleagues were waging their own heated battle with the military for increased rank and authority.

The Medical Profession on the Eve of War

The second decade of the twentieth century was a time for optimism for medical women in the United States. As the nation entered the war, women physicians could point to progress in educational opportunity and occupational variety. In 1910 women physicians reached a peak of approximately 6 percent of the medical profession (about 6,000 women practitioners), and a 1916 study showed that 1,313 American women physicians in active practice were specializing. Two-thirds did so in what were considered women's specialties such as obstetrics and gynecology; one-third of women physicians were making inroads into fields considered to be male territory.[2] There were still many reforms to be made, especially in access to medical education for women of color, and in internship and professional opportunities for all women. Here the medical profession mirrors the patterns Margaret Rossiter studied for women in the sciences during this period. After women achieved some access to medical education, institutional gatekeepers such as the American Medical Association (AMA) raised the stakes for professional success to include internships, hospital residencies, and research publications.[3] To combat these barriers women physicians worked within the AMA and local medical societies and in 1915 organized a separate professional organization for support and advocacy, the Medical Women's National Association (MWNA).[4]

Many medical women had great expectations that wartime needs for medical services would expand their opportunities and enhance their claims for more complete citizenship. Physician Mary Sutton Macy asserted that "medical women as a body" were "better equipped to do practical service than any other one class of women" in the United States. And Dr. Frances C. Van Gasken told students and faculty at the Woman's Medical College of Pennsylvania in December 1917:

> Today we are overlooking the Promised Land. . . . [I]t is for *you* to enter this Promised Land, this land of equal opportunity. . . . [I]t does not take a prophet to read the writing on the wall for the woman of today. In letters of light it says to her: "Come on! Here is work! Here is opportunity! Here is equality of reward!" The war that has opened "Pandora's Box" has also set free Hope. And, when the "world is made safe for democracy," Democracy will be made safe for women. . . . The demand for women physicians is, and will be, a constantly increasing one.[5]

Male physicians also saw the First World War as an opportunity, in their case to increase the rank and authority of the medical corps within the military hierarchy. Medical men under the direction of Dr. Franklin Martin of the General Medical Board of the Council of National Defense waged a legislative campaign for almost the entire length of the war itself. The result of their efforts was the Owen-Dyer Bill, which passed in both houses of Congress in July 1918. Owen-Dyer gave medical officers the same status as other military officers of the same rank from lieutenant to major general and provided them with increased authority over sanitary regulations and recommendations.[6] Over the course of the war male physicians struggled for increased rank at the same time that they enlisted for wartime service to demonstrate their professional and patriotic service. At the time of the Armistice, 30,591 physicians were serving in the military medical corps.[7] This concept of service with continued emphasis on reform was the general response of African American men in the profession. Leaders of the African American medical community urged male physicians to serve. "Racially, this war spells for us the most glorious word in the vocabulary of freedom—opportunity," Dr. C. V. Roman told his audience at Meharry Medical School in Tennessee in December 1917. Others echoed his hope that service in the face of prejudice would bring honor.[8] The editors of the *Journal of the National Medical Association* urged male readers to "be a man in every dimension . . . [and] convince the other fellow that you are the 'Real Stuff.'" Thirty African American doctors entered the Medical Officers' Training Camp at Fort Des Moines, Iowa, in the fall of 1917, and others followed them into service.[9]

The structural gains within the military represented by the Owen-Dyer Bill were part of male physicians' broader struggle for professionalization and legitimization in American society. In the early twentieth century public confidence in the profession increased, as the American Medical Association continued to strengthen professional boundaries and as the Flexner Report, published in 1910, graded medical schools and established stricter standards for medical education. Whereas a medical education in 1890 was equivalent to one or two years of undergraduate college study, by 1920 the medical degree was comparable to a Ph.D. By 1925 a survey of high school students and teachers in the United States asked respondents to rank professions in order of prestige. Physicians ranked third, behind bankers and college professors, ahead of members of the clergy and lawyers. By 1933, the medical profession ranked first among other professions.[10]

The Medical Women's National Association War Service Committee

For women physicians, the Medical Women's National Association provided a logical organizational context for maximizing the civic and professional possibilities of women's medical war service. When the program committee was looking for a speaker on the topic "The War Work of Women Physicians and Surgeons in the European War" for their second annual meeting in the summer of 1917, Dr. Rosalie Slaughter Morton seemed a natural choice. On her own due to the death of her husband, Morton was traveling in Europe when the war broke out in 1914. By the spring of 1916 she had secured an appointment as a special commissioner of the Red Cross to carry supplies from the United States to the Serbian army. This commission allowed her to travel and work with an official status, even after the supplies had been delivered. During her travels in Europe in the spring and summer of 1916 Morton studied the wartime medical work of British women physicians. She was especially interested in the all-female hospital units of the Scottish Women's Hospitals in France and Serbia organized by Dr. Elsie Inglis and supported by the National Union of Women's Suffrage Societies of Great Britain.[11] For several months Morton provided medical care to soldiers and refugees in tent hospitals along the Salonica front in Serbia. She returned with detailed notes concerning the war hospitals she had visited. Through the fall and winter of 1917–18 Morton developed plans and made inquiries in Washington concerning the possibility of forming a hospital unit of American medical women to serve in Serbia or France. When the United States entered the war, her plans took on a new dimension as "the thought of medical women was turning toward war service."[12]

Medical women at this June 1917 meeting of the Medical Women's National Association discussed the question of war service formally in sessions and informally among clusters of interested women. The general session featured reports of war service activities by women physicians in Illinois, Maryland, Massachusetts, and New York.[13] British physician Kathleen Burke, on a speaking tour to raise funds for the Scottish Women's Hospitals, addressed the eager group while dressed in her uniform and told of the effective service of these units of British medical women.[14] And as the featured speaker, Rosalie Slaughter Morton made her own observations concerning the need for medical women overseas.[15] A purposeful audience unanimously approved a resolution by California women physicians to be sent to Secretary of War Newton D. Baker, calling for equal access to military service.[16] In this atmosphere of enthusiasm for the possibilities of American medical women's war service, the women present supported the creation of a War Service Committee that they hoped would translate their desires for service and recognition into concrete plans and positive results.[17] There were some three hundred women present, and the new organization was less than two years old, but the women of the MWNA believed that they constituted a quorum to act on behalf of the women physicians of the United States.

The assembled women asked Rosalie Slaughter Morton to chair the War Service Committee, but she was reluctant to take on the post. Morton was in the process of creating an all-women medical unit, and she believed she could sail within a short time for either France or Serbia. She wanted to serve at the front as a surgeon, and definitely did not want to push papers and visit administrators in the States. But eventually she acceded and accepted the position. Morton renamed the War Service Committee the American Women's Hospitals (AWH), binding the new American organization to the strength and accomplishment of the Scottish Women's Hospitals already at the front and signifying her wish to bring American medical women to the war zone to make their own mark on military medicine.[18] She asked trusted colleagues and friends to serve on the executive committee: Emily Dunning Barringer as vice chair,[19] Mary Merritt Crawford as corresponding secretary,[20] Frances Cohen as recording secretary, Belle Thomas as associate secretary, and Sue Radcliffe as treasurer.[21] As New York practitioners, members of the Medical Women's National Association and the American Medical Association, and as women willing to work for the cause of women physicians in war service, they took up headquarters in donated office space at 637 Madison Avenue and went to work.

Morton also established the work of the AWH in the context of women's civic roles and responsibilities. Just after the women of the state of New York achieved the vote in November 1917, the AWH executive committee sent the following resolution to President Woodrow Wilson:

> WHEREAS, the privilege and responsibility of full citizenship has been extended to the women of New York State, and
> WHEREAS, the physicians of the American Women's Hospitals residents in New York State realiz[e] what full citizenship means, especially now in time of war, therefore be it
> RESOLVED, that our first official act of business as enfranchised citizens be to forward to the President of the United States our pledge of undivided loyalty.[22]

As loyal and now fully enfranchised citizens, the New York–based executive committee of the AWH offered its civic and professional services at a new level of political commitment and meaning.

Rosalie Slaughter Morton and the American Women's Hospitals were gaining recognition and an authoritative voice in the medical community, and they hoped to build a coalition of support for medical women's wartime service. Soon after the AWH was organized, Dr. Franklin Martin asked Morton to present an outline of the work of the AWH to the General Medical Board of the Council of National Defense. Morton visited a board meeting on June 24, 1917, and presented information on AWH activities and plans to the assembled male physicians. Soon after, Martin invited Morton to become a member of the General Medical Board of the Council of National Defense and to form a Committee of Women Physicians as part of that important policy-making body.[23]

War Service Registration

Leaders of the American Women's Hospitals believed that they might prepare the way for the acceptance of women physicians into the military medical corps by conducting a nationwide survey to determine the numbers of medical women who could and would serve and the specific skills they possessed. Census results would show Washington policy makers that medical women were ready and organized for wartime service. And AWH leaders hoped that by holding and controlling this information, they would be recognized as authoritative by military medical men and would be called upon to set policy and oversee the activities of all women physicians. The *Woman's Medical Journal* published registration forms, and the AWH mailed similar forms to individual medical women asking if they were willing to serve and in what capacity at home or abroad.[24] The registration was both a practical measure and a political one, like a nationwide petition directed to the federal government, the War Department, and the Medical Department of the Army calling for officer status for medical women qualified for military service. Women physicians returned thousands of registration cards to AWH headquarters and to the offices of the Committee of Women Physicians in Washington, D.C., from the summer of 1917 to early 1918.

The registration effort did not result in the acceptance of women into the military medical corps as officers. Yet through this war service registration, medical women expressed their sense of responsibility as members of the medical profession and as citizens. They made a claim for equal opportunity with male colleagues in the military medical corps and in the profession of medicine, and demonstrated their skills in public relations and lobbying for political action. The AWH published the results of the registration with other information on 5,991 women licensed to practice medicine in the United States as the *Census of Women Physicians* in 1918.[25] According to its data, almost one-third (1,830, or 30.5 percent) of the medical women in the country in 1917–18, active and retired, signified their willingness to provide medical service as part of the war effort. The significance of this percentage of registrants is amplified when we realize that this one-third comprised not simply those medical women who believed in the principle that women physicians should have the opportunity to participate in wartime service but those who were willing to register personally for such service. This point is particularly significant, because women were the traditional caretakers of extended family members, and many of these medical women had family responsibilities as well as professional responsibilities that might encumber a decision to register for war service. Rosalie Slaughter Morton believed that "nearly all the women [who registered for war service] had dependent, aged parents, invalid relatives, brothers or sisters, nieces, nephews, or their own children to educate." The one-third also does not include those women who supported wartime service but refused to register "unless they were first commissioned in the military medical corps."[26]

A commitment to medical professionalism was an important factor in the war service registration of women physicians.[27] Forty percent of medical women who were members of the American Medical Association registered for war service, 58 percent of the members of the Medical Women's National Association registered, and 62 percent of those women who were members of both the AMA and the MWNA registered for war service, twice the average for the *Census of Women Physicians* as a whole.[28] Only 27 percent of the women with no professional affiliation registered for war service. These figures indicate that those medical women who were most concerned with women's professionalization, those who were active in organizations and perhaps believed that they had the most to gain in a bid for equality with male colleagues, registered for war service.

The war service registration rates of the medical women in the *Census of Women Physicians* are significant when we compare them to the war service of male physicians. According to the army surgeon general's office, there were 30,591 physicians in the medical corps at the time of the Armistice in November 1918, which means that approximately 20 percent of the male physicians in the country were in military service in 1918.[29] Another contemporary listing of physicians, *History of Medicine and Surgery and Physicians and Surgeons of Chicago* (1922), gives information on civilian and home-front war service for 1,507 Chicago medical men. Almost half of this group (734, or 49 percent) reported no war-related service, civilian or military. Twenty-six percent reported some form of civilian service, and 25 percent reported military service in the war.[30] These figures suggest that medical women committed themselves through the avenues open to them in substantial numbers and compared favorably to the service rates of male colleagues.

Contract Service and Service with Voluntary Organizations

At the same time that the AWH's registration of women physicians got under way in the summer of 1917, officials in Washington received numerous letters and other inquiries regarding women and the medical corps. Many women applied for acceptance to the army's Medical Reserve Corps. Some physicians made personal visits to government and military leaders that summer, and prominent women and men outside of the medical field urged army surgeon general William Crawford Gorgas and secretary of war Newton Baker to admit women physicians to the medical corps on equal terms with male colleagues. Medical men were developing their own legislative campaign for increased status and authority in military medicine. Pressure from many sides mounted and placed the question of medical women's military service and status in public debate.[31]

While medical women and their supporters petitioned for officer status in the medical corps, there was one official avenue open for medical women to serve in the military. Several women—including Dr. Anita Newcombe McGee, who had served as the first director of the Army Nurse Corps—had served in the army as contract surgeons. A contract surgeon was a civilian consultant employed by the military to perform medical duties without the benefits of rank or status. Physicians in the Civil War had been employed as contract surgeons performing "part-time work, the individual doctor so employed maintaining his own private practice at home and at the same time giving some hours of each day to his Army hospital duties." Now, as male physicians were struggling for increased status within the medical department, the position of contract surgeon seemed to be an anachronistic "curiosity," one that lacked any rank, professional prestige, or authority to command deference.[32] The surgeon general still had the power to appoint as many contract surgeons as might be needed in "emergencies," and "at places which did not justify the expense involved by the detail of a medical officer." Only 2 men served abroad with the American Expeditionary Force as contract surgeons; the other 887 men employed during the war years as contract surgeons served on the home front in part-time, limited capacities. Chicago neurologist Peter Bassoe, for example, contracted with the army to teach a course in neurosurgery.[33]

Given contract work's lack of rank and status and its temporary nature, many medical women across the country thought that it represented inferior status and strongly opposed such terms of service for women physicians in the war. Philadelphia surgeon Caroline Purnell believed that accepting contract work "would mean our ability to be under the cook, the head nurse, or others, and be ordered around." Following a trip west, Chicago physician Martha Whelpton reported that "very few of the Coast women, and few of the Colorado women also, will go as Contract Surgeons. They object with all their might." Chicago women believed that their "professional dignity" was at stake, and "absolutely opposed" contract service.[34]

In response to pressure regarding women's medical service in the world war, Washington officials announced a new purpose for contract service. In August 1917 Acting Judge Advocate General Blanton Winship handed down his interpretation of military regulations regarding contract surgeons. "The statute does not prescribe that contract surgeons shall be males," he wrote, "and, in the absence of such a limitation, I am clearly of the opinion that it is allowable by law to appoint female physicians as contract surgeons in the United States Army."[35] Many medical women saw this decision as an attempt to create a separate and unequal category of military service for women physicians and a "halfway measure" in response to their call for equal opportunity and officers' commissions. Regulations dealing with regular service in the medical corps contained the same phraseology as did those outlining the qualifications for contract work. Yet that same month the acting judge advocate general had decided that the medical corps regulations pertained only to men.[36] It seemed that although women would be accepted only as what many termed "day laborers," men would be given the status, rank, and pay of officers in the medical corps.[37]

Caroline Purnell did not support the argument that contract work was a step along the road to equality in military service. "As a woman and as a physician and as a surgeon, I think our days for crawling are over," she said. "I cannot see why women should demonstrate their patriotism in any different way from men. If the men respect themselves and demonstrate their patriotism according to their training and experience, why should not women do the same thing? Why should we have to have a different way when our ability is just the same? We would be more self-respecting if we should stand upon this. . . . Our brains are not in our sex." Apparently, the majority of medical women in the country agreed. In the fall of 1917 Dr. Caroline Towles of Baltimore attempted to register medical women's opinions on such service. When asked, "As the only manner of serving, would you consider contract practice if this form of service can be made less objectionable?" most medical women responded "No."[38]

Some women physicians held notions of patriotism and professionalism that allowed them to view contract service with the military in a more positive light. Such service would make it possible for them to use their professional skills to serve their country, the wounded, and the sick without delay. Some believed that if contract service was the place where women could push the boundaries of military service, then they would join and push. And a few women found contract service to be the only way that they could circumvent military restrictions and still serve as members of the hospital units that they had joined for overseas work. Physician Esther Pohl Lovejoy summed it up: "They were without commissions," she wrote, but "they were on the job."[39]

The surgeon general asked Washington, D.C., physician Emma Wheat Gilmore, who took the place of Rosalie Slaughter Morton as chair of the Committee of Women Physicians in 1918, to recommend women for contract service. Over the course of the war, fifty-five medical women engaged in contract service with the United States Army, all, apparently, with her approval. They came from all parts of the country—nineteen from the East, twenty-three from the Midwest, seven from the South, five from the West, and one from Puerto Rico—and from urban areas such as Brooklyn, Boston, Memphis, and San Francisco as well as smaller towns and rural communities from Kalamazoo, Michigan, to Gilmore City, Iowa. They had been educated at both large and small medical institutions, in "regular" medicine, homeopathy, and psychiatry. And although more than half graduated from medical school after 1908, they represented a range of age groups. Gertrude Mitchell Streeper of New York served three months, from May to August 1918. She had been practicing medicine for twenty-six years, having received her medical degree from the Woman's Medical College of Pennsylvania in 1892. Nell Carney of Ada, Oklahoma, graduated from the Medical School of the National University of Arts and Sciences in St. Louis in 1918 and then went quickly into service as a contract surgeon from September 1918 through January 1919. The average length of service for the group was seven months, with two women serving only one month and one serving longer than eighteen months.[40]

Eleven medical women (20 percent of the total) served as contract surgeons overseas. Dr. Frances Edith Haines worked as an anesthetist with a medical unit at Limoges, France. Cincinnati physician Elizabeth Van Cortlandt Hocker entered the army as a contract surgeon in May 1918 and served until August 1919. She was particularly proud that after the Armistice she was placed in charge of two hospital wards of forty-two beds each that were for women personnel of the army at Savenay, France. Forty-four women contract surgeons (80 percent of the total) performed their military duties while remaining in U.S. territory, some serving in administrative posts and others at military hospitals, many caring for convalescent soldiers. Dolores M. Pinero had received her medical degree in Puerto Rico and was practicing in the town of Río Piedras when the war began. She became a contract surgeon with the army in October 1918 and was immediately assigned to the base hospital at San Juan, the only woman serving in the army in Puerto Rico. She did anesthesiology and laboratory work and helped to open a four-hundred-bed hospital in Ponce during the influenza epidemic in the fall of 1918.[41]

Whereas these medical women accepted the terms of contract service, other women physicians wished to provide immediate war service overseas without the onus of contract work, and volunteered with the Red Cross and other civilian organizations in Europe. They made individual contracts with these organizations, and their work ranged from service in private hospitals to service in civilian communities and locations near the front. They provided medical and surgical care and worked in public health with civilians and refugees. By November 1918 there were at least seventy-six medical women serving abroad with various organizations. Forty-nine percent of them were from the eastern United States, 21 percent from the West, 17 percent from the Midwest, and 13 percent from the South. A comparison of the average graduation year for these women who went overseas with that of all women physicians in the 1918 *Census of Women Physicians* indicates that the overseas group was younger. For all medical women, the average year was 1899, and for these seventy-six overseas women the average year of graduation was 1904. Sixty percent of the overseas women had graduated between 1902 and 1914.[42]

Medical women of color found voluntary service with organizations other than the U.S. military to be more accessible due to racial and gender barriers. Most African American women physicians worked within their communities to provide wartime health care service, but two African American medical women served overseas. One of them was Dr. Mary L. Brown, who was commissioned by the Red Cross for wartime service in France. A graduate of Howard University Medical School who had received advanced training in Edinburgh, Brown was living in France and received her assignment in the spring of 1918. Harriet Rice of Newport, Rhode Island, an 1891 graduate of the Women's Medical College of New York, was living in France with her brother at the outbreak of the war. Rice gave distinguished service in a French military hospital, where she served for most of the war. In August the French presented Rice with the Reconnaissance Française medal for her meritorious service with the French wounded.[43]

Yet service abroad in the military without the authority and rank of officer status could lead to vulnerability for women physicians. The question of the treatment of women workers in the war zone was the subject of much discussion among medical women in the States. Jessie Fisher, a doctor working with the Red Cross in Paris, sent a letter to a woman colleague in the States. It appears that numerous copies of the letter were made and passed around the women's medical community. Fisher wrote in the spring of 1918 as women physicians were in the midst of their campaign for commission as officers in the medical corps. She had chosen to go to France for wartime medical service as a civilian doctor employed by the Red Cross. In her letter she described the "anomalous" and "embarrassing" situation she and other women physicians in France were experiencing. "We are not saluted nor have we any authority," she wrote. She found allies in the "older men in the R.C. and Army" who were "as courteous as at home." But the younger men were a problem. She confided that she had "struck" a young U.S. Army Medical Corps lieutenant "who made me feel my lack of rank" and lamented that the "soldiers do not have the proper respect for us." Fisher was uncertain about how French officers would treat her and promised to provide more information as she served with them. In general, she said, "I think we are usually taken for army chauffeurs." Her account reinforced concerns that women physicians without military rank were vulnerable to a hostile working environment. "My advice to you, and to all women M.D.s, is to stay in the U.S. and fight for commissions for the women. They need us badly and if the women will refuse to come without commissions they will be compelled to give them to us."[44]

The Campaign for Medical Corps Commissions

Whereas some women served as contract surgeons and others with private organizations, many women physicians focused their actions on gaining officer commissions for medical women in the military medical corps. At least two groups of women, and many others as individuals, applied directly to the medical corps for military service. They took the position that they were professionally prepared citizens who had all the qualifications required by statute to be accepted as medical officers. In their view, military regulations outlined the necessary credentials and experience necessary for physicians to be accepted in the medical corps, and the language of the regulations included the term *citizens* without explicit reference to gender.[45] Here they followed the interpretive and practical strategies of Susan B. Anthony, Virginia Minor, and other late-nineteenth-century suffrage activists who presented themselves at the polls as citizens eligible to vote under the protection of the Fourteenth Amendment, which established the definition of citizens as "all persons born or naturalized in the United States." These women, as Ellen Carol DuBois suggests, "marched into power directly, through the main political entrance."[46] As Susan Anthony declared to audiences prior to her 1872 trial for attempting to vote, "In voting, I committed no crime, but simply exercised my 'citizen's right,' guaranteed to me and all United States citizens by the National Constitution, beyond the power of any state to deny."[47] Virginia Minor, president of the Woman Suffrage Association of Missouri, sued the St. Louis registrar who refused to let her vote in 1872. Her case, *Minor v. Happersett* came to the Supreme Court in 1875. In a unanimous decision, the justices decided against Minor, stating that "if it had been intended to make all citizens of the United States voters, the framers of the Constitution would not have left it to implication."[48] Now these medical women, many of whom lived in states that granted women the right to vote by 1917, continued to refine the definition of women's citizenship rights and obligations. They challenged their exclusion as citizens from military service to the state and used their professional credentials to attempt to enter through the front door of the military medical corps.

One group who claimed the status of citizenship through direct action consisted of Portland, Oregon, medical women who drove to the Vancouver, Washington, training facility for medical officers in the spring of 1918 to present themselves as eligible physicians desiring commissions. Drs. Katherine Manion, Mae Cardwell, Mary MacLachlan, and Emily Balcom came representing many other women physicians of the area. "There is no word in the war department regulations that bars women," one of them told a reporter for the *Oregon Journal* after their attempt, "and away we went to the officers' training camp." They had prepared themselves so that they could not be turned away because of a lack of credentials. "We looked up the requirements very carefully," they explained. "We armed ourselves with our certificates, our references, our diplomas from reputable universities, our personal testimonials from citizens and a dozen other details." They presented themselves to an astonished major in charge of the camp, "ready and armed to take the examinations, don the uniforms and salute the privates." The women stated their intentions, arguing that in their community women had full suffrage, that they were citizens and ready to meet the professional and other requirements necessary for acceptance into the Medical Reserve Corps. The major examined their documents and after "a long debate" told the group that he could not examine them because "it hasn't been done." After more discussion he asked them if they wouldn't like to go overseas as nurses. They replied firmly that they would not, and asked the male physician-officer, "'Would *you*?'" The major finally said that he would telegraph Surgeon General Gorgas for an answer, and the negative reply came from Washington the next day. Gorgas also sent separate letters to each of the four women declining their application for service as medical officers in the army.[49] Katherine Manion, who had been active in the campaign that brought votes to Oregon women in 1912, considered it a distinction to have mounted the challenge even though the army refused to grant the women commissions on account of their sex.[50]

Another coalition constructed a more elaborate test case to assert the right of medical women as citizens and trained physicians to serve as medical officers in the military. The newly formed Colorado Medical Women's War Service League met in September 1917 and formed a Committee on Recognition of Medical Women. Mary Elizabeth Bates, a prominent Denver gynecologist, MWNA officer, suffrage activist, community organizer, and secretary of the league, was asked to chair the committee and to "take up the question of the appointment of women physicians in the Medical Reserve Corps of the U.S. Army."[51] The committee had two tasks: first, to identify and study the regulations governing the service of physicians in the Medical Department of the Army and, second, to recommend and implement the actions necessary for women physicians to gain equal access to the Medical Reserve Corps.

Bates and her committee members began an investigation of the status of the regulations concerning service with the Medical Reserve Corps. Section 37 of the National Defense Act of June 3, 1916, prescribed the following qualifications for appointment in the Officers' Reserve Corps: "Such citizens as, upon examination prescribed by the President, shall be found physically, mentally and morally qualified to hold such commissions."[52] The *Manual for the Medical Department* required applicants for appointment in the medical corps to be between twenty-two and thirty years of age, citizens of the United States, with a degree from a "reputable medical school legally authorized to confer the degree of doctor of medicine, and must have had at least one year's hospital training." The requirements for service in the Medical Reserve Corps were similar: commissions were to be given "to such graduates of reputable schools of medicine, citizens of the United States . . . [who shall be found] physically, mentally, and morally qualified to hold such commissions." Such officers were required to be between twenty-two and forty-five years of age and to be qualified to practice medicine in their state or territory of residence.[53]

Gender was not an explicit category for acceptance in any of these regulations, and there were hundreds if not thousands of women who could meet the professional and physical qualifications necessary for service. Based on their examination of military regulations, Bates and her committee concluded: "The word 'citizens' must include women, since women are citizens." In the opinion of the committee, "it was obviously not necessary to seek the enactment of a law to permit the appointment of women."[54] Unlike nurses who would need to get new legislation passed to allow them as a professional group to gain officer status, medical women had to deal with the interpretation of laws that, in explicit language at least, were not gender specific, and already granted officer status to their professional group.

Yet the interpretation of a law could be just as powerful as the absence or presence of a law. On August 30, 1917, Acting Judge Advocate General S. T. Ansell had written an official interpretation of military regulations regarding the service of women physicians in the Medical Reserve Corps. His interpretation was based on the same premise as the actions of the major in Vancouver—"It hasn't been done"—but his decision carried more powerful consequences because it was supported by legal precedent and the authority of his office. After quoting the National Defense Act of 1916, which stipulated the service of citizens, Ansell referred to an opinion of the Massachusetts Supreme Court in a case dealing with the appointment of women as notaries. This decision in turn employed as precedent another Massachusetts court decision that raised the question of whether women could serve as justices of the peace:

> There is nothing in the Constitution which in terms prohibits women from being appointed to judicial offices, any more than from being appointed to military offices, or to executive civil offices, the tenure and mode of appointment of which are provided for in the Constitution. It was the nature of the office of justice of the peace, and the usage that always had prevailed in making appointments to that office, that led the justices to advise that it could not have been the intention of the Constitution that women should be appointed justices of the peace. . . . In our opinion the same considerations apply to the office of notary public.

Claiming these rulings as precedent, Ansell concluded, "For similar reasons it is the view of this office that it is not allowable by law to appoint female physicians to military office in the Medical section of the Officers' Reserve Corps of the Army."[55]

In the body of his decision, the acting judge advocate general stated four main reasons, in his opinion, that women physicians should not be commissioned as officers in the Medical Reserve Corps. First, as we have noted, was his belief in "the usage that has always prevailed" (or, again, in the words of the Vancouver medical officer, "It hasn't been done"). Legal precedent and Ansell's conclusion that because it had not been done before "it could not have been the intention of the Constitution" bolstered this contention. Second, he referred to other legislation (without being specific) that required soldiers to be males. In other words, because some statutes used the word *male* to refer to soldiers, women physicians could not become part of the Medical Reserve Corps, despite the fact that regulations for this corps did not specify gender. His third reason to bar women was a physical one: "I think women physicians would not have the physical qualifications which would be required for the performance of some duty which may be required of a medical officer," he wrote. And his fourth reason was also part of the justification for creating a separate and unequal sphere for women as contract surgeons: service as medical officers was qualitatively different from service as contract surgeons, because medical officers in the Medical Reserve Corps "have a military status as officers in the army."[56] For Ansell, women were not to have the status of officers in the military where they would have authority, including the authority to command men.

Mary Bates and her committee developed, along with their ally Colorado senator John Franklin Shafroth, a plan to test the medical corps regulations that called for the appointment of citizens. It was a plan, Bates wrote, that would "achieve the result desired with the minimum amount of trouble for the War Department." The War Service League would select from six to twelve women physicians who would apply as a group for service with the Medical Reserve Corps. The medical women in this test case were to come from states that granted women the right of suffrage, presumably because women in these states had already crossed an important conceptual and practical boundary of citizenship. These women were to be professionally prepared and have all of the qualifications necessary to "make good" if appointed. Along with the standard documentation of education and accomplishments, the women were to secure recommendations from "prominent and influential persons." They would enlist the support of senators and representatives from their states to cooperate with Senator Shafroth and Colorado representative Edward Keating, "who enthusiastically endorsed the plan." The alliance between Shafroth and women working for the cause of female citizenship was an enduring one: in the House of Representatives, the *Woman Citizen* recalled, "he helped Miss Anthony in the days when he was almost the only friend suffrage had in Congress."[57]

To select these important individuals, the Colorado Medical Women's War Service League consulted with other women working for entrance into the medical corps. They sought the advice of the California Medical Women's League for the Recognition of Women Physicians in the U.S. Army, a group that was primarily working on a petition drive for legislation that would include women physicians in the medical corps. And the committee sought the recommendations of Charlotte M. Conger, the recently named executive secretary of the American Women's Hospitals in New York City, who had access to the war service registration information on women physicians interested in service. Eight women physicians were chosen to present themselves to the surgeon general and secretary of war for service in the Medical Reserve Corps: Myra L. Everly of Seattle, an 1893 graduate of Northwestern; Julia P. Larson of San Francisco, an 1898 graduate of Berkeley; Mary McKay of Macon, Georgia, an 1897 graduate of the Woman's Medical College of Baltimore; Mabel A. Martin of Livingston, New York, a 1912 graduate of Cornell Medical College; Regina M. Downey of Beaver Falls, Pennsylvania, a 1914 graduate of the Woman's Medical College of Pennsylvania; Marion H. Rea-Lucks of Philadelphia; M. Jean Gale of Denver, an 1889 graduate of the Woman's Medical College of Pennsylvania; and Helen Craig of Denver, a 1913 graduate of Rush Medical College of Chicago. All were from suffrage states except for McKay of Georgia and Downey and Rea-Lucks of Pennsylvania, who, it appears, were chosen to round out the regional and institutional representation of the group.[58]

By February 1918 the applications were in order, and the league put the test case in motion. A group of eleven members of Congress, led by Shafroth, went to the office of Surgeon General William Crawford Gorgas.[59] Anita Newcombe McGee, who had served as a contract surgeon in the Spanish-American War and had been appointed head of the Army Nurse Corps at its creation in 1901, accompanied the delegation. As the woman physician most closely associated with actual experience in military medicine, McGee's presence was both symbolic and practical. In her account of the proceedings, McGee reported that the league representatives included the application of Mary Bates with those of the other eight women and then presented all of the completed applications to the surgeon general for his approval.[60] By all accounts Gorgas was sympathetic with the movement. McGee reported that he told her he personally favored commissions for women physicians. But he was bound, he said, by the decision of the judge advocate general opposing women in the Medical Reserve Corps. He suggested that the next step for the group was to take the matter up with Secretary of War Baker. McGee believed that if Baker could be persuaded, then "the Judge Advocate General's Office would doubtless reverse its decision, and the Surgeon-General be given a free hand."[61]

On February 4 the same group went to the office of Secretary of War Baker, hoping to convince him to support commissions for medical women. Baker was on record opposing women in military service. In a letter to the military committees of both houses of Congress considering a bill to commission women in the Signal Corps, Baker wrote that he did "not approve of commissioning or enlisting women in the military service." The group presented the women's applications to Baker, read the decision of the judge advocate general, and explained their position on the matter. Baker replied that "his main thought was to win the war, and that he did not think that commissioning women physicians would contribute to that end, nor did he want to make any unnecessary innovations now." Shafroth and McGee both argued that there was a need for the service of women physicians, McGee stating that the surgeon general wanted them especially for work as anesthetists and pathologists. Baker ended their conversation by saying that he believed that women physicians were not needed by the military but that he would consider the matter further.[62]

The test case was at a standstill, with the applications shelved in the office of the secretary of war. At the close of her account of the meeting with Baker, Anita McGee asked her readers in the *Woman's Medical Journal*, "Shall we accept the Secretary's views, and stop 'bothering people,' or shall we say that the need for at least a few of us will surely come if the war lasts, and we should fight for the principle of equal recognition for equal work?" Mary Bates urged medical women across the country to take action. "We ask that all the influence possible be now brought to bear," she wrote, "to prevent the consummation of the great injustice of allowing this opinion to be the final judgment of this administration of the real question at issue—the rights of citizenship as applied to women." The editor of the *Woman's Medical Journal* expressed the hope that the convincing case of the medical women would persuade the secretary of war to change his mind. However, she wrote, if the War Department should decide against the medical women, "there will be no cessation of this effort, but renewed activity to bring about this obviously just action."[63]

Medical women also mounted a campaign to bring the question of women's entrance in the medical corps to the formal attention of the American

Medical Association. They hoped that the association would use its influence to support commissions for women physicians. Women physicians were successful in achieving a voice, although it was a voice filtered through male allies, at the AMA National Convention in Chicago in June 1918. Colleagues introduced three resolutions on behalf of women physicians. Dr. H. G. Wetherill, a Colorado physician and colleague of Mary Bates in gynecology, introduced one resolution; Dr. George Kress, a California physician active in tuberculosis work and professor of hygiene at the College of Medicine of the University of California, introduced another that specifically reflected the views of the Medical Association of the State of California; and Dr. E. O. Smith, professor of urology at the University of Cincinnati, introduced a third supportive resolution.[64]

The language contained in these three AMA resolutions reveals a great deal about the way in which medical women and their allies constructed a case for women's service. It also reveals that they were responding to the objections made by the judge advocate general and the secretary of war, opinions that in turn reflected social concerns about women's military service. In a broad sense, medical women employed the same two arguments that Aileen Kraditor identified as the basic rationales in the call for woman suffrage: expediency and justice. According to the AMA resolutions, it would be expedient for the military to commission women physicians: they were "fitted and equipped" to provide "valuable service," they were graduates of medical schools and qualified to practice medicine, and "most if not all of them have signified their readiness" for service. With the demands of war, all available skill should be utilized, and commissions would "further the utilization of women physicians in service." The resolutions also called for women's entrance into the medical corps based on the idea of justice. Women physicians in all fields, including surgery, one resolution emphasized, render service that is "as efficient and valuable as can be rendered by men." Medical women serving overseas with such groups as the Red Cross had "performed invaluable services" and demonstrated their loyalty, employing, in the words of another resolution, "their skill and energy in our common cause." For these reasons, the resolutions called on the secretary of war to bring women physicians into the medical corps "in full standing" with the same rank and pay as male medical officers.[65]

The AMA resolutions also addressed objections to service based on a supposed physical weakness or unsuitability for military service. American women physicians serving "in the war zone" with the Red Cross and other organizations, and women physicians from other nations, one resolution stated, "have demonstrated that it is possible for women to endure the hard-

ships of life in the war zone and still do creditable work."[66] Here, as well as in
the other aspects of their argument, they made the implicit claim for service
as citizens who were equal in their abilities to serve the state, even while facing the dangers of the war zone.

Members voted to forward the resolutions to the Reference Committee
on Legislation and Political Action for the AMA. This committee returned
an opinion that appeared to be both supportive and cautious, and drew the
line for women's service at the boundary of "soldiering." "The very character
of military service and women's natural limitation for such service must
require wise discrimination in their employment in war work," the committee members wrote. Women physicians, in other words, were not to be
placed in situations in which they might have to perform as soldiers due to
the "natural limitations" of gender. However, they continued, the "principle
of equal rank and pay for equal service is inherently just without regard to
sex, and the committee feels this should be unhesitatingly approved by the
House [of Delegates of the AMA]."[67]

Although it appears that some male colleagues were supportive of commissions for women physicians, the committee's decision can also be seen
as a cautious one. As we have seen, male physicians were fighting their own
battles for increased status and authority in the military in this same period.
They were interested in strengthening and maintaining the military status
of their profession both during and after the war, and could stand on such
principles as "equal pay for equal work" without conceding much overall
ground to women.[68] This stance was especially true when the disclaimer
regarding the "natural limitations" of women's military service was included
in their resolution. According to this AMA committee, women physicians
could serve in the military without actually being soldiers, and therefore they
avoided the issue of women's military service as combat service, a threshold
most Americans were unwilling to cross. Yet in denying them soldier status,
the AMA perpetuated a less-than-equal place for women in the medical
corps. Caroline Purnell believed it. "The men are not just ready to give us
the ground yet," she told her colleagues. "They got in on the ground floor
first; they are going to get all out of it that they can for the sacrifices they
have made."[69]

The committee recommended the resolutions to the AMA membership
for action, but before it could take place the war was over, taking with it the
expediencies that had made the arguments for women's service possible.
Like the applications of the women brought to Secretary of War Baker by the
Colorado coalition, the resolutions, petitions, and other calls for legislative
action were not formally acted upon before the end of the conflict, yet they

helped to set new definitions for what was possible. Officially buried, they lived in the memories of the women and men who had made their claims until another war broke out in Europe twenty years later. In April 1943, with the passage of the Sparkman-Johnson Bill, women physicians gained the right to be officers in the military medical corps, thanks to heightened wartime need and their successful, strategic hard work.[70]

* * *

The women physicians who made claims for wartime service in the military medical corps based their campaign on a vision of women's citizenship that included economic and professional equality. The juxtaposition of their campaign for wartime service with important professional gains and the final stages of the woman suffrage campaign encouraged them to link their professional and civic arguments for service and equality. The women who served as contract surgeons and with voluntary organizations, those who registered for wartime service, members of the Colorado Medical Women's War Service League, the four Oregon women who took direct action to apply for service, the hundreds of women who sent in applications and inquiries, and the thousands who signed petitions to Washington officials seem to have agreed with Colorado physician Mary Bates. The real question, or, perhaps, the all-encompassing question, was "the rights of citizenship as applied to women."

6. Helping Women Who Pay the "Rapacious Price" of War

Women's Medical Units in France

Warfare is much worse for women than for men. Men have the right of death and they die fighting gloriously for their ideals. But women must live and be confiscated with the goods and the chattels.
—Esther Pohl Lovejoy, M.D., 1919

[Women physicians have priorities for treating the] suffering of noncombatant populations, particularly women and children, in war-stricken countries.
—Eliza Mosher, M.D., 1917

In addition to their campaigns for fuller civic and professional roles with officer status in the military medical corps, many medical women responded to the information they received about rape and violence against women in the war. Some took action to challenge the violence of war on women by providing care for women and children who had experienced the violence of the war zone and enemy occupation. Oregon physician Esther Pohl Lovejoy worked with the Red Cross and other organizations in Europe to provide medical care for refugees and civilians in France in 1917. She returned to the States in 1918 for a successful speaking tour to raise awareness about the devastating effects of war on women and children and funds for their medical care. And in 1918 two groups of women physicians created all-female hospital units to serve women's health needs abroad in the wake of wartime violence and occupation. With staffs of women with various surgical and medical specialties focusing on gynecology and obstetrics but also in general medicine and public health, they would treat not only soldiers wounded in combat but the women and children who were victims of the physical and sexual violence of the war and its devastation. These medical women sought to combine their struggle for equality with male colleagues with a challenge to violence against women in wartime. Their actions emphasized the specific consequences for women in war: sexual assault, impoverishment, and lack of resources. Their wartime vision highlighted these definitions of violence against women and motivated them to new activism. This chapter will explore the responses of these women physicians to violence against women in the war zone.

Esther Pohl Lovejoy and the Violent Consequences of War for Women

Physician Esther Pohl Lovejoy publicized the violent consequences of war for women by drawing on her firsthand experiences during five months in wartime France from September 1917 to January 1918. Lovejoy, an Oregon physician, was born in a logging camp in Washington Territory in 1869, graduated from the Medical School of the University of Oregon in 1894, and practiced obstetrical medicine in Oregon and Alaska before the war. An active suffragist, Lovejoy became involved in public policy and administration when she joined the Portland Board of Health in 1905 and served as the Portland city health officer from 1907 until 1909, the first woman to hold such a position in a large city in the United States.[1]

Lovejoy was in New York City for the second annual meeting of the Medical Women's National Association the first week of June 1917 at which the War Service Committee (shortly to be called the American Women's Hospitals) was formed. She attended the first meeting of the War Service Committee on June 9 and "volunteered for service overseas." Her colleagues authorized her to consult with suffrage leader Anna Howard Shaw who had recently been appointed chair of the Woman's Committee of the Council of National Defense, an umbrella organization for wartime activities. And they asked Lovejoy to represent the MWNA in Washington and to "go to Europe as the official representative of the War Service Committee of the Medical Women's National Association," with particular attention to the needs of women and children in France.[2] Ten days later Lovejoy attended a Washington, D.C., conference of the Woman's Committee that included the representatives of fifty-nine women's organizations. The Woman's Committee supported her visit to France "to study conditions there" and "gave her letters of introduction to the American officials in France."[3] By the time she sailed for France and began her work there in September 1917, Lovejoy had secured the support and sponsorship of the American Red Cross and the American Fund for French Wounded in addition to the Women's Committee of the Council of National Defense and the Medical Woman's National Association.[4] With

Esther Pohl Lovejoy, ca. 1918. Esther Pohl Lovejoy Collection,
Oregon Health & Sciences University Historical Collections &
Archives, Portland, Oregon.

this substantial, multilayered organizational backing, Lovejoy spent the next
ten months gathering information for a speaking tour in the United States
and for a book titled *The House of the Good Neighbor.*[5]

While in France Lovejoy worked with a variety of institutions and observed
the war's effects on women and children. The "House of the Good Neighbor"
that provided the title for her book was a settlement house, the Residence
Sociale, administered by Marie-Jeanne Bassot in the working-class factory
district of Levallois outside of Paris. For a decade before the war the Residence Sociale had served the local community, and its role intensified and
expanded with the loss, poverty, and need of working women and children

in wartime Paris. The residence provided job training, health care, day care, and inexpensive and free meals and served as the liaison between government contract garment cutters and women who did finishing work by the piece at home. In particular, the number of single mothers needing help from the residence increased due to wartime conditions. "After their accouchements," Lovejoy wrote, "suitable employment was found for them, and if they could not earn enough to support themselves and their babies, their earnings were supplemented by ways and means provided by societies organized for that purpose." One single mother, pregnant, with a small child in her arms and without hope, was rescued after jumping into the Seine. The staff of the residence cared for her and her children until she gave birth and helped her find work and a place to live with her children.[6] Lovejoy also visited other institutions for single mothers and the large public maternity hospital in Paris. In the city and its outskirts she also found dental and public health clinics, and *crèches* that provided day care and long-term care for children.

At the Residence Sociale Lovejoy also met refugees from northern France who had been forced from their homes by the advancing German armies at the start of the war. Their stories of violence, violation, and loss made her want to see more, firsthand. She spent some weeks in Évian-les-Bains on Lake Geneva near the Swiss border "through which the intermittent streams of human war wastage that had passed through the military mill in the invaded provinces was emptied" back into France. Here she found the resort baths and casinos of former days occupied by *repatries* who had spent the past several years as wandering refugees and were now trying to heal and find a way to make a new life. The things that she witnessed at Évian chilled and angered Lovejoy. It was here that she felt that she confronted the ultimate horror of war. The German invaders, she said, had sifted and sorted the residents. "Those without military value were robbed of their earthly possessions, evicted en masse from their native towns and villages, herded together, and finally deported," and "those with military values were detained by their conquerors." But just what are "military values"? "Are they not fighting values, labor values, and breeding values?" She discussed the separation of families at the time of the invasion, including what she understood as the German policy of keeping "strong boys over fourteen" for labor value and "strong girls over sixteen" and "strong young women" with less than one child for labor and "breeding" value.[7]

Lovejoy's experiences in Évian among the refugees expanded her understanding of the consequences of war for women. Women suffered the consequences of war not only from being "selected" for labor and "breeding" at the time of invasion, not only from the "brutal soldier who breaks down the

door with the butt of his rifle," but also from the soldier who "comes in kindness with a loaf of bread for her and her children and who actually affords
her protection against all save himself." Women suffered the consequences
of invasion, violence, desperate impoverishment, and disease, and some,
she said, could turn only to the enemy as Protector. "Warfare is much worse
for women than for men. Men have the right of death and they die fighting
gloriously for their ideals. But women must live and be confiscated with the
goods and the chattels." Women had to pay the "rapacious" price in war and
sacrificed everything. "The inhumanity of this war to little children and their
mothers cannot be described. It involves a series of horrors surpassing the
possibilities of human language," she concluded.[8]

Lovejoy returned to the United States in early February 1918. That spring
and summer she went on a speaking tour as a representative of the Woman's
Committee of the Council of National Defense to raise awareness concern-

"War Babies," in
*House of the Good
Neighbor,* by Esther
Pohl Lovejoy, facing
p. 180.

ing the status of women and children in the war zone and to report on the work of the Red Cross and other organizations working to provide support. On this successful tour she developed the material for her *House of the Good Neighbor* published a year later. Accounts of her stops suggest that she was an effective speaker and that her focus on the effects of war on women raised strong reactions. W. I. Eyres, her escort at the Wilson Shipbuilding Company in Astoria, Oregon, for a speech on August 20, was clearly impressed. "She held her audience with rapt attention," he reported. "This brilliant and talented woman in her protrayal [*sic*] of German frightfulness as evidenced by her in devastated France, and Belgium, appealed to her hearers as only a woman could; certain parts of her address owing to her pathetical description of events which have come under her own personal observation, caused many of those present to yield to their emotions perceptibly." C. W. Tebault, a National Service representative for Oregon, wrote to Lovejoy, "Your addresses to the men in our shipyards have been productive of wonderful results because they have brought home a phase of the war which has been only vaguely understood and only meagerly comprehended—that of the terrible sufferings of the women and children. I testify to the effectiveness of your addresses both from personal observation and from testimonials. Your message is truly an eye-opener. I have seen husky workmen in your audiences actually wipe away tears."[9]

Lovejoy's message in speeches and in print was that war presented particular violence for women. They suffered violence and rape, dependence, dislocation, and desperate poverty. In addition to her speaking tours and book, Lovejoy provided reports on wartime "conditions affecting women and children" to the Medical Women's National Association, the Woman's Committee of the Council of National Defense, the Red Cross, and the National American Woman's Suffrage Association during the war.[10] By these observations and with her reports she would influence the creation of all-women hospital units abroad to assist women and children who were the victims of war's violence. After the war Lovejoy took the leadership of one of these organizations, the American Women's Hospitals, a position she would hold for almost fifty years. Lovejoy's leadership after the war would be built on the foundation of her own pathbreaking observations and the important work of medical women and their supporters during the conflict.

The Women's Oversea Hospitals

Women physicians were mindful of the wartime rape of women and the impact of war's violence on civilians as they made their plans to provide medical service in Europe during the war. One group of physicians under the direction of Caroline Finley, a 1901 graduate of Cornell Medical School and a surgeon with the New York Infirmary for Women and Children, organized a complete overseas medical unit known as the Women's Oversea Hospitals (WOH) in July 1917. The National American Woman Suffrage Association agreed to be the official sponsor of the unit and publicized its activities in the *Woman Citizen*. Local suffrage groups nationwide raised funds to support the venture. Finley and the WOH staff planned their unit to provide primary care for women and children whose lives had been devastated by war. They offered the unit to the U.S. government for service overseas, but because women were not accepted as officers in the military, the government refused. In September 1917, however, the French government officially accepted the unit for service. The editors of the *Woman Citizen* made the announcement and also informed readers of the goals of the WOH:

> Primarily this work, which will follow closely the lines carried out by the New York Infirmary, will be among women and children in the devastated area and as close as may be necessary to the actual firing line. But upon request, in times of necessity, the unit has agreed to extend its activities to include the care of the military wounded. Owing to the pressing needs of the army upon the medical profession, women and children in the occupied districts have been altogether without medical aid.

The WOH planned to establish a hospital of one hundred beds somewhere in France, and medical women on staff would provide service to outlying villages "over a wide territory" by means of ambulances donated by two women's clubs, Sorosis and Civitas. The personnel included "gynecologists, general surgeons, obstetricians, a radiologist, bacteriologist, dentist, pharmacist, 21 nurses, 20 nurses' assistants, chauffeurs, laboratory assistants [and] a bookkeeper." When the unit finally sailed for France in February 1918, the *Woman Citizen* announced that "the women surgeons in the unit will do the gynecological operative work that has been so greatly neglected in France since the war began."[11] The WOH was the first all-female unit established by women physicians of the United States for wartime service abroad, and it carried with it women physicians' concerns for the women of France who had suffered the violent consequences of war.

There was strong competition and tension between the organizers of the WOH and other women physicians who were working with the Medical Women's National Association to establish all-female units for service in France. The American Women's Hospitals would soon sponsor its own units for service. The conflict appears to have been organizational in nature in ad-

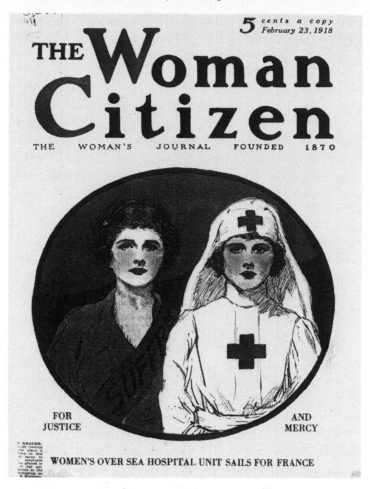

Women's Oversea Hospitals, cover of *Woman Citizen* (February 23, 1918).

dition to being influenced by personalities and loyalties. As Esther Lovejoy wrote forty years later, "Dr. Shaw and many of the women doctors concerned felt that the two groups should be united under the Medical Women's Association, but efforts to effect a merger were unavailing."[12]

The medical women of the WOH soon experienced tension between their desire for equal service with male colleagues, symbolized by the care of wounded soldiers and traditional military medicine, and their desire to put women's wartime priorities in place through the care of women and children civilians. When the unit arrived in France in early March 1918, there was some confusion about the location for their work, and the staff members were occupied for several weeks in examining several other possible sites. On March 26, during the German offensive on the Somme (March 21 to April 5), the French Service de Santé asked for a group of women physicians and support personnel to give immediate service at a French military evacuation hospital at the Château Ognon. They were to work with male physicians under the direction of the chief surgeon, Dr. Courvelier, and provide care for soldiers coming directly from the front.[13] Such service was an opportunity for women doctors to provide surgical and medical care to soldiers in a military hospital. They could prove their worth as medical women side by side with male colleagues, and the publicity would support other efforts to have women accepted in the medical corps of the American army. But accepting the request would break up the group for an indefinite period of time and disrupt plans for the establishment of a hospital for women. And it would also mean that those who went to the evacuation hospital would be under the authority of male physicians. Caroline Finley and her associates decided to accept the invitation, and fourteen members of the unit went directly to the French evacuation hospital. Those left behind, under the direction of Dr. Alice Gregory, soon established a unit for the medical relief of refugees in the town of Labouheyre south of Bordeaux. Throughout the summer and fall of 1918 more medical women and support personnel arrived in France with the WOH to establish several other units that included dispensaries and outpatient care.

In a letter reprinted in the *Woman Citizen* in early May 1918, Caroline Finley emphasized the opportunities that service with the evacuation hospital provided for women physicians to demonstrate equality with male physicians. "This is not only the most wonderful opportunity to serve our country," she noted, "but also the first chance of its kind to serve the cause of women in just this way. . . . [T]he first actual work of the Women's Oversea Hospitals has been with men fresh from the trenches." She justified her decision to serve under male military men by emphasizing conditions of professional equality. "It seems a fine thing," she wrote, "for women to work side by side with the military surgeons in a strictly military hospital, under the same conditions, exposed to the same risks and having the same criticism of our work, as have the men."[14]

But Finley also had to confess to her readers that she and her associates were not actually working "side by side" in surgical work with the male military surgeons in the evacuation unit. "The surgeons have been doing military surgery for nearly five years," she explained tentatively. "We are quite new to it and it will take some time for us to get the requisite experience. So we have been given other medical work than the operating with the understanding that if we remain with the military hospital that will come later." At first the women doctors were given work that was "little more than nurses' work." After several weeks Finley was given charge of a shock ward, and Dr. Anna Sholly reported that she and the other women doctors at the evacuation hospital were doing triage, having "charge of the reception, sorting out and preparation of the patients for operation." As one report put it, "Doctors worked like nurses," and "nurses worked like orderlies."[15] Even though the women who went to the Château Ognon evacuation hospital gained more responsibilities in the coming months, they could not entirely disguise the fact that they were under the authority of men. They were not serving side by side with male colleagues, nor were they operating a military unit on their own in which they could set priorities for the medical care for women.

The medical women and supporting personnel of the Women's Oversea Hospitals demonstrated equality with men, and at the same time they brought women's priorities to war. The service decisions of Finley and other medical women of the WOH physically separated those in official military service and those in civilian work, but the WOH embraced both in its total plan and vision. These patterns continued until the units returned to the United States in the summer of 1919. The Finley unit continued its military work, serving in association with the French Army of Occupation in Metz, Germany, caring for prisoners of war with influenza and other medical problems. Other units continued to operate among refugees until French physicians returned to their local practices. The WOH opened one last civilian hospital unit in January 1919 at a former boarding school for young women in the town of Nancy, France.[16]

The American Women's Hospitals Overseas Units

Another group of women physicians, working in association with the Medical Women's National Association, established the American Women's Hospitals to provide civilian and military service overseas in 1917. AWH leaders were particularly anxious to emphasize women's medical priorities at the same time that the organization fought for equal service with military men. Discussion in a general AWH meeting in July 1917, for example, focused on the need for medical care in Europe for women who were the victims of rape in the wartime climate of fear, destruction, and invasion. Physicians reported that there were many women who were pregnant as the result of rape by soldiers, in their terms "pregnant by force," and the discussion at the meeting emphasized "that these girls need very great care, physically and mentally." Members reported that a number of groups were interested in sponsoring "a maternity unit abroad at an early date."[17] One of the first items on the agenda for the Medical Women's National Association annual meeting in June 1917 was "Maternity Units to Devastated Part of Allies' Countries."[18] Dr. Eliza Mosher of New York joined Esther Pohl Lovejoy to represent the AWH at the national conference of women's organizations chaired by former NAWSA president Anna Howard Shaw to discuss wartime service. Mosher outlined the problems women physicians were having with access to military medical service and summarized the development of the AWH. The meeting focused on the women physicians' priorities for treatment of the "suffering of non-combatant populations, particularly women and children, in war-stricken countries" and provisions for "maternity service."[19]

An early tally of the registration of women physicians for wartime service suggests that the majority of women registrants supported women's priorities for wartime medicine. By early fall 1917, 592 women physicians had registered with the AWH for overseas work. Their service preferences indicate that 14 percent specified maternity and public health care in "devastated regions," and that another 4 percent specified "village practice" with civilians, for a total of 18 percent. In addition, 270 women, or 46 percent, preferred service in all-female units, whether with the French or Serbians who would accept such units or with other sponsorship. The all-female units planned to provide maternity care and dispensary service to aid local communities affected by war as well as to practice more traditional military medicine in the treatment of wounded soldiers. Therefore, women's selection of these categories of service suggests they shared the desire to transform military medicine to provide care for women in the war zone. It is also possible that many of the women who indicated that they would serve in any of the five situations were in sympathy with such women's priorities but wished to demonstrate a strong desire for patriotic service by responding that they would do whatever was most needed.

By the end of May 1918 Dr. Caroline Purnell, director of the AWH Committee for Foreign Service, had selected the personnel for the first AWH overseas unit, and they assembled in New York ready to sail for France. The director of the first unit was Maine gynecologist Barbara Hunt, a Johns Hopkins graduate who worked in surgery with her father in Maine and left a post at the Bangor State Hospital and private practice to sail with the unit. Two other women doctors accompanied her: Margaret Ethel Fraser, a gynecologist from Denver, and Mary Getty, a Philadelphia ophthalmologist. The dentist for the unit, Kate Doherty of Wisconsin, had been a nurse in the Spanish-American

Table 1. Foreign Service Preferences of Women Physicians,
September 1917

Maternity units in devastated regions	84 (14 percent)
Village practice	25 (4 percent)
All-female units	160 (27 percent)
All-female units to Allies' armies	110 (19 percent)
Established units (male and female)	103 (17 percent)
Any of the above without choice	110 (19 percent)
Total	592

Source: *Report of the American Women's Hospitals, June 6th to October 6th, 1917*, 4, Box 1, Folder 2, AWH Records.

War before pursuing her dental training. Three registered nurses went with the first group, all from Pennsylvania: Nora Annette Merrick, Lillian Pettingill, and Pauline Whittaker. Support personnel included Lida Touzalin as assistant administrative superintendent, interpreter, and purchasing agent; Ada Tobitt, a Nebraska teacher, as secretary; and two drivers and mechanics, Mrs. Victor M. Braschi of Ohio and Mme. Lenoir-Lehman, who "speaks French fluently and knows the people well."[20]

By the end of August members of the AWH unit established residence in a reconstructed château in Luzancy, France, along the Marne River less than one hundred miles from the trenches. The Luzancy unit combined the dual goals of providing military and civilian care by planning for what the French military called an *hôpital mixte*. This was an officially designated hospital with a ward of fifty beds for the care of wounded soldiers and a separate ward of fifty beds for civilians. The staff would provide medical care to outlying villages by ambulance, and the unit planned for a dispensary service. Whereas the personnel of the Women's Oversea Hospitals served in separate military and refugee units, the AWH women at Luzancy constructed their hospital to contain both the "male" and the "female" spheres of military medicine as a complete whole. French military officials inspected the Luzancy unit on several occasions and declared it ready to receive military patients in the fall of 1918. But the Armistice, declared on November 11, 1918, cut short the group's plans for the care of wounded soldiers. "The Armistice has changed all conditions," Barbara Hunt told the executive committee in early December. "The French will not continue to use any of their [auxiliary] hospitals for military purposes."[21] The women of the AWH continued to hope that their goals for an *hôpital mixte* would see actual expression, but for most it was enough that they were prepared to offer both services in a redirected vision of military medical service.[22]

The promise of the *hôpital mixte* enabled the women of Luzancy to avoid the dilemma in which their colleagues in the Women's Oversea Hospitals found themselves. They could provide military surgery without having to place themselves under the direct authority of men in service that was hardly equal. On several occasions French military leaders asked the AWH medical women of Luzancy to send medical teams to assist in military hospitals in need of surgeons during heavy military drives. They were able to go, operate and assist with distinction, and then return to their original unit because they believed that they would soon have their own military cases.[23] Pride in the ability of the AWH units to avoid the problems encountered by the WOH is evident in the records of the organization.

Soon after the Armistice the executive committee of the AWH sent camera and film to the new director of the Luzancy unit, Rochester, New York, surgeon Dr. Louise Hurrell. Chair Mary Crawford wrote, "We have need for all the picturesque publicity which you can send us, including photographs of interior views, patients and doctors at work." Hurrell's photographs of the AWH women were reprinted widely in AWH literature. They provided viewers then as well as viewers now with representations of skilled women physicians bringing their own priorities to military medical service, providing care to women and children in the wake of war and invasion. One is a photograph of the women's ward at Luzancy, with nurses at work and physicians in consultation. The woman in the bed closest to the camera looks stoic and well cared for, and she represents the health care goals of the AWH.

The medical women of the AWH provided statistical evidence of their public health service to match the photographic representations of their work in France. From their arrival in August 1918 through March 1919 the eight physicians and three dentists of the Luzancy Unit treated 420 hospital cases, 254 surgical cases, and 472 dental cases at the château-turned-hospital. Their surgical cases included hysterectomies, uterine and cervical operations, and a cesarean delivery as well as more general operations such as tonsillectomies. The women physicians tallied 3,344 dispensary calls during this period, treating a total of 1,552 dispensary patients. They established formal dispensaries in twenty villages (including Luzancy) and had a twice-weekly rotation for such medical service. In these seven months they made 3,626 house calls to these twenty villages and to forty-five other villages in the area, reaching sixty-five communities of French civilians whose lives had been affected by war.[24] The AWH had several ambulances for this mobile work, each staffed by a physician, a nurse, and a driver, "with all medicines that are needed, even the container for sterilizing and a stove for boiling water are taken along, so desolate are the homes visited."[25]

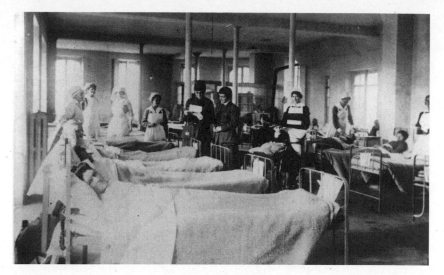

Women's Ward of the American Women's Hospital, Luzancy, France, AWH Collection, a144-048, Archives and Special Collections on Women in Medicine and Homeopathy, Drexel University College of Medicine, Philadelphia, Pennsylvania.

American Women's Hospital services, ambulance and staff, Luzancy, France, 1917, AWH Collection, a144-002, Archives and Special Collections on Women in Medicine and Homeopathy, Drexel University College of Medicine, Philadelphia, Pennsylvania.

Many civilians in the area were refugees returning to villages and homes after some of the final battles of the war that had been waged nearby, including Château-Thierry (just fifteen miles from the Luzancy hospital unit) and Belleau Wood across the Marne River. The AWH women called them "bad lands" for good reason. Esther Pohl Lovejoy explained the plight of these refugees: "Twice during the war they had been driven from their homes, and for four years had lived from hand to mouth in strange places. In the fall of 1918 they had crept back behind the advancing American and French armies, and had taken refuge under any sort of shelter they could find near their ruined homes." Many of the villages had been occupied by troops in the spring and summer of 1918, and the soldiers had scoured the area for anything edible. They had also left an unhealthy mess of human waste, or, as Lovejoy phrased it, an "insanitary state of affairs," behind.[26] Villagers living on the edge of physical survival combined with these unsanitary conditions led to a severe typhoid epidemic that lasted for three months that fall. In the same period residents of the region suffered from the global influenza epidemic and local outbreaks of diphtheria and scarlet fever.

During these epidemics AWH physicians and staff in Luzancy established regular visits to the villages they so carefully documented in their reports. They created dispensaries and clinics in "ruined houses with paper windows and shelled roofs" and "in the ruins of . . . cellars." The medical personnel used these areas for treatment and also for a night's sleep when the "circuit had expanded to the limit of [their] motor capacity." They treated the sick, provided inoculations for those who had not yet contracted typhoid (and were willing to undergo the procedure), and worked to clean up the "insanitary state of affairs" by organizing public health cleanup campaigns. "Streets and courtyards were cleaned, decaying debris dug out of holes and corners, and these disease breeding spots liberally sprinkled with disinfectants," one physician recalled. They also attempted to deal with the disposal of human and animal waste to prevent further outbreaks.[27]

The AWH women proudly forwarded letters of thanks for this service from French women, and public addresses from local French officials were reprinted in the *American Women's Hospitals Bulletin* in the States. A letter from "A French Woman Who Will Never Forget You" thanked the women for their strategic medical service and kindness. "For years we have been unable to receive visits from the doctors," she wrote. "It is to you that we owe our lives; you have also helped our many sorrows. It is by your courage that we know that ours is kept up." Pauline Dragin, a teacher in Saint-Aulde, wrote to thank the AWH women for their "generous attendance" to her students and to her own daughter during the typhoid epidemic. She was grateful for their assistance, she said, when the community was "deprived of everything" during the war. The mayor of Luzancy memorialized the medical women and communicated an understanding of their role and priorities in military medicine. He told the women physicians of the AWH that they were completing the liberating work of the Allied soldiers, putting "the science of your medicine at the service of our people."[28] These were testimonials of which the medical women were extremely proud: their work in France had put the health care of women and children at the forefront.

AWH physicians also worked with other American women and their organizations to establish health care for wartime refugees. Mary Breckinridge served with the Red Cross Children's Bureau in France and the American Committee for Devastated France. She reported that her organizations established ties with the AWH physicians at Luzancy, taking first the emergency cases and then civilians with more chronic medical or surgical needs to be treated by the medical women there. A coalition of leaders of women's voluntary organizations in France, including the AWH, supported a "program for the war-devastated children, with special care to those under six and to pregnant and nursing mothers."[29] The AWH associated its organization with the American Committee for Devastated France, providing the professional expertise in a coalition of women who sought to provide assistance for the civilian victims of the conflict.[30]

When the war was over, the AWH Executive Committee received word that the new units they had ready to sail would not be needed. They felt "as though a bomb had burst in their midst." And by early 1919 French doctors were returning home from the war to Luzancy and other villages nearby. One of them met with the mayor of Luzancy and asked him "how long those American women were to take the bread out of the French doctors' mouths." Clearly, the AWH leaders and staff had to make decisions about their postwar activities. Staff members saw a clear need for continued work among women and children in France and planned accordingly. The AWH moved the Luzancy unit north to Blerancourt, and as some medical and staff women returned to the United States, others came to take their places. The AWH expanded its overseas work to the Balkans, with a continuing emphasis on refugee and public health.[31] As they demobilized along with the rest of the Allied forces, women physicians worked to leave institutions in place that would carry on with their public health priorities.

* * *

With the achievement of national woman suffrage in sight, members held the last "victory" convention of the National American Woman Suffrage Association in Chicago in February 1920. Esther Pohl Lovejoy was there. Since the staff of NAWSA's Women's Oversea Hospitals had returned to the States and there was some money left in the WOH budget, Lovejoy suggested that the funds be transferred to the American Women's Hospitals for their continuing work among women and children in the postwar period. NAWSA members agreed.[32] It was a harmonious end to a competitive wartime relationship.

Esther Pohl Lovejoy assumed the directorship of the American Women's Hospitals in this postwar period and built the organization's financial base and its extensive clinical work among refugees until her death in 1967. By the 1920s the AWH was operating nine clinics in Greece, the Balkans, and the Near East with the same philosophical and practical foundations of the Luzancy and Blerancourt units.[33] Under Lovejoy's direction, the AWH established cooperative relationships with the American Committee for Devastated France to continue work among the French; the Near East Relief Committee for clinics and dispensaries in Armenia, Turkey, and Greece; and the American Friends Service Committee during the postwar conflicts in Russia.[34] And many AWH members, like Lovejoy, participated in the newly founded Medical Women's International Association as a way to reach across national boundaries to build services for women and children with medical women of other nations. The AWH maintained its commitment to providing health care for women and children in the wake of war and in the conditions engendered by war and its aftermath—local conflicts erupting on the shifting sands of boundaries imposed by postwar commissions, famine, and refugee conditions. The AWH was created, Lovejoy wrote in 1933, "for the purpose of utilizing the services of American women physicians in a great emergency." And the AWH had met that challenge and more. "This committee has fulfilled its function, developed opportunities, and maintained important medical work." From the perspective of a decade and more, Lovejoy believed that "our post-war and peacetime activities have been far more important than anything we got a chance to do during the war."[35]

As women, as physicians, and as citizens, the medical women of the Women's Oversea Hospitals and the American Women's Hospitals embraced a vision of medical service in wartime that included both the idea of equality with male counterparts and the necessity of providing medical care to women and children in the wake of wartime violence. While they struggled to enter the military on equal footing with men, each organization established medical units to focus on the care of women and children in regions devastated by war. War's violence had many effects on women's health and well-being, including sexual and physical assault, destruction of homes and property, poverty, and dislocation. It included typhoid in the wake of occupying armies, the life-threatening implications of a delayed operation, malnutrition, parasites, and infection. All were health and wellness issues for women of international import that stemmed from wartime violence. As such, their activities and the institutions they created are an important part of the history of women's antiviolence activism.

7. A Base Hospital Is Not a Coney Island Dance Hall

Nurses, Citizenship, Hostile Work Environment, and Military Rank

[Medical officers were] inclined to treat the base hospital as a kind of Coney Island dance hall or something of that sort.
—Sara E. Parsons, former chief nurse, Base Hospital no. 6, 1919

It is a calamitous thing to place women in such an anomalous position, with men as absolute monarchs over them.
—Daisy Urch, former chief nurse, Base Hospitals no. 12 and no. 103, 1919

This advertisement for Walk-Over Boot Shops in November 1917 captures the paradoxes and possibilities of nursing in the First World War with remarkable clarity. The "solace model" suggests the daintily crossed feet of a woman dressed in white holding the hand of a dying soldier on a hushed hospital ward "somewhere in France." The "cavalier model" covers the feet of an adventurous woman in khaki marching in military formation or tramping through muddy fields and trenches. These "models" of footwear signify two modes of female action and identity in wartime. Nurses could maintain and promote their role of nurturers of men wounded by war—the Protected comforting their Protectors—by clothing themselves in the traditions of female deference and sexual purity to maintain their reputations even as they became "women in public." Or they could put on the panoply of war as cavaliers, forfeiting the supposedly protective shield of submissive womanhood to claim a measure of equality with male comrades in the military struggle. Each of these models had an institutional base. The first was within the carefully constructed rules of professional or "trained" nursing that supported a code of middle-class respectability and True Womanhood of the nineteenth century. The second model took women into the male institution of the military, where authority was based on rank and where, as yet, women nurses had no official rank and no official place.

Nurses—as individuals, as members of a "women's profession," and as a group of women needed urgently by the military for service—faced wartime questions that concerned women's place within institutions and the complex relationship among professional, civic, and gender identity; equality; and workplace safety. The campaign for military rank for nurses that lasted until after the war was over focused on the importance of rank for nurses as a part of full female citizenship. It also highlighted the problems of a hostile, sexualized workplace environment. Military nurses did not disrupt gender conventions by shouldering guns as did the women-at-arms, but their claims for rank to protect them from workplace harassment did draw on a critique of the idea of the Protector and the Protected and affirmed the importance of

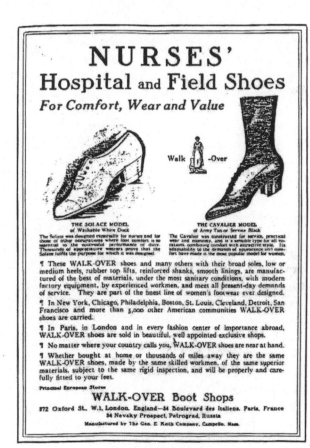

Walk-Over Boot Shops advertisement, *Red Cross Magazine*, November 1917.

workplace safety as part of women's full citizenship rights. Like women physicians, they sought an authoritative place within the military as part of the fabric of female citizenship. And they also sought to transform the military as a place that would provide a safe working environment for women and protect them from gender-based discrimination and hostility. This chapter will address nurses' civic expectations in wartime and also their drive to end a hostile military workplace through military rank.

Nursing has always been a part of war, yet military leaders have been extremely reluctant to create an official place for nurses as women in the male military. Historically, members of religious sisterhoods with an emphasis in the healing arts provided care for wounded soldiers, but their institutional affiliation was with their religious orders, not with the military. Before the modern period the wives, partners, and widows of soldiers provided essential nursing care as part of traveling military encampments and drew military rations. In the American Revolution, for example, women nurses were a vital part of the entourage of the Continental army and performed the often overlapping tasks of washing, mending, cooking, and nursing.[1] Yet hospital matrons and nurses, as Linda Kerber has shown, were "paid less well than stablehands," and although George Washington asked for better wages for female nurses, he also gave strict instructions that "not a woman belonging to the army is to be seen with the troops on their march." In the American Civil War, as Jane Schultz demonstrates, "nursing" was still a fluid category that encompassed a wide spectrum of women. This ranged from elite women volunteers with civilian organizations and members of religious sisterhoods to middle-class white women in Dorothea Dix's nursing corps and newly freed black women who were given the title of "laundress" or "cook" and paid accordingly.[2]

Nurses served by individual contract as temporary workers in a medical emergency during the Spanish-American War.[3] By 1898 the army reluctantly received nurses from two rival sources: Dr. Anita Newcombe McGee, representing the "Hospital Corps" of the Daughters of the American Revolution (DAR), and the American Red Cross. The extreme resistance of army men to accept women in official capacities and the absence of any regular military organization of nursing led to acrimonious competition between the Red Cross and McGee and the DAR. Consequently, women did not come into the military on nursing contracts until August 1898, when the "war" was over and nurses were urgently needed to fight disease epidemics among the troops.[4] Out of this experience McGee fought for a regular nursing corps within the army. But when the War Department formed the Army Nurse Corps in 1901 to supply nursing staff for hospitals and bases in the growing military bureaucracy, male leaders placed women as auxiliary workers who had no clear status and rank in the military.[5] They were still heeding George Washington's instructions to make women in the military as invisible as possible.

The "torchbearers" of a new age in nursing—Florence Nightingale, Clara Barton, and Dorothea Dix—formulated their calls for professionalized nursing in the crucible of the Crimean War and American Civil War. Responding to the poor treatment of women who provided nursing care in these wars and seeking a "respectable" career option for women in an industrializing age, they envisioned a trained corps of nurses made up of middle-class women pledged to perform their work within the genteel bounds of social propriety and moral obligation of the cult of True Womanhood. They would form a new professionalized sisterhood dedicated to the restoration of health through "the proper moral, environmental, and physical order."[6] Training schools for female nurses, which opened in Boston, New York, and New Haven in 1873, were at the heart of this new professional vision. By 1915 there were 1,509 professional nursing schools in the United States, with 46,141 students and 11,118 graduates.[7] White nursing leaders who espoused the new professionalism envisioned a "respectable" cadre of nurses who were daughters of the middle-class or women who rose to the ranks of the middle class through their training. The emphasis on obligation, service, and sexual purity was the key to their program of public acceptance. Whereas nurturing and care of family members were the duty of all women in the gender contract, nursing for pay was still associated with poor women who were sexually available to men. Popular images of nurses in the nineteenth and early twentieth centuries often focused on their sexuality and sexual availability rather than their training or skill.[8] The new professional nurse would use respectability and a spotless sexual reputation as her weapons to gain institutional status and to combat a hostile work environment.

Women of color, particularly African American women, figured ambiguously in white nursing leaders' programs for the professionalization of the field. Indeed, in the post–Civil War years, the African American "doctor woman" or "Mammy" symbolized the "primitive" role of women as healers to white nursing leaders, a role that was antithetical to their "modern," professional goals. Rather than seeing women of color who nursed in private homes and in various institutions as colleagues who were particularly vulnerable to workplace coercion and sexual violence, most white nursing leaders were influenced by racist images, especially those images of black women as sexually voracious Jezebels.[9] Many of them believed that African American nurses enhanced the dangerous association of nursing for pay with prostitution in the public mind. Consequently, only six African American women received training in primarily white facilities in the nineteenth century. As Darlene Clark Hine shows, African American community and medical leaders cre-

ated separate hospitals and nursing schools, and by the turn of the century
more than a dozen institutions offered training specifically for black women
nurses.[10] Throughout the First World War, African American nurses, led by
Adah Thoms and joined by community members and organizations, worked
for the acceptance of black women in the Red Cross and Army Nurse Corps.
They claimed victory when eighteen African American women were accepted
for Stateside service at two army training camps, Camp Sherman in Ohio and
Camp Grant in Illinois, during the influenza epidemic in the fall of 1918.[11]

On the eve of the First World War medical care was moving to the hospital,
and white nursing leaders had formed a profession that was based on training
and skill but also on a class- and race-based code of True Womanhood that
they hoped would legitimate their work and protect them from associations
with prostitution and sexual availability. Many nursing leaders who traced
the coming of age of nursing to the Crimean War and the American Civil
War placed great faith in the promise of the First World War to demonstrate
the success of nursing professionalism. Many of them believed that wartime
service in this new conflict would put the trained nurse and her skills on
the public stage and could be a crowning demonstration of the efficacy of
professional nursing. They knew that the military needed them. Indeed,
white nurses were the only group of women formally invited to service by
the U.S. military for the entire length of the war. More than 21,480 women
served in the Army Nurse Corps during the world war, 10,660 of them with
the American Expeditionary Force.[12]

The military called nurses to assist in war but not to be warriors, and because they were entering a hierarchical institution, their "difference" meant
inequality. Male military leaders praised the selfless service of Florence
Nightingale, Clara Barton, and those women who had nursed the sick in
previous wars, but they used the ideal of selfless female service as permission to maintain nurses in an auxiliary, ambiguous position in the military.
Women nurses were subject to military discipline and regulations but had
no official rank in a hierarchical system that depended on it. As neither
enlisted personnel nor commissioned officers, nurses were "hired extras" in
the business of war,[13] invited to accompany the military because they were
women practicing the indispensable women's work of nurturing.[14]

The Nurse as Citizen

As the United States entered the world war, many nursing leaders and their
suffragist allies linked the campaign for full female citizenship with a campaign for military rank for nurses. As white nurses were literally gathering

on the docks to embark for military service in France, the editors of the May 1917 issue of the *American Journal of Nursing* provided space for discussion of the wartime role of nurses. They chose a significant title: "The Nurse as a Citizen." And in an accompanying article, Isabel Stewart affirmed that as citizens, nurses had the responsibility to use their professional skills in service to the nation. Indeed, nurses could provide better service than "amateur volunteers of equal patriotic devotion," because they were trained to meet "critical situations" and had learned the "ready subordination of self which is essential to good cooperation." At a time when "good citizenship" was a highly valued social goal for groups desiring acceptance in American society, and at a time in which many feminists called for increased civic and professional equality through wartime service, Stewart argued that it was crucial for nurses to respond to this civic duty with care and readiness.[15]

Many nursing leaders shared Stewart's vision. As Sandra Beth Lewenson has noted in her study of nursing and suffrage in the United States, "The vote meant more than personal equality: the vote represented the avenue for professional advancement and autonomy as well."[16] For many nurses, this civic and professional vision extended logically to wartime nursing service. And many nurses came to believe that military rank was an important extension of the rights of citizenship for nurses. M. Adelaide Nutting and her colleagues on the Committee on Nursing for the General Medical Board of the Council of National Defense were active lobbyists for military rank for nurses in Washington. The *American Journal of Nursing* printed updates on the struggle, and nursing leaders and their supporters organized the National Committee to Secure Rank for Nurses in 1918. Their goal was to change military regulations so that all nurses in military service would be commissioned as officers, from the entry level of second lieutenant to the rank of major for the superintendent of the Army Nurse Corps. This campaign for rank for nurses was waged throughout the war and continued until 1920, when nurses received a halfway measure, termed "relative rank," that gave them quasi officer status without many of the benefits and without the complete authority of command in the military.[17]

Suffrage supporters outside the profession linked their own fight for institutional equality and the vote with the struggle for military rank for nurses. In viewing the situation of military nurses without rank, suffragists saw a reflection of their own concerns for voteless women as pseudocitizens who had an ambiguous and auxiliary relationship to the state. For them, the question of rank was an explicit debate about the definition of women and their relationship to men and men's institutions. Suffrage organizations offered a clear, active endorsement of rank for military nurses. The National American

Women's Suffrage Association adopted a resolution asking Congress to give military rank to army nurses.[18] The *Woman Citizen* and the *Suffragist* ran frequent supportive editorials during the war and as the struggle continued in the immediate postwar years.[19] Many suffragists were active on the Committee to Secure Rank for Nurses. Harriot Stanton Blatch chaired the New York committee, and Helen Hoy Greeley worked as legal counsel and general secretary for the organization.[20]

As founder of the Equality League of Self-Supporting Women, later the Women's Political Union, Blatch had a vision of reform that included active efforts to improve the lives of laboring and professional women, and she saw the war as a clear opportunity for women to advance their reform goals.[21] Her letter to the editor of the *New York Times* dated March 4, 1918, represents the committee's arguments in favor of military rank for nurses. Blatch first appealed to national pride. American women, she said, were the only nurses among the Allies without "military recognition." She also argued that the efficiency of a hospital in the business of saving lives was compromised if orderlies did not consider the nurse "as holding a position commanding their respect and obedience." Surely "every mother . . . who knows the value of the nurse to the well-being of her wounded boy . . . [would] wish nothing omitted which adds to hospital efficiency," she affirmed. Blatch then called attention to the fact that nurses were serving with skill and devotion to the nation in the midst of "hardship and danger," and so they deserved rank for their equal sacrifices. Quoting a nurse serving abroad, Blatch insisted, "If Uncle Sam knew his skillful and devoted nurses were being discriminated against and shabbily treated, he would quickly set the matter right."[22] Blatch and other supporters gave these same arguments in testimony before the House Committee on Military Affairs in favor of rank for nurses in April 1918.[23]

Committee members gathered an impressive repertoire of expert opinion in favor of rank from nursing leaders, civilian medical authorities, and military medical men. Dr. Franklin Martin, chair of the General Medical Board of the Council of National Defense; William C. Gorgas, surgeon general until October 1918; Dr. Victor Vaughan; and Dr. William J. Mayo all went on record in favor of rank, as did numerous physicians who served with the American Expeditionary Force. Their written testimony, along with that of nursing leaders such as Jane Delano (director of Red Cross Nursing who died in April 1919), Clara Noyes (her successor), and M. Adelaide Nutting of Teachers' College, Columbia University, was an integral part of the committee's legislative and public relations campaign. Former president William Howard Taft endorsed rank for military nurses, and he became the honorary chair of the Committee to Secure Rank.[24]

The *New York Times* also endorsed military rank for nurses in March 1918 as a measure that would increase efficiency in wartime military hospitals and therefore save the lives of soldiers. The paper also acknowledged that "to a considerable extent they share the dangers of the front and they often die for their country as bravely and in the same way as the active combatants."[25] In May 1918 the *Stars and Stripes,* the newspaper of the American Expeditionary Force in Europe, included the proposal for military rank for nurses as part of a story on women's increased activity on the home front. Along with more women police officers, mail carriers, conductors, and women members of New York's Tammany Hall political machine, the paper reported the request for "federal legislation permitting Red Cross war nurses on the same footing regarding rank as are the men in the military establishment" as evidence of broad claims for women's rights.[26]

Vulnerability in the Wartime Workplace

Over the course of this campaign for rank, military nurses themselves added a new dimension to the discussion. Many of them saw military rank as a tool to prevent the hostile working environments they experienced in wartime nursing. Nurses were among the many women workers who experienced unwanted sexual advances and a hostile environment from male coworkers and supervisors before the war.[27] And military service in isolated units far from support networks and with few constraints on the power of male officers meant that nurses experienced a heightened vulnerability to systematic workplace hostility during wartime. The solution, for many nurses, was the achievement of military rank as a way to ensure a safe workplace for women nurses in wartime and beyond.

In 1918 no group named workplace conditions like those experienced by military nurses as "harassment" or "workplace hostility." But women nurses did identify behavior that resonates with Vicki Schultz's definitions of "gender-based hostility" in the workplace. These actions include "denigrating women's performance or ability to master the job," preventing women from training or opportunities to gain expertise, "deliberate work sabotage," using "taunting, pranks, and other forms of hazing designed to remind women that they are different and out of place," "isolating women from the social networks that confer a sense of belonging," and "discrediting" a woman's "mental stability or sanity." Such hostility can also take the form of unwanted sexual attention or threats of assault. Gender-based hostility in the workplace in this view emphasizes the power to define work and workers to preserve male privilege.[28] As we will see, many nurses provided reports of a hostile work environment on base hospital units in Europe that would fuel a debate about the best ways to provide a safe workplace for women nurses in the military.

The rapid growth of the size of the Army Nurse Corps during the war and the visibility of nurses' wartime service to the nation created a strong context in which to make the argument for military rank. But many military nurses did not feel safe in discussing the discrimination they experienced until they were no longer in the military. The demobilization process made it possible for them to tell their stories, but it also meant that there were far fewer nurses in the military. Yet this ability for nurses to tell their stories when no longer in service provided essential information about workplace hostility that was crucial to the campaign.

At the beginning of the war many nursing leaders expressed great faith in their institution of professional nursing, built on the vision of proper behavior and sexual respectability as well as skill and training. Isabel Stewart identified three main characteristics of the "nursing spirit" that she believed would enable nurses to use their attributes and skills for a civic purpose in time of war: the mother spirit, the fighting spirit, and the sister spirit. Stewart based the third characteristic, the "sister spirit," on the caregiving tradition of the religious sisterhoods. But she now assigned it the important secular function of controlling gender relations and providing workplace safety for nurses against unwanted sexual advances, defining a particular kind of relationship "between the woman-nurse and the man-patient." Before the professionalization of nursing, "it was necessary to wrap the nurse round with a special robe of sanctity, and to hedge her about with vows and prohibitions," Stewart wrote, "in order that she might carry on her work with safety and dignity and might continue to retain public confidence in her moral character." Without this protection, the "secular nurse of the servant type" had been unable to keep her reputation because of the "special moral dangers" of caring for the bodies of men who were not part of her family. But modern nurses could be protected by a new professional relationship between the woman-nurse and the man-patient (and the men with whom the nurses worked) as "distinguished from the religious or the servile or the ordinary personal relationship." Based partly on professional responsibility and integrity, and "partly on the idea of the family relationship which is expressed in the title of 'sister,'" she wrote, this "sister spirit" would protect nurses from sexual danger and would protect the collective reputation of the nursing profession. "Such a relationship is not incompatible with good friendship and mutual confidence," she continued, "but any suggestion of romantic philandering or sex-adventure destroys its whole meaning and tears down the carefully built-up structure on which public confidence and professional integrity rest." Stewart suggested that American nurses should adopt the European nursing title of "sister" to enhance the control of gender relations implied in its use.[29]

Stewart knew that although nurses would enter the military as trained professionals, they would also enter it as women, and her faith in the protection of professionalism did not obscure her understanding that society and policy makers and male coworkers and patients would judge women by their gender. Nursing leaders like Stewart were concerned with the sexual danger to individual nurses in time of war, accusations that they were "public women," and consequently the reputation of the nursing profession itself. The protection of professionalism was fragile: a "carefully built-up structure" based on public confidence and community acceptance. The work of elite women nursing leaders to "lift" the profession to institutional acceptance through training but also through adherence to middle-class values of respectability and moral purity would be tested in this great public event of the war. And while nurses were now "wrapped round" with a special robe of professionalism instead of sanctity, no robe was substantial enough to obscure the woman underneath. Stewart located much of the responsibility for the control of gender relations and gender-based violence on the nurses themselves. As women, they would have to prove themselves not only capable but also respectable for nurses as a group to gain a safe place in the military structure.

Yet as women nurses left their home communities to serve at hospitals in the states and overseas, they left behind the institutional framework, community support, and administrative allies that had all provided protections for them. Over the course of the war most nursing leaders and many of the rank-and-file nurses serving with the armed forces came to believe that genteel codes of behavior were not enough. They called for military rank for nurses to gain institutional equality and particularly for protection from hostile work environment harassment.

In the spring of 1916, a year before the United States would enter the war, medical and nursing personnel around the United States began to organize base hospital units in civilian hospitals under the direction of a Red Cross committee of prominent medical men, including Dr. George Crile of Cleveland and Dr. William J. Mayo of the Mayo Clinic in Minnesota. Crile originated this medical unit–preparedness campaign, believing that the esprit de corps among hospital personnel who worked together as civilians should be preserved, even to the point that "'mediocrity well organized is more efficient than brilliancy combined with strife and discord.'"[30] The nurses from each group enrolled as reserve nurses through the Red Cross and medical men enrolled in the Medical Reserve Corps, and they trained together in weekly educational and practical sessions on military medicine. When the United States entered the war a year later, the War Department activated many of these base hospital units for service in France with the British Expeditionary Force. Then more units accompanied the American Expeditionary Force as they embarked for service, and others were formed overseas during the course of the war. The majority of nurses served with these base hospitals during the war and the period of demobilization. Those who had been enrolled as Red Cross nurses joined the Army Nurse Corps for the duration of their service.[31]

Medical and administrative personnel formed these base hospital units around existing workplace, social, and community relations. The medical director of the unit was usually a prominent surgeon, and he helped to select the chief nurse from among those nurses with administrative experience and prestige at his hospital or at a companion institution. In consultation with the medical director, the chief nurse selected the unit's nursing personnel and had charge of their training and administration. The nurses knew and most worked with the medical men who became officers in the unit.[32] In theory, when the medical units went overseas these familiar working relationships would be transplanted to a new military and geographical context. This original organization of base hospital units illustrates the success of nurses who had struggled for authority and a place within the medical institutions of their communities, the fruition of the program of respectable professionalization and institutional access begun by the post–Civil War generation of nursing leaders. The administrative nurses selected to be chief nurses of the units were respected in the hospital environment, were given the power to select and train the nursing corps for the group, and had supporters in the community such as board members whose advocacy held medical men in check. They had achieved institutional power and "place" in the American hospital.

But when these units left for the European front the addition of new personnel, the incorporation of the units into a military structure that did not give nurses rank, and the transformation of relations of power and authority in this new environment away from home and community support created conflict and made nurses vulnerable. When called to war, base hospital organizers had to add another group of personnel for the units to be completely functional. These were enlisted men who would serve as orderlies. When the chief surgeon and chief nurse received notification that a unit was being activated, they opened these positions to local men who were interested and eligible. In the case of the Lakeside unit in Cleveland, for example, organizers set up an enlistment office in the hospital dispensary, and men from around the city and from colleges in Ohio and Pennsylvania "poured in, and 155 were enrolled in a few days." They joined sixty-four nurses, twenty-seven officers, and four civilian employees and left Cleveland on May 8, 1917, for Rouen, France.[33]

The addition of male enlisted personnel to the hospital unit transformed the relationship between male physicians and female nurses. As the group entered the military, medical officers, female nurses, and enlisted men now occupied the three points of a social and professional triangle. And nursing and military leaders did everything possible to make these relationships conform to the figure of an isosceles triangle—with nurses and officers occupying the two larger and more closely linked angles—rather than an equilateral one. It was against army policy for nurses to associate socially with enlisted men, but regulations permitted and even encouraged their social relations with officers.[34] Dora Thompson, superintendent of the Army Nurse Corps during most of the war, shared the view of most nursing leaders that the professional training of nurses gave them the status of officers, even if that status was unofficial. The association of nurses with enlisted men, she wrote to a chief nurse in December 1917, "would render it quite impossible to establish a status of the nurse above the enlisted man if the nurse persists in associating with him."[35] As women in the military, nurses had to guard against the image of the sexualized camp follower, and most nursing leaders supported these regulations for reasons of social respectability and professional standing. Such regulations only added to the "robe of professionalism" that Isabel Stewart and other leaders favored for protecting nurses from harassment, an extension of their class-oriented program for nursing professionalism. They assumed that nurses would be safest with officers.

Military leaders encoded these assumptions in the arrangement of the physical space of the base hospital. Living space for officers and nurses was located at the front of the unit, which reinforced their privileged place in the hierarchy of the group. The quarters for nurses and medical officers were separated only by a walkway, suggesting the desirability of social relationships between them. On the other hand, quarters for enlisted men were located far to the rear of the hospital, next to the large latrines and the unit's "feces destructor shed." Spatially, this discouraged their social contact with nurses and officers and marked them as the group with the least privilege in the unit, at the far distant point of the isosceles triangle of ideal gender relations.[36]

As wartime demands escalated, the home community relationships of the base hospital units abroad eroded further with new arrivals of medical, nursing, and enlisted personnel who had no previous ties with the group. Increasing numbers of women were assigned to duty as transient "casual nurses," meaning that they were not assigned to a specific post but served at various locations when needed. And there were constant changes to meet the

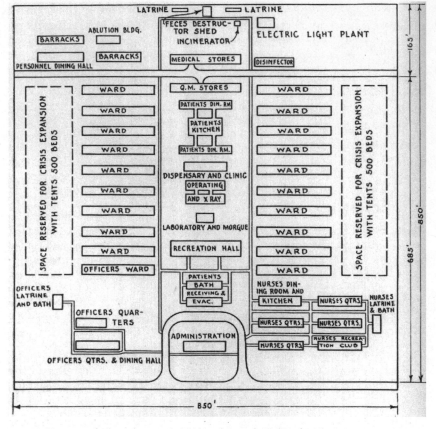

General layout of a base hospital. (Colonel Joseph H. Ford, *Administration,
American Expeditionary Force,* 242).

needs of the numbers of wounded at various points along the war front. New
medical officers, unfamiliar with the nurses or their supporters back home,
took command of some units. Male orderlies came and went. And the ideal
plans for the spatial organization of the base hospitals were often modified
when units were located in old chateaux and in large public spaces such as
racetracks and stadia. Women and men arrived by the trainload to live and
work together miles away from home and family. Consequently, the social
and professional relationships among nurses, officers, and enlisted men most
often depended on personality and the views of the participants rather than
institutionalized rules or established relationships.

These changes in the organization and workplace of the base hospital
meant that nurses were increasingly vulnerable to workplace hostility.[37] Even

those who trained with male officers before leaving for the war front found themselves at risk. Without the safety net of other protections such as a supportive nursing and hospital community and the organizational structure built up at home, nurses faced hostile actions from the men who supervised and worked with them.

Daisy Urch faced this situation and became a strong supporter of rank for nurses as an important protection against a hostile workplace as a result of her experiences as a nurse serving with the U.S. military in France. In the fall of 1916 as an experienced, accomplished nursing administrator at the Illinois Training School for Nurses, Urch agreed to serve as chief nurse for a base hospital unit made up of Chicago medical and nursing personnel from the Northwestern University Medical School, the Cook County Hospital, and the Illinois Training School for Nurses.[38] Dr. Frederick Besley, a professor of surgery at Northwestern Medical School and attending physician at the Wesley Memorial and Cook County Hospitals, was director of the unit.[39] With additional personnel from Northwestern and Cook County Hospitals, the group was one of the first six units called to active duty in May 1917 as Base Hospital no. 12.

The members of Base Hospital no. 12 were assigned to service with the British Expeditionary Force at a hospital site along the English Channel in Picardy near a large British army base some forty miles from the front. Major C. C. Collins of the U.S. Army Medical Corps had general command of the hospital on their arrival. Only one hundred of the eighteen thousand hospital beds were housed in wooden structures; the rest of the hospital and quarters was a sprawling tent city. Running water was limited, housing and working conditions primitive, and the climate damp and harsh. Urch wrote home about a wind that "threatened to blow the entire hospital into the sea." The storm carried fifty-five tents away, scattered equipment, and exposed patients and personnel to a "drenching rain."[40] In spite of these conditions, Urch praised the work of her "nice family of nurses" and their "wonderful organization," citing instances of bravery, clearheaded thinking in emergencies, and skillful patient care.[41]

Due to a technicality that would later harm her, Urch was officially only a "temporary chief nurse" because there had not been time for her to pass the necessary written examination before sailing for Europe. Because she was a reserve nurse who came into the Army Nurse Corps through the Red Cross for "the period of the war only," the Army Medical Department considered this temporary status to be sufficient for Urch, especially since she would receive the same pay as a chief nurse. Yet, as Urch would soon discover, there was a catch: a "temporary chief nurse" could be removed at the direct and complete discretion of her commanding officer, whereas only the surgeon general could relieve a chief nurse of her duty.[42] A "temporary chief nurse" was at the mercy of local conditions and personalities with no official recourse.

As soon as they sailed, Urch found herself in personal and administrative conflict with Dr. Besley, the medical director of the unit. In the contest for authority over the nurses Urch stood her ground, and she paid dearly for her position. In a later investigation of the matter initiated by the surgeon general's office, Besley testified that he believed that Urch was "disloyal" and "critical" and manifested "antagonism to any directing or controlling authority." In the fall of 1917 Besley recommended that she be removed from service. Major Collins, the commanding officer, believed that he could resolve the issue by placing Urch on the sick report and sending her away "for a period of recuperation." He later testified that "during her absence a marked improvement in the attitude of the nurses on duty here was noticed." When Urch returned from her "recuperation," Collins recalled, she "showed plainly by her actions and words that she could not serve in her capacity as Temporary Chief Nurse and give me her loyal support and cooperation." With the encouragement of Dr. Besley, Collins asked Urch to resign, and she refused. So, using his power to remove a "temporary chief nurse," Collins relieved her from duty on Christmas Eve 1917 and assigned her to work as one of the regular nurses of the unit. "Her work as a nurse has been satisfactory," he said in his later testimony, "but she still maintains an attitude of hostility to me personally."[43]

After an investigation of the case that did not include any consultation or communication with Urch, officials in the office of Merritte Ireland, the chief surgeon of the American Expeditionary Force, recommended that she be transferred to another unit.[44] The woman who had been in a position of authority and esteem as a Chicago nursing administrator found that in the transition to service in the military overseas, she was silenced, demoted, and transferred away from the only community left to her—the nurses she had gathered and trained for duty. She was at the mercy of male supervisors, placed on sick leave, and not allowed to participate in any way in her own defense during an investigation of the matter.

Daisy Urch vindicated herself by her service record, her subsequent position of authority in the military, and the honors she received for skillful military service. After her transfer from Base Hospital no. 12 she served in several different hospitals and eventually gained an appointment as chief nurse at Base Hospital no. 103 at Neuilly, France, a post she held until her honorable discharge in July 1919. From this position, Urch continued her advocacy for better military nursing conditions.[45] Her story demonstrated the vulnerability of women nurses serving away from community and professional support networks on isolated base hospitals in a marginal and ambiguous position in the military hierarchy.

Jane Ransom volunteered for military nursing service with the unit that would become Base Hospital no. 41, mobilized in early 1917 for wartime medical service in Saint-Denis, France. By October 1918 she was serving as chief nurse at Base Hospital no. 81. In the first weeks "everything was pleasant," but things soon changed.[46] In her official grievance, Ransom reported that she began to be "treated with discourtesy, indignity, and injustice" by the administrators of Base Hospital no. 81, including the commanding officer, Lt. Colonel P. J. H. Farrell; Captain Heatherly; and Major Morse, the chief of medical services. To Ransom, the reason for this change in circumstances was obvious. "Subsequent to the Adjutant's social attentions to the nurses being rejected, the nurses were made to suffer many indignities and annoyances. I defended the nurses and tried to look out for their interests. Indignities were then offered me."[47] At the end of December, Farrell recommended that Ransom be relieved of her position as chief nurse and that she be transferred to "some other organization for duty."[48]

Ransom saw nothing short of a "plot to get rid of me" in Farrell's actions. "Though not sick I was ordered to bed," she reported, and then examined by the chief of medical services at Base Hospital no. 81, who then prepared "an erroneous report of my health" that supported Farrell's request for her demotion and transfer. Farrell recommended that Assistant Chief Nurse Margaret Lydon ("a friend of the Adjutant's," as Ransom noted in her grievance) be promoted to chief nurse in her place. Ransom charged that she then experienced "numberless indignities" and was placed in a "false position with both officers and nurses." Farrell made orderlies follow her and watch her office, she reported, and he denied her permission to visit AEF officials like Julia Stimson. He removed Ransom from her post as chief nurse and sent her to Base Hospital no. 103 at Neuilly. From there, Ransom filed a formal complaint in February 1919 and asked the chief surgeon of the AEF for a full investigation.

Over the next several weeks AEF chief nurse Julia Stimson gathered evidence in the case, and Ransom visited her at least once. Stimson noted that Lieutenant Murray of Base Hospital no. 81 "would uphold" Ransom and that he considered the commanding officer to be "crazy" and "brutal." And Stimson received a lengthy letter from Daisy Urch, who was now serving as the chief nurse of Base Hospital no. 103 at Neuilly. Urch reported that she had talked with Ransom several times and had also talked with several nurses from Base Hospital no. 81. "I am glad you are looking into the matter," she wrote. "I really think it needs investigation." She told Stimson about several conversations that she had had with Ransom, and stressed, "I am afraid for her sanity if something is not done for her soon." She closed by saying that she had written at length about Ransom, "for I feel that she is a very fine woman in many ways, and she aroused my sympathy to an unusual degree."[49]

By the first of March, Jane Ransom was in the embarkation port of Brest, waiting to sail back home to Arlington, Virginia, discharged from the army for health reasons. From Brest, she wrote to both Julia Stimson and Merritte Ireland, the chief AEF surgeon, that she had intended to prepare another draft of her grievance. "I have no desire to injure anyone," she told Stimson, "only to clear up my own records." She wanted her file to be clean, and she "felt that she had a right" to that. Now about to sail for home, Ransom asked that the investigation be stopped. She was not willing, she wrote, "to have an investigation when I was not there to look after my own interests. No one else could possibly know the ordeal through which I went." She told Stimson that she was going home to heal and move forward with her life. "In a month or two I hope to be quite myself again, though it is going to take a little while to recover from the nervous strain."[50] After this last letter Jane Ransom does not appear in the American Expeditionary Force files.

Daisy Urch's and Jane Ransom's experiences with some officers in authority over them were replicated at other base hospitals in Europe. Eighty-one nurses from Base Hospital no. 7 sent a petition to the superintendent of the Army Nurse Corps in September 1918 protesting the impending transfer of their chief nurse, Emma M. Nichols. "We who have worked with her know the difficulties which she has had to meet. We know how untiringly she has worked and how loyally she has shared whatever hardships have fallen to our lot and we wish to express our appreciation of the efforts she has made to provide for the comfort and the welfare of the nurses under her," they wrote. "We feel that her withdrawal at this time would be most unfortunate and leave a lasting stigma on the good name of the Unit."[51] The signatures of 122 nurses from Base Hospital no. 69 appear on another petition protesting the demotion and removal of Chief Nurse Anna H. Johnson. The nurses objected to "the proceedings against her" and wanted to "express our appreciation and loyalty to her." Emma Byrne passed the chief nurse examination and went to her assignment at Base Hospital no. 52 in Le Mans only to find that the commanding officer refused to recognize her status.[52]

Military nurses found common cause as they shared their experiences together and with a wider nursing audience. In December 1919, Daisy Urch wrote a long letter to the editor of the *American Journal of Nursing* to reveal publicly the "inconceivably anomalous position our nurses found themselves in when they answered the call to service." Home now, and honorably discharged from the military, she felt it was her duty to speak out. Military rank, Urch insisted, would give the army nurse the "proper protection" so that she could do her job "and not be harassed by the petty jealousies and vagaries, peculiar to the temperament of some officers and corps men."[53]

For Urch, the most important aspect of rank was that it would replace arbitrary conditions for women nurses with specific, recognized authority and power to control relations with military medical men. "Our greatest difficulties lay in the insecurity and unstability [*sic*] of every nurse's position from the Director of the Nursing Service, (yes, I may say from the Superintendent of the Army Nurse Corps), to the nurse on duty in the ward," she wrote. "The better type of commanding officer" supported nurses, she continued, "but we had no protection from the other types." Without rank, nurses occupied only a "false position" in the military hierarchy. "It is a calamitous thing to place women in such an anomalous position, with men as absolute monarchs over them," she affirmed. "Incalculable harm was done to the morale of the nurses because of that one condition." Rank would promote secure workplace relationships and enable the medical staff to focus its energy on helping patients. "We would have more and better cooperation," she wrote, "if the officers understood that they could not intimidate the nurses with threats, and the nurses knew they did not have to expend their best energies courting the good will of the officers." Urch also advocated a structure for grievances and additional administrative personnel to provide assistance. Nurses would "indeed be short sighted and selfish," she concluded, "if we allowed another group of women to be subjected to similar indignities."[54]

The discussion concerning rank for military nurses escalated in 1919 as women demobilized from wartime service and felt more freedom and safety to speak out about their experiences. Postwar demobilization brought a rapid decrease in numbers of nurses in the ANC. At the end of June 1919 just 9,616 women were in active duty, and by June 1920 only 1,551 nurses remained in the corps.[55] In this public debate about rank, many nurses joined Daisy Urch in a critique of what they referred to as their anomalous position in the military and testified to the need for military rank for nurses to protect them from workplace hostility, particularly in isolated base hospital units. Others shared their concerns about workplace safety but questioned whether rank would solve these problems. Their views published in the *American Journal of Nursing* in the form of letters to the editor, in reports of professional papers and discussions, and in letters to the *Trained Nurse and Hospital Review* provide a wealth of information and bring us nurses' own voices concerning this issue.

When members of the National League of Nursing Education met for their annual conference in Chicago in June 1919, the meetings turned into a referendum for military rank for nurses. Sara E. Parsons, who served as chief nurse of Base Hospital no. 6 from Massachusetts General Hospital in Boston, told her audience that the nurses she had worked with had all been models of proper behavior. "You would be proud of the relation they established with the patients, the sisterly and the motherly spirit, shown to the men." But this was not enough to protect the nurses from workplace hostility. Large numbers of officers "coming and going" were "inclined to treat the base hospital as a kind of Coney Island dance hall or something of that sort," Parsons reported. An officer at each base hospital had to censor nurses' letters, and "usually the youngest officers were detailed to look after the nurses' mail." These young men frequently discussed the "social life and personal things" contained in the nurses' letters. She was also critical of the orderlies, who often refused nurses' instructions and showed hostility. For nurses' "self-respect" and workplace protection, Parsons advocated military rank in the strongest possible terms.[56]

In the less-formal discussion session following her paper, Parsons noted, "We hear much said about the necessity for rank for nurses on account of the enlisted men. My experience is that we need the rank for nurses much more on account of the officers. I think the officers were at a complete loss as to how nurses should be treated, except where they had a personal interest in a particular nurse or a particular group of nurses." "I felt like clapping for Miss Parsons," an army nurse wrote to *American Journal of Nursing* editors after reading Parsons's comments about officers. "All chief nurses, I am sure, think so, but all have not the courage to say so." Nursing leader Clara D. Noyes agreed. "It is an embarrassment, because we women of America had always felt that we occupied rather an unusual place. We are beginning to feel somewhat different at the present time."[57]

More letters followed. M. Adelaide Nutting, director of nursing education at Columbia, wrote that without rank, nurses had no power "to guarantee courteous or respectful behavior" from men and had suffered unprecedented "humiliations and indignities." M. M. Riddle, former chief nurse at Camp Devens, Massachusetts, believed that rank was necessary for safety. A nurse should not be secure in the workplace only if "she is tactful, amiable, and winning." "If a nurse happened to have spirit enough to insist on her rights, we all know the results," "An Old Army Nurse" wrote. "She was branded . . . and her life was anything but pleasant." "We in the Navy are just as anxious for Rank as the Army Nurses," a navy nurse wrote to the editors. "Not because it will mean more respect from the enlisted personnel, but because it will make the officers appreciate that we are women of refinement, as well as members of a profession."[58]

R. Inde Albaugh conducted interviews with some fifteen hundred nurses as part of her work with the Bureau of Information of the Nursing Service of the American Red Cross. "The subject of military rank for nurses is one that they discuss very freely and frankly with the personnel of this bureau," she wrote in a letter to *Journal* editors. These nurses "felt the lack of protection" and were "solidly for something, *anything*, that will prevent a repetition of their experiences."[59]

Most military nurses agreed that they had experienced a hostile workplace, but some working nurses questioned whether rank would help the situation. And they voiced concerns that rank would separate them from enlisted men and would not protect them from officers. Although they wished to serve their country as part of the nursing profession, they had other reasons for choosing military service that included seeking new opportunities and experiences, and also the possibility of forming social relationships with military men.[60] An army nurse still serving in France wrote to the editors, "To us, who for some years have catered to pampered people for a sum of money, it has meant much to have known the American boys over here." She and other nurses were "always sure of absolute courtesy from enlisted men. God bless them!" Whether "on the ward" as patients "or on leave or at any social gathering," they showed appreciation to the nurses. But medical officers were another matter. Nurses "suffered so much humiliation at the hands of officers," she wrote, that "if I were doing private duty again I should hesitate to take a case" if it meant working with or treating a former medical officer.[61] This nurse was "vague" about rank, but said she intended to continue to study the matter.

A nurse from Maryland also opposed officer's rank for nurses because it would continue to separate military nurses from the men with whom they wished to associate. "We are not allowed to be on social relations with the men in the ranks," she wrote, "but more than two-thirds of the nurses who married in the service have married from sergeants down." Furthermore, she wrote, "the officers would not change even if we had Rank. They would continue to treat us as dirt under their feet." Another nurse argued that "95 per cent of nurses both at home and overseas" believed that enlisted men "are the most loyal institution that the nurse has met."[62] These nurses took exception to the class-based views of nursing leaders who believed that professionalism would make all nurses genteel and respectable women on par with officers rather than enlisted men. They applauded professionalism but not the elitism that leaders assigned to the process. Military rank, they suggested, would only strengthen the barriers between enlisted men and nurses and would not address the problems posed by male officers.

Rank-and-file nurses were not the only ones to question the efficacy and results of military rank. Indeed, the woman who became the most authoritative military nurse during and after the war was also the most vocal in her opposition to rank. Julia Stimson brought with her a faith in the elite, class-based code of honor and respectability that was the foundation for the professionalization of nursing in her generation. Her own success as a military nurse seemed to support her position dramatically. In what other nursing leaders described as a "meteor-like ascendancy," Stimson, a graduate of Vassar and the New York Training School for Nurses, began her military service as chief nurse of Base Hospital no. 21 in Rouen, France, in the summer of 1917. She became the liaison in charge of Red Cross Nursing in France in April 1918 and in November 1918 was appointed director of the Nursing Service for the American Expeditionary Force. In the fall of 1919, the surgeon general appointed Stimson as the superintendent of the Army Nurse Corps, making her the most powerful nurse and the most powerful woman in the military.

Stimson was the daughter of prominent New York clergyman Henry A. Stimson and Alice Bartlett Stimson, and the cousin of Henry L. Stimson, the former and future secretary of war who had assisted 1913 Washington, D.C., suffrage parade marchers and spent part of the First World War fighting at the front.[63] Her parents instilled in their seven children the imperatives of a socially conscious Christianity, high educational standards, and encouragement in professional endeavors. Henry A. Stimson believed that history taught that women are either goddesses or slaves, "and there is no stationary position midway. Men will either look up to women, or they will look down on them." Stimson advised male readers of his 1905 advice book, *The Right Life and How to Live It*, to consider every woman either mother, sister, or wife, "being in the order of nature other and finer" than men. Anything other than the pedestal, including equality between the sexes, would mean the "certain degradation of both women and men" and an end to civilization.[64]

As Julia Stimson entered the nursing profession and the military, she fashioned these familial views about the importance of the genteel rules of gender relations into her understanding of the workplace and professionalism. Although she broke with her parents in some of her views—supporting woman suffrage, for instance—she carried with her much of the substance of their philosophy. When her first letters home to her family were published in early 1918 as *Finding Themselves: The Letters of an American Army Chief Nurse in a British Hospital in France*, she dedicated the book to "all my Majors whose kind helpfulness was never failing."[65] Stimson shared the view held by some nursing leaders that the proper social relations between men and women were central to professional roles, and proper individual behavior was the surest means of control and protection in the workplace. As chief nurse she was proud that she persuaded the nurses serving under her not to drink or smoke, and she strictly enforced the ruling that prevented social relations between nurses and enlisted men. Outings with medical officers were strictly chaperoned, and she rigidly monitored nurses' leave. *Finding Themselves* constructs a picture of a group of men and women following the prescribed code of genteel gender relations from her father's book *The Right Life and How to Live It.*

Stimson's success in the military came in part from her ability to negotiate personal power through her influence with individual men. She explained to her parents that when talking with chief surgeons at army hospitals in her role as director of nursing for the Red Cross in France, "I always introduce myself by saying that I have been sent by the Chief [AEF] Surgeon General Ireland to make inquiries about the nurses and to see if there is anything I can do for them. General Ireland told me to do that and it always assures me of the most polite welcome." Male Red Cross officials and army officers shared Ireland's high opinion of Stimson. At a farewell dinner held when she left her Red Cross post and accepted the position of director of nursing for the AEF in October 1918, assembled male officers and officials applauded as she rose to give a speech. She had to wait for some time "for the dear old things to stop clapping." She told her parents, "They are so funny, these men, they act as tho they owned me and are so proud of me and have an air as tho to say, Just see what we have done with her." Stimson was "beginning to understand" her "army backing" six months later when she wrote to tell her parents that army officials were asking her to accept the position of the superintendent of the Army Nurse Corps.[66]

As she rose in the military nursing hierarchy, as she herself became more militarized, Stimson continued to enforce genteel behavior as a means of protection for nurses in the corps. She was appalled at reports that some chief surgeons were relaxing the rules preventing social relations between enlisted men and nurses, but she focused on nurses' behavior, not the chief surgeons' choices. "I shall be glad if you will let me have the names of nurses, no matter how many, who are not obeying the regulations about enlisted men," she wrote to Isabelle Carson at Base Hospital no. 50 in February 1919. "I think we can show them that they are not too many to be dealt with." It was "difficult to show a great many of the nurses that a ruling which precluded social relations with enlisted men was for their protection and the good of the corps," she later wrote in her history of the ANC. To remedy the "continued disquieting reports about the conduct of nurses on leave," she sent out a list of detailed instructions to all chief nurses with specific regulations for nurses' behavior.[67]

Stimson believed that in a system where women lacked official power, they had to depend on the goodwill of men. But she also realized that not all men were adherents to the code of *The Right Life and How to Live It*. In *Finding Themselves* she acknowledged that "other Chief Nurses do not always get the kind of help and cooperation that I am getting. What would I do," she asked, "if I had forbidden my nurses to do something which I felt was wrong or inadvisable and then the director of the Unit reversed the action? It is an unbearable situation to conceive, but I am afraid some Chief Nurses may have to face such difficulties." Stimson later spent a great deal of her time visiting various hospital units. "Some C.O.s are such devils," she wrote to her parents. They "countermand the orders of the Chief Nurses right over their heads." Her visits led her to believe that some officers cared very little for "what kind of trouble they get the nurses into."[68]

Although her analysis of the situation was similar to the views of most other nursing leaders and military nurses, Stimson did not feel that rank was the answer. In her mind, instead of structural, institutional protections, nurses needed to act as respectable ladies in order to protect themselves. In an article titled "Nursing Overseas" in the October 1919 issue of the *American Journal of Nursing*, Stimson, now acting superintendent of the Army Nurse Corps, appalled and offended most nurses and nursing leaders with this attitude. She defended the military and claimed that "the clashing of personalities that occurred so often; the times when chief nurses failed to develop in Commanding Officers a confidence in their cooperativeness and common sense; when nurses in wards were unable to secure the cheerful assistance of corpsmen; when from the top down a sense of harmony and esprit de corps was missing . . . when, in short, the leaders forgot their opportunity to keep up morale of the whole group—such times could not have been prevented by rank." Stimson concluded her article with an extremely weak endorsement of military rank for nurses that hardly seemed genuine when weighed with her other comments.[69]

To make matters worse for supporters of rank, Stimson's lack of support surfaced directly in Surgeon General Merritte Ireland's testimony against rank for nurses during congressional hearings. Ireland told a subcommittee of the Senate Committee on Military Affairs on September 4, 1919, that after Stimson's return from France, he had "asked her what foundation there was for so many of these reports [concerning nurses' problems with workplace hostility by officers and enlisted men], and she said there was none whatever.

She said that she did not believe them at all." He echoed Stimson's focus on nurses' behavior rather than structural difficulties. "I hate to be in opposition to or opposing anything these splendid women want, but I think their idea of securing rank to better their position would be altogether wrong—altogether wrong," he told the committee members. "I think that one of the nurses in a ward with a certain amount of tact will get generally what she wants."[70]

Many nurses expressed outrage that Stimson and Ireland were blaming them for the problems that resulted from a lack of military rank and penalizing them for waiting until they returned home to air their grievances. "After reading the article by Miss Stimson and the replies of General Ireland to the Senate committee, I am forced to reply to each one of them personally," wrote a military nurse now home in Nebraska. "I do not feel that they are fair or just to the nurses who earnestly tried to do their duty in obedience to orders issued them in the A.E.F., and who have made no complaint in the treatment they received, from officers in particular, while in the service. The war is over and we do not want to come back grumbling and complaining," she wrote. "But there is no denying that the present system in the army has many flaws in it." She believed that there was a place for constructive criticism to help the nurses in the service. "If rank for nurses will accomplish this, then I am surely in favor of it. . . . Service under the present system is surely unfair, unjust, and unreasonable for a nurse serving under a commanding officer who does not hold up her hand and assist her in every possible way," she wrote. "Unfortunately there are many of that kind in the army."[71]

Daisy Urch wrote her influential letter to the editor in part because of the Stimson and Ireland statements. Military nurses "have not come home and trumpeted their deeds to the world," she asserted. "I have yet to hear of any nurse complaining of the hardships that were due to the exigencies of the war, but they certainly are justified in objecting to the unnecessary indignities and false position that I am ashamed to learn the War Department is unwilling to remedy." "I do not think it was a 'clashing of personalities,' a forgetting of 'opportunities to keep up the morale of the whole group,'" Chief Nurse May Vroom wrote in reply to Stimson's article. The reason for conflict was, in Vroom's estimation, "eternally striving to achieve the impossible because of a wrong system."[72]

Military rank for nurses failed to pass congressional muster in 1919. Members of the Committee to Secure Rank for Nurses made the decision to modify their demands and ask only for "relative rank." This would confer a pseudo officer status on nurses and allow them to wear the official insignia from second lieutenant to major, but without corresponding pay and official position in the hierarchy. Congress granted this modified relative rank to military nurses with the passage of the Jones-Raker Bill, signed into law by

President Warren Harding on June 4, 1920, as part of the Army Reorganization Act. In a public ceremony that many nursing leaders must have observed with great ambivalence, the War Department selected Julia Stimson to be the first woman in the Army Nurse Corps to receive a commission, in her case the relative rank of major.[73]

Six years later Stimson offered nurses an olive branch in a public acknowledgment that rank for military nurses was an important institutional reform. In "Rank for Nurses: What Have Five Years of Rank Done for the Army Nurse Corps?" published in the *American Journal of Nursing,* she also included the results of a survey of military nurses on the question of rank. Stimson now believed that "there seems to be no question that relative rank has dignified the Corps—made its status in the Military Establishment definite, unmistakable and unquestionable, and brought about an ease and celerity in the mechanics of the administration that cannot be disputed." The seven hundred army nurses serving "all over the United States, in the Philippines, in Hawaii and in China" who responded to her questionnaire on how military rank affected their lives and their service were "almost unanimous" in their praise of rank in peacetime. They believed that rank "would be of immeasurable help in another emergency such as the World War." A chief nurse wrote that with enlisted men, "'even relative rank has helped us to secure better cooperation and more prompt compliance with requests.'" She believed that rank helped to overcome the view that "'women are men's servants.'" Rank seemed to make a difference with patients as well. Another nurse wrote that rank seemed to impress the type of patient "'who demands a little more than the fact that he is dealing with a woman or a nurse to enforce the necessary discipline.'" According to Stimson, most nurses who responded believed that "'soldiers carry out an order more willingly when they know that the nurse ranks as an officer and must be obeyed.'"[74]

Nurses were not so confident about the effect of their "relative rank" on officers. "'There was a strong tendency on the part of many officers, the first few months after the bill had gone through, to shift much of their responsibilities upon the nurses,'" said one nurse. And a chief nurse told Stimson that officers were "'jealously guarding their rank against invasion.'" Though most military nurses believed that officers resisted their rank, they expressed hope in institutional pressure. "'The lack or possession of [rank] cannot but affect the attitude of [army] members,'" some argued. "'Gradually the feeling is being overcome,'" wrote a chief nurse, "'and as time goes on greater benefits may be obtained.'" Interestingly, some nurses responding to the questionnaire also told Stimson that rank had a very definite effect on their relationships or standing with officers' wives. When the wives of officers needed health care they were treated at base and post hospitals by military nurses and other members of the medical corps. Several respondents detected an important shift in the attitudes of military wives toward them. "Rank has evoked a more cordial attitude on the part of [these] women patients, wives of officers," Stimson reported.[75]

Nurses surveyed praised other more tangible benefits of rank, including additional insurance privileges, increased travel allowances, and access to officers' clubs. But Stimson concluded her remarks by emphasizing benefits that were on "the personal side. It has been a source of great satisfaction that [army] nurses have the right to a defined status, and are not dependent on courtesy that might or might not be extended to a working woman."[76]

Nurses and their supporters campaigned for commissioned rank again during the Second World War and received temporary commissions for the period of the war as a result of legislation passed in 1944.[77] Eleanor Roosevelt, Massachusetts representative Edith Nourse Rogers, and Maine representative Margaret Chase Smith joined other supporters in the creation of legislation leading to the passage of the Army-Navy Nurses Act of 1947 along with the Women's Armed Services Integration Act of 1948. With this legislation, military nurses received commissions and pay and benefits commensurate with their rank.[78]

* * *

This case study of nurses' responses to a hostile military workplace in the First World War is an important chapter in the history of women in the military and also in the history of women's activism to create a safe and equitable workplace environment. The campaign for military rank had many successful elements. Nursing leaders were able to draw support from outside the nursing profession and outside the military, including members of women's organizations and civic groups. They also gained endorsements from prominent military, medical, and civic leaders. Their success was also influenced by the large numbers of women nurses serving in the military—21,480 at home and abroad in November 1918 by Julia Stimson's reckoning. Theirs was a very public stage upon which many women worked for the war effort.

But nurses still had to contend with the power of the masculine world and institution of the military when they asked for the right to officer status to command other men. Nurses who advocated rank as a way to resolve a hostile military workplace were directly challenging the structure of power and authority within the U.S. military. And as we will see in the next chapter, they did so in a repressive climate of postwar backlash. But rank, even relative rank, indicated that women had achieved a place in this most masculine of institutions. In Cynthia Enloe's terms, they had begun to unsettle the masculinized military.[79]

8. "Danger Ahead for the Country"

Civic Roles and Safety for the Consumer-Civilian in Postwar America

Having her to provide for will keep many a young veteran off the soap-box platform of the agitators and disruptors of our national life.
—Corra Harris, "Marrying Off the American Army"

All over the country the readers of the daily newspapers note the trial of some frenzied woman righting her imagined or real wrong with the revolver.
—William McAdoo, *When the Court Takes a Recess*

The world war presented Americans with models of male and female citizenship as part of the continuing dialogue concerning the definition and qualifications of civic roles in American life. The participatory civic model of the Progressive Era evolved for many Americans into an obligation for participation in wartime service. Both men and women, including supporters of fuller female citizenship and those who opposed such advances, adopted and adapted the "bullets for ballots" model to suit their vision of citizenship during the conflict. Various groups used different interpretations of "patriotic motherhood" as a foundation for wartime civic claims. Women-at-arms, military nurses, and women physicians all acted to redefine the meaning of service with the military and in national defense in this fluid civic matrix.

In the period of demobilization and reconstruction after the war, a complex series of images, fears, events, and debates erupted over the roles of returning soldiers and the women who had struggled for and achieved many gains during wartime. Civic leaders, policy makers, and the popular media found a solution in the form of a new postwar model for citizenship: former soldiers would have to be transformed into consumer-civilians. Married, with "congenial" employment and the purchasing power to attain and maintain middle-class status and "respectability," they believed that veterans would

turn from violence to conformity. They would not participate in labor radicalism or embrace the Bolshevik threat. They would be healed from the potential
violence of shell shock and postwar trauma. And although these men would
be civilians, they would still be serving their country in their reinvigorated
role of Protectors.

Embedded in the male role of consumer-civilian was the powerful suggestion of a necessary postwar bargain for women. They would, as a group, need
to exchange wartime gains for protection from male violence at home and
in the community. And the popular press, civic leaders, and policy makers
fixed their calls for women's support in the rhetoric of patriotic civic service.
Although not all women could or would adhere to this postwar bargain, this
new social and cultural construction of the threat of male violence was part
of the "demobilization" of woman power after the war. Now that the war
was over, men needed to protect home and community for the safety of the
home front. Women's patriotic duty in the postwar world was to marry men,
reinstate the roles of Protector and Protected, and embrace the role of the
consumer housewife.

Scholars of the interwar years in Europe have found similar messages about
containing women's wartime gains in traditional roles. Mary Louise Roberts,
in her study of France in the decade after the war, demonstrates that many
leaders and culture makers structured French motherhood into an idealized
civic role to reinvigorate and preserve the French nation. French women as
loyal wives and mothers supported a traditional France for which soldiers
had sacrificed, enabled men to regain their manhood lost in bloody trench
stalemates, and provided an antidote to massive social changes symbolized
by the sexually free New Woman.[1] Susan Grayzel examines the cultural role
of mothers of soldiers and mothers of soldiers' sons in postwar commemo-
rative rituals in France and England. "Elevating the status of the implicit
maternal mourner and making all women synonymous with mothers" in
these rituals, she concludes, "demonstrated the cultural power of women as
mothers, not as 'citizens' in their relationship to the costs and experiences of
the war." And Susan Kent finds that for Britain, postwar stability and order
were to come through marriage and family and a satisfied heterosexuality.
"Violence, war, and conflict could only be avoided," in the dominant script
of British postwar society, "if separate spheres for men and women were re-
drawn." The consumer citizenship and maternalism of the post–First World
War years provides a prelude for the onslaught of consumer citizenship in
the post–Second World War era analyzed so fruitfully by Lizabeth Cohen
with the United States as a focus and Erica Carter in her consideration of
West German society.[2]

In the U.S. military, nurses and their supporters made their case for rank in the medical corps as this new model of citizenship was taking hold in the postwar negotiations of civic roles. Women physicians made plans for continuing medical relief and also returned to postwar practice and public health activism under the heavy shadow of the consumer-civilian model and its implications for women. Yet both groups had institutional and organizational support in place, and both could hold claim to the cultural role of healers in a devastated world. The military would have need for nurses; continuing crises in the Balkans, Russia, and Europe meant refugees and the need for medical relief and women physicians' international cooperation. Yet women-at-arms did not have this same organizational or professional support or postwar roles to continue their claims. The process of demonization that had cast female soldiers as "bad girls" would be strengthened and deepened with the return of the male Protector in the role of the consumer-civilian. This final chapter will consider the elements of the construction of the new postwar civic role of the consumer-civilian to provide a context for understanding the challenges to women's wartime claims in the immediate postwar world.

The "Reflex from the Violence of War Time": The Threat of Dangerous Veterans

Like veterans from other conflicts, soldiers of the First World War faced monumental challenges as they returned to what veteran Willard Waller called an "alien homeland."[3] Psychiatrist Jonathan Shay suggests the homecoming of Odysseus as a metaphor for the struggles all veterans encounter on their return journey home. For many, the journey is fraught with stress, pain, vulnerability, anger, instability, and lack of trust in people and institutions. Physical and mental disabilities compound the struggle for many others. Shay and other scholars and veterans provide important contributions to our understanding of the traumas and challenges of returning soldiers and also of the historic and contemporary failures of states and communities to provide support and assistance to them.[4] Following the First World War, veterans returned to an "alien homeland" in which fears of radical labor, Bolshevism, and a weak postwar economy clashed with claims that the economy could be robust enough to welcome all wartime workers and returning soldiers. They returned disabled, shell-shocked, and searching for a way to resume civilian lives. This chapter does not seek to analyze the varied experiences of returning soldiers in detail. Rather, it highlights the fears of policy makers and community and institutional leaders about the dangers of returning soldiers in the months after the Armistice and analyzes some of the consequences of those fears for gender roles and policies in this period of demobilization.

Many Americans feared that demobilizing soldiers might bring habits of violence with them as they returned to their homes and communities, a "reflex from the violence of war time."[5] From the beginning of the war observers commented on a decline in crime in the Allied nations; authorities warned that it could be explained to a great extent by the enlistment of criminals in the Allied military forces. The Commissioners of Prisons for England and Wales believed that the "marked decline in crime" in 1914–16 was due in large measure to the fact that the "country's call for men appealed as strongly to the criminal as to other classes." Prison officials in Scotland and Ireland drew similar conclusions, and Professor Roux, an expert on criminal law at the University of Dijon, reported that "war has emptied the prisons of France."[6] J. K. Codding, warden of the Kansas State Penitentiary, reported in April 1918 that "we are not receiving at the penitentiary any more the adventurous, daredevil type of criminal," and concluded that these "adventurous" criminals had all gone to war. Dr. William Healy, an American specialist on juvenile delinquency, asserted that "the very qualities which make a good soldier, such as fearlessness and love of adventure, have led some of our offenders into crime" and "produced heroes in warfare."[7]

These reports reinforced concerns that wartime service might not only attract "adventurous" men who might be criminals outside of the military but even develop criminal behavior in soldiers and the use of violence among veterans upon their return. France's Professor Roux warned that war "is not a school that teaches respect for the person or property of others." And in her study "Crime and the War," Edith Abbot of the University of Chicago reported that criminologists feared "the habit [soldiers] have formed of violent solutions and of acts of force."[8] The *New York Times* reported in September 1916 that a discharged veteran in Glasgow, Scotland, named James O'Hara threw a grenade in the midst of a noisy group of neighbors at the rear of his tenement when they did not heed his call for quiet. He "learned the art of bomb throwing at the front and grew callous in regard to the results," the *Times* reported. When officials searched his apartment they found that O'Hara had "a quantity of ammunition" stashed there. Other press reports during the war years raised the alarm about rising crime rates in Germany and Austria. "A band of former jailbirds and deserters appears to be terrorizing the suburbs of [Berlin]," the *Times* reported in front-page headlines for March 13, 1918. All parts of Austria and Germany appeared to be in the midst of violent "calamity," and "men and women" were "attacked on the streets" every day. No place was safe. Criminals and deserters were creating chaos across the countryside and in city and suburban streets, all part of the lawlessness of wartime conditions. Susan Kent reports newspaper accounts of British soldiers rioting and assaulting civilians as they returned home from the conflict.[9]

Subsequent investigations suggested a high percentage of crime among veterans of the world war, an indictment of "military habits" as well as institutional and judicial failings. In December 1922 Wisconsin governor John J. Blaine found the "pleas of the soldier boys" for pardons "ringing in his ears" and commissioned an investigation of Wisconsin veterans in prisons that was published in 1923.[10] The study found that 20 percent of the veterans in prison had some physical disability related to military service, and 23 percent were "criminals because of facts associated with alcoholism." In addition, 62 percent of the veterans at the state prison and 40 percent of the veterans at the state reformatory were "mentally abnormal," and at both institutions 40 percent of the veterans had "physical diseases that need medical attention." Seventy percent of the offenses for which the veterans had been imprisoned at both institutions involved property or money. "The investigation of the crime wave among soldiers," wrote journalist Fred Holmes in his review, "has . . . definitely ascertained that war has a damaging influence that leads to after-war criminality by persons not criminally inclined, in all likelihood, under peace-time conditions." And, Holmes concluded, the investigation "disclosed the evils that follow the neglect of the individual through failure to restore him to a remunerative civilian occupation." Willard Waller's research suggested that twenty thousand veterans "served time in prison within four years of the end of the war." And he cited a 1922 study of twelve state reformatories and nineteen prisons that showed that veterans were 18.12 percent of these prison populations. Waller believed that the actual rate of crime for veterans was much higher because of two additional factors. First, "many serious crimes of ex-soldiers go un-punished because of sympathy for the accused," and second, "only a small percentage of felony charges result in convictions." Therefore, he concluded, "veterans in prison constitute a small fraction of the veterans who commit serious crimes."[11]

In addition to presenting information about veterans as criminals during and after the war, the popular press advised that the postwar world would feature a large percentage of soldiers who had been traumatized and disabled by their wartime experiences. Shell shock and other disabilities were pressing concerns for the army and the nation. Jennifer Keene's investigation of army psychiatric sources suggests that "veterans suffering from shell shock filled three out of every five beds in government hospitals in the interwar period." During and after the war many military medical officials refused to consider the validity of what we today know as posttraumatic stress disorder and considered it to be "slacking" or effeminate behavior. As Keene notes, men who were shell-shocked "did not receive wound chevrons to mark them as suffering from a legitimate war injury." The official and popular rhetoric about the importance of providing rehabilitation and services for veterans who were disabled was not matched by the extensive services and support needed, and the scandals of Charles Forbes and the Veterans Bureau uncovered in 1923 capped this postwar problem.[12]

For this study it is important to note that the popular press presented Americans with the prospect that all returning soldiers might be volatile shell-shock victims with unpredictable and violent behavior. Stoddard Dewey, reporting from Paris for the *Nation* in July 1918, highlighted the prevalence of shell shock in a variety of forms among soldiers and civilians. "The United States will have plenty of these cases," he wrote. Nerve shock, in Dewey's view, would present a great danger to communities by "unfitting . . . hundreds of thousands of soldiers for immediate resumption of the effort of civil life." American psychiatrist L. Pierce Clark warned in a *New York Times Magazine* article in June 1918 that 90 percent of returning Canadian soldiers were suffering from some form of shell shock and urged Americans to prepare for a similar situation. Neurologist M. Allen Starr advised that shell shock produced a mental state of depression and confusion and "a state of half-consciousness or of moody brooding" in the returning soldier. But then, he observed, "this passes off and in the course of time he becomes emotional and excited." This could include unpredictable fits of terror, distress, and nightmares. In November 1918, as demobilization efforts were under way, Dr. H. R. Humphries told the readers of *Touchstone* that the thousands of soldiers returning with shell shock would "seem almost like strangers in the homes in which they have been born and reared and to which they have so longed to return." Mary C. Jarrett, chief of social services at the Boston Psychopathic Hospital, believed that the medical establishment in the United States was vastly ill-prepared to handle the numbers of shell-shock cases among veterans. It "will not be long before we shall have, coming every month from overseas, three thousand invalid soldiers, of whom . . . 400 will be suffering from nervous and mental diseases," she reported. Army psychiatrists were "discovering nervous and mental disorders at the rate of 2,000 a month for which there are almost no means of treatment," and shell-shock cases were overwhelming the few institutions prepared to deal with those suffering from the disorder. Present institutions were "completely inadequate," she told social work colleagues. Psychiatrists specializing in the treatment of shell shock were "scarce," and "dispensaries for mental disease are still conspicuously rare," she told the readers of *Touchstone*.[13]

There were other worries about the problems of readjustment for returning soldiers. At a conference of social workers in 1917, Helen Reid of Montreal, director of the Ladies' Auxiliary of the Canadian Patriotic Fund, was invited to provide a perspective on the challenges Canada was facing with returning soldiers and their families. "The biggest problem for which we have not yet found any solution is that of the men who are not disabled and crippled, but who have been discharged and after three years out of civil life have lost their sense of family responsibility and find it difficult to take root again," she said. "Apparently they are physically fit to take hold, but the stress and strain of war has made them unfit to make quick adjustments.... The men become chronic grumblers, and that means danger ahead for the country." John Shillady of the Department of Charities and Corrections in Westchester County, New York, voiced concerns about the problems of employment for "unadjusted people." James Tufts, professor of philosophy at the University of Chicago, referred to "something as yet undefined, a certain disturbance of all values, a certain shaking loose from older foundations and an uncertainty as to things once settled, which as yet cannot be precisely described or estimated," that "marks the men who for four years have lived away from home and native land and have been led to measure many things with a different standard."[14]

In addition to these fears about crime, shell shock, and readjustment, the popular media and policy makers raised the specter of labor agitation, Bolshevism, and violence in association with returning soldiers. As Jennifer Keene points out in her thoughtful study of American soldiers in the First World War, the U.S. military failed to create an overall plan for the demobilization of troops at the conclusion of the conflict. The Armistice came upon army officials while they were attending to plans for strengthening American forces for what they believed would be a much longer conflict in the fall of 1918. Then the Wilson administration's attention was on the upcoming peace conference. The War Department, by default, "simply discharged men when the military rationale for their mobilization had ceased to exist." As Keene demonstrates, the demobilization process was chaotic, and soldiers perceived it as unfair and frustrating. At the time of the Armistice, she notes, army administrators of the American Expeditionary Force quashed spontaneous peace celebrations and ordered troops to conduct drill and training because "until a peace treaty was signed, the army wanted to maintain an obedient, combat-ready force." Some soldiers acted with their feet by going AWOL, and many others complained forcefully to family and friends and to members of Congress. Many of the five thousand troops stationed in Russia protested and refused orders, asking for an explanation of their military purpose there. All this raised the "worrisome possibility that military service had radicalized citizen-soldiers."[15]

On February 16, 1919, the *New York Times* featured excerpts from letters written by soldiers critical of the demobilization process "read before Congress in large numbers of late." The complaints, for most letter writers, focused on postwar employment and class and status differences between enlisted men and officers. Representative John Tilden (R-CT) noted that the "dissatisfaction of the writers seemed largely due to their belief that they were being kept for the purpose of insuring the jobs of officers," and he provided numerous examples. With a "record as clear as mine," wrote a carpenter with the rank of sergeant, "I am still denied the right to go home to support my wife and child." A "machine-gun man" wrote, "If Colonel _____'s morals of holding these men to hold his job is any different from those of the Kaiser, who used men to sustain his ambitions, I can't see it." He reported that the skilled workers in his unit were "red hot" and worried about postwar work. "There is hardly a man in the machine-gun school who doesn't earn $35 to $50 a week in civil life. Many of them have been urged by their former employers to get released. Some will lose their jobs if indefinitely detained. All will lose familiarity with their professions and businesses that get further away every day." This soldier warned that something "should be done to punish these militarists. They are breeding bolshevism, anarchy, and socialism in the souls of men who were sterling patriots."[16]

Veterans were returning home to a complicated postwar economic and political scene. Although industrial wages rose during the war, prices rose even higher. When the Armistice was signed in November 1918 the government began to cancel some war contracts immediately. The Wilson administration acted to end all price controls and limits on profits that had been part of the control of the wartime economy. A recession ruled for the next six months, with fast declines in employment, manufacturing, and wholesale prices. Even though there was a partial postwar boom that lasted from the summer of 1919 to the summer of 1920, consumer prices rose faster than during the war years. The consumer price index rose over 1916 levels by 77 percent in 1919 and 105 percent in 1920. And in the year following the war some four million workers struck for better wages and hours and for continuing recognition of wartime union gains. These ranged from members of the Industrial Workers of the World in their strongholds in the Pacific Northwest and Massachusetts to the United Mine Workers in the Southwest and East. As David Montgomery notes, "Bold visions of social change and strikes for a few more pennies per hour fed on each other." The Seattle general strike of early 1919 was the most prominent general strike in the nation's history.[17] Mine workers, factory workers, and agricultural workers all hoped to maintain wartime gains in the troubled postwar economy. There were wrenching and destructive race riots across the country in 1919.

At the same time, the congressional elections of 1918 brought Republican control to Congress, combining, as Montgomery notes, a "law-and-order electorate" with a "lower prices electorate" that continued to repress civil liberties, embraced the Red Scare, and supported a strengthened Justice Department that surveilled "dangerous radicals" across the country. At the same time this Republican Congress lobbied to hold wages down in an inflationary economy.[18] The revolutionary hopes and actions of workers, political progressives, and radicals came face-to-face with this postwar corporate and political powerhouse in strikes, at the bargaining table, and in political contests and challenges for the maintenance of civil liberties. Attorney General A. Mitchell Palmer arrested and deported suspected radicals in 1919 and 1920, wartime restrictions on civil liberties remained for months and even years after the Armistice, and immigration officials joined with local authorities and corporations in continued surveillance and deportation.

Press accounts expressed concerns that veterans might be radicalized by the problems of reconstruction and readjustment and tied their situation to these larger aspects of the antilabor, anti-immigrant Red Scare. The *Portland Oregonian* reported in January 1919 that troop demobilization was a "serious problem," and editors feared that "idle men" with time on their hands and pay allowances and transportation money would "increase both unemployment and crime" in their communities. "Present conditions furnish fertile soil for agitators of whom there are seemingly many. They are well provided with money, said to come from Russian Bolshevist sources." Walton Hamilton, writing in the *Dial* in May 1919, warned about visible veteran unrest and increasing alarm about it. "In more than one city soldiers have already paraded their status of being among the unemployed. In many localities unrest is finding expression in strikes. . . . A certain barometer of the change is to be found in the attitude of officials. The indifference of November had become a grave concern by March." Veterans joined workers to form Workmen and Soldiers' Councils in Portland, Oregon, and Tacoma, Washington, to advocate for solidarity among workers whether they had served in the military or in factories or had logged timber for the war effort.[19] The *Portland Oregonian* warned that Bolshevik doctrine was spreading in Portland and that agitators tailored their radical message to soldiers' ears. The council meeting, the paper noted, "was called by radicals who felt that the return of soldiers and sailors had created a problem with which existing organizations were not dealing effectively." In the Seattle general strike of January and February 1919 three hundred veterans served as the "War Veteran Guards" on eight-hour patrol shifts to protect strikers, and refused to be deputized in order to maintain their allegiance to workers rather than to the city.[20]

Veteran unrest seemed to spill over factory walls and strike committees and into communities. The *New York Times* ran a first-page story and follow-ups in May 1919 about a "raid on the Yale campus" by "some 300 soldiers" who "invaded the campus and punched two or three students before the police arrived," claiming "that from campus dormitory windows students ridiculed [the soldiers] in their parade that afternoon." A week later "rioters" and a "mob" of "more than 5,000 persons joined some 200 discharged soldiers" in another attack on Yale students. The students tried to repel the mob with "clubs and baseball bats." New Haven's mayor called out the Connecticut Home Guard the next evening, and they turned a fire hose on a crowd of "about 15,000 persons" that "quickly melted till at 10 o'clock not more than 3,000 remained." The *Times* concluded that the "outbreaks . . . are clearly instigated by the local Bolsheviki" whose "ringleaders were roughly-dressed characters who spread propaganda of the wildest description."[21]

Fears about Postwar Gender Relations: Divorce and "Public Women"

Layered over these concerns about dangerous and violent veterans were worries about the susceptibility of the home front and the negative impact of the war on marriage, the family, and gender roles. These combined with fears about the extent to which women's wartime activities strengthened their claims to postwar equality. One of the most scathing critiques of the consequences of militarism on men's attitudes toward women came from the future historian Frank Tannenbaum in an article published in the *Dial* in April 1919. Tannenbaum's experience as an officer convinced him that army life encouraged soldiers to objectify women, and he sounded the alarm about the effects of this objectification on postwar gender relations and community life. He deliberately used the term *woman* to suggest this objectification. "The search after woman is one of the great games the soldier plays," he wrote. "It is the game of a huntsman, and like a good hunter he displays persistence, energy, avidity, and resourcefulness in the chase. . . . And in this process he reduces all social institutions within his reach, from the church to the gambling house, to an instrument for his end, and does so deliberately." The chase was an objectification. "But the interesting thing in the present connection is the soldier's attitude towards woman as that attitude is affected by his life in camp and the narrow outlets which it forces upon him. This attitude is unexpected. It is the attitude of the scientist. It is an attitude shorn of modesty, morals, sentiment, and subjectivity. It is immodest, unmoral, objective, evaluating, and experimental. Men will sit," he wrote, "till late at night in a darkened tent, or lie in their cots, their faces covered with the pale glow of a tent stove that burns red on cold nights, and talk about women—but this talk is of the physical rather than the emotional, of the types, the reactions, the temperaments, the differences and the peculiarities of moral concepts, the degrees of perversity, the physical reactions, the methods of approach—in fact, as if it were a problem in physics rather than morals." Tannenbaum told of young boys who advertised the services of prostitutes near the army camp at which he was stationed in the States. One of them called to Tannenbaum and asserted, "'Look a here, Soldier, I tell you it is clear, fresh, and good.' These were the very adjectives, and others like them, which are on the lips of the men in camp when discussing the problem of sex," Tannenbaum wrote, "an attitude applicable not only to the public woman, but to all women in general."[22]

Such fears about postwar gender relations combined with women's independence were magnified by discussion of the "divorce evil." Both the number of divorces and the divorce rate rose in the United States directly after the war, making the conflict a "watershed" in the history of divorce. The annual national average of divorces in the period 1914–18 was 111,340, but in the period between 1919 and 1921 divorces rose to 155,070, a 40 percent increase.[23] The increase was part of a pattern of rising numbers of divorces in Western nations, with the United States "between 1910 and the mid-1940s" on "an ascending curve that surpassed the divorce rate in all other nations."[24] Analysts have explained this "ascending curve" in terms of increased expectations for marital happiness,[25] as evidence of increased cooperation between spouses to get around legal barriers to divorce, and as evidence of the consequences of the "divorce reform" movement.[26]

There are a number of specific explanations for the rise in divorce rates and numbers in the immediate aftermath of the First World War. Many wartime marriages were contracted hastily after brief courtships. The numbers for the beginning months of the war are quite telling. For the first three months of 1917 the monthly average number of marriages was 74,000 nationally. The United States entered the war in early April, and marriages rose to 112,000 in April, 93,000 in May, and 130,000 in June 1917, a monthly average of 112,000 across those first three months, a 50 percent increase. Many of these marriages did not last after the war was over. In addition to these quick wartime marriages the stresses of wartime undoubtedly led to a rising divorce rate after the war. Separation and sexual experimentation on the home front and the war front contributed. Roderick Phillips suggests that "the separation of husbands and wives by war made divorce proceedings more complex, and moreover, the very fact of separation would have made the need to dissolve a marriage that much less urgent."[27] In the United States, Congress passed legislation in the fall of 1917 that placed a moratorium on civil actions against soldiers for the duration of the conflict. President Wilson signed this Soldiers' and Sailors' Civil Rights Bill into law in March 1918. The law was primarily for the financial protection of members of the armed forces and their families, and civil proceedings such as divorce were included. This legislation also contributed to delays in divorces until 1918 and beyond when soldiers demobilized.[28]

Many contemporaries explained the rise in divorce rates by pointing to an increase in women working for wages during the war and to statistics that showed that women initiated the majority of divorce cases in the States.[29] When the Census Bureau released a major study, *Marriage and Divorce, 1916,* in the spring of 1919 that showed that one in every nine marriages ended in divorce and that the rate of divorce had increased 55.5 percent, the "divorce evil" became a hot topic. Many commentators worried that the war would accelerate this upward trend and feared chaotic consequences in postwar society.[30] Oregon had the third-highest rate, after Nevada and Montana, in the 1916 study, and the Oregon press carried numerous stories about the rising rate that continued in 1918 and 1919. Oregon lawyers "put themselves on record as being opposed to the ever growing divorce evil," and in August 1919, "as a means of lending their efforts toward curbing the promiscuous granting of divorces," they increased the minimum fee in noncontested cases from forty dollars to seventy-five dollars.[31] They took these increased fees, of course, all the way to the bank.

The Consumer-Civilian as Protector

And what was the solution to the chaos of this postwar world? Policy makers answered, overwhelmingly, that it was jobs, marriage, and families for homecoming veterans. Employment would enable returning soldiers to ease into the role of the consumer-civilian. This would be the antidote for Bolshevism and labor radicalism, on the one hand, and the maladjustment of postwar trauma, shell shock, and "restlessness," on the other. Although this solution had important consequences for all Americans, women were targeted as those responsible for shepherding men into these roles and for standing by them as supportive spouses and family members. They were not to be men's competitors. And the stakes—safety at home and in the community—were high. Many writers cast this as women's patriotic duty, assigning it a stature of civic sacrifice equal to the wartime mobilization of woman power. The call for full employment for men to avoid violence and to protect home and community reinforced the return of the traditional gender conventions of the Protector and the Protected, roles that some women had contested during the conflict. In this context, and in this construction of male violence, women's safety would not come through armed self-defense, provisions against gender-based hostility in the workplace, or actions to challenge rape and domestic violence. Rather, it would come by surrendering to the reinvigorated patriarchal consumer-civilian family.

The popular press and women's magazines underscored the necessity of "congenial" employment for men and also women's responsibility to help men have such employment. To compete for this "congenial work" with men would mean that they were putting themselves and their communities at risk because such work was the antidote to postwar violence among veterans. Advice columns in women's magazines directly after the war provided guidance for women readers whose men were returning home. During the war the "Soldiers All" department was a monthly column on women's war work and relief activities written by Anna Steese Richardson, published in the *Woman's Home Companion* from the summer of 1917 until April 1919. The last installment represented a complete transformation of the nature of the column and was titled "Now That They're Back." Now the "work which during the past two years has been done by a nation in cooperation and through established centers," Richardson wrote, "becomes individual and local." Women would now be required to understand and support their returning men and sacrifice for their own well-being. "Unless he was exceptional," Richardson noted, "he saved little of his pay . . . so . . . will have no funds except the pay given him the day he is mustered out, nothing to tide him over until he secures a position and draws his first week's salary. The Government is trying to find positions for its fighting men through its department of labor, but not all men wish to go on farms, to lumber camps, to huge industrial plants. Some of them desire to resume their former occupations, for which they are eminently suited; but their places have been filled by non-combatants. It is good citizenship, true reconstruction work, to help such men find congenial positions and to tide them over the financial embarrassment."[32] Evelyn Newman, a former wartime canteen worker, wrote an article titled "Old Husbands for New!" in the *Ladies' Home Journal* that placed responsibility for postwar harmony solidly on the shoulders of women. "The past is dead; the world is new; and whether it becomes a new heaven or a new hell depends largely upon you, the women, who must live with and love these returned men."[33] Good female citizenship required women to make certain that the returning soldiers were employed and happy. If they did not take on this duty, the consequences, quite literally, could be hellish.

Within these advice columns came warnings about men's violence and lack of desire for employment. Women would have to find ways to help men overcome these problems. "The fact that a man comes back unscratched by bayonet or shell does not mean that he is physically and nervously normal. War leaves strange, hidden scars, which even physicians cannot always find," Anna Steese Richardson told *Woman's Home Companion* readers. "You may find that he is restless. He does not wish to remain in the regular army, neither does he feel satisfied with the old industrial system under which he worked in pre-war days. He may not express any desire to travel, to roam from the old home, yet its very walls seem to irk him. He may find fault with what you do, with what you say," and express "irritation."[34]

Advice columnist Laura Spencer Porter responded to a letter from "Eleanor" about the way her returned soldier was behaving: smoking, drinking, treating women in less respectful ways. Porter suggested that the problem was not with the soldiers but with the women to whom the soldiers were returning. "You can mistake all this; you can quarrel with him if you like, about his smoking; you can disagree sharply with his 'broader views;' you can disapprove of his present attitude toward religion; but I do not believe that you will uproot in this way his deep and new determinations. The most and best you can do as to those is to try to understand them, and to follow them, and, if you are worthy of them, to share in them."[35]

Some writers insisted that women had a civic duty to marry veterans and to encourage them to work. In her article "Marrying Off the American Army," Corra Harris told readers that only marriage and male employment would save the nation, communities, and individual women from the consequences of male violence and Bolshevik agitation. Writing in the *Independent* for February 1919, Harris asserted that it was "time to announce the engagement and approaching marriage of all young American soldiers to all young American women." Why? Because the "one immediate and most intimate problem in this country today is what we shall do with these young American veterans. . . . So, everything is arranged except the details of more weddings than we ever had before." Marriage would stabilize returning veterans and reinstate them as Protectors. "Having her to provide for will keep many a young veteran off the soap-box platform of the agitators and disruptors of our national life." Harris also spoke of the "young American women" she was consigning to this bridal fest. "And these girls they left at home are not the same. They are finer, braver, more dutiful women. They have a new sense of responsibility, for they also have accomplished their part in this war. More than a million of them enlisted for service, not in the army, but for the men in that army. They have served for them, knitted for them, made bandages for their wounds, prayed for them. Therefore they are also in love with these returning soldiers. It is natural and it is right, the best kind of righteousness."[36]

"Congenial" Work

In the long run, the federal government, states, and voluntary organizations did not keep pace with the rhetorical calls for employment and other types of support for veterans. William Breen demonstrates that the politics of internecine and extra-agency conflicts kept crucial funding of the wartime United States Employment Service (USES) from passing Congress in 1919.[37] The Soldiers' Bonus Bill, passed in 1924, was the end of major actions on behalf of veterans. But in the short run the fears of veteran unemployment and concerns about the period of readjustment fueled direct action at the federal, state, and community levels. In the first six months of 1919 (the period for which funding remained) the United States Employment Service registered almost 3 million workers for positions and reportedly placed 1,884,499 workers in positions of employment.[38] The USES created advisory boards at the state and community levels in November 1918, and these boards worked with state employment offices to provide assistance to returning soldiers and male and female war workers. The military also funded plans to use the period of demobilization to provide soldiers with "education enough to make them self-supporting and self-respecting members of the civilian community when they return to it."[39] The Army Educational Commission in cooperation with the YMCA took the lead in these demobilization educational efforts.[40] These programs were responses to fears about radical influences on soldiers who could not fit into the world of work after the conflict. Job training would counteract radicalism, Major Alexander Powell asserted. The "anarchists and the agitators will find their numbers rapidly dwindling. . . . Education and remunerative employment, contentment and self-respect, will do more than rifles and machine guns to check the spread of the theories of Comrades Trotzky and Lenin."[41]

When the Council of National Defense published its survey of reconstruction activities for 1919 it reported that all forty-eight states and the District of Columbia had active employment offices, some with more than one office in cities and towns with federal, state, and community sponsorship.[42] All forty-eight states and the District of Columbia had information services for returning veterans, all the states had public works projects through the construction of highways and other projects, and forty-seven (minus Rhode Island and the District of Columbia) had land grants for veterans or were considering them by the end of 1919.[43] Twenty-one states had some provision for veteran housing. Forty-six states (minus Arkansas and New Mexico) and the District of Columbia provided specific vocational education and training for veterans. States enacted a variety of programs to provide exemptions and preferences for veterans. Eighteen states had policies for preference for returning service men in public employment. Sixteen had some kind of tax exemption for returning veterans. Many had property tax exemptions, most for a year, that ranged from New Jersey's exemption for five hundred dollars to South Dakota's exemption of property worth up to five thousand dollars. Indiana, Minnesota, and Montana law made service personnel exempt from delinquent tax charges for varying periods after the war. Vermont excused veterans from paying all taxes for 1917–19. New Hampshire, New York, Massachusetts, and Delaware made returning veterans exempt from paying the license fees required for "hawkers" and "peddlers." Fourteen states provided some kind of educational benefit for returning veterans, often with scholarships to state universities and teaching colleges. The Oregon legislature, for example, passed a law in 1919 that "honorably discharged soldiers, sailors, and marines, enlisted or inducted into the service from Oregon, may attend any institution of learning, public or private, in the State and have their necessary expenses, not exceeding $25 per month nor $200 per year, paid by the State for four years."[44] Five states passed laws that allowed veterans to count their time in the military as years toward teaching certificate renewals or teacher retirement pensions. By 1922, the World War Veterans' State Aid Commission of Oregon reported that "with the exception of Alabama, Georgia and Mississippi, every state in the union has passed legislation, or has pending legislation giving to or authorizing for World War veterans' aid, exemptions, or benefits of some kind."[45]

Local communities organized to provide employment and other services to help returning soldiers find "congenial work." Many larger communities set up canteens for enlisted men and community centers for returning veterans[46] and employment offices under the auspices of reconstruction committees. In Portland, Oregon, representatives gathered for a statewide "Reconstruction Conference" in January 1919. The conference brought labor, management, and voluntary organizations together with state agencies to develop strategies to combat the "unemployment menace" through a census of the unemployed, incentives for businesses, and support for public works programs.[47] Like those in many other states, Oregon policy makers supported preferences for returning veterans in public employment, hiring, and firing policies that provided preferences for soldiers in industry and short-term emergency relief funds.[48] The *Portland Oregonian* published editorial cartoons supporting jobs for veterans, praised the legislature for appropriating funds for veteran employment, and offered veterans free advertising.

This focus on the civic necessity of employment for returning veterans as a deterrent to violence was part of an ongoing struggle to define who had the right to work and in what ways women and men of various classes and races would be part of the workforce. Prior to the war, court cases and legislation most generally related to women as mothers or potential mothers. They were to be protected, and were considered less than equal partners in economic citizenship. From the time of the Supreme Court's 1908 *Muller v. Oregon* decision in favor of limiting women's work hours through 1917 when the United States entered the war, eighteen states passed laws regulating and circumscribing women's wage work. As Alice Kessler-Harris notes, such legislation "reinforced the sex-segmented structure of the labor force without regard for individual desire or need or marital status" and "gendered the terms" of women's economic citizenship.[49] After the war, the debate over "protective" labor legislation for women workers formed one of the central conflicts among women's groups in the postsuffrage era and was a part of organized labor's platforms and conferences.[50] When the American Federation of Labor drafted a "reconstruction program" at its annual meeting in St. Paul, Minnesota, in June 1918, its points about women workers had a familiar ring. "Women should receive the same pay as men for equal work performed," they wrote. "Women workers must not be permitted to perform tasks disproportionate to their physical strength of which tend to impair their potential motherhood and prevent the continuation of a nation of strong, healthy, sturdy and intelligent men and women."[51]

The postwar scene had some room for debate and discussion, including the nuanced sponsorship of the continuation of the wartime Women's Bureau of the Department of Labor, and a variety of grassroots claims for the right of certain groups of women to be employed or not employed. The war accelerated trends that increased women's wage work in white-collar jobs and in job mobility. In the interwar years the number of women who were wage workers and mothers rose 25 percent.[52] But as Alice Kessler-Harris notes, with "few exceptions, jobs returned to male control when the conflict ended." Maureen Weiner Greenwald in her study of women and wartime work demonstrates that women's opportunities for job mobility and the satisfaction of work in new kinds of jobs most "frequently ended upon demobilization or soon after." She shows that the postwar power of management combined with hostility from male workers worried about full employment created powerful barriers to women's postwar wage-work aspirations.[53] In the postwar decade from 1920 to 1930, the number of women who were in the wage labor force remained steady at about 25 percent.[54] For Kessler-Harris, the postwar period still "left to men the moral claim to the sphere of work."[55]

In addition to the issues identified by these scholars, it is important to understand that fears about veteran violence were also influential in shaping ideas and messages about the postwar workforce. In the immediate postwar period the construction of messages about violence and returning veterans became a way for policy makers in government and the corporate world, supported by the popular press, to try to shape men's and women's behavior. They also served to reinstate the gender-role conventions of the Protector and Protected in popular discourse as well as in official policy. Individual women and men and various organizations supporting women contested these visions. But the cumulative power of this "redefinition"[56] of male violence may certainly have been a factor in pressuring businesses and communities to participate in the demobilization of women in wage work at the close of the conflict. It perhaps influenced some women to think in terms of a postwar bargain: safety in exchange for wartime gains in the workplace.

Employers, civic leaders, and business owners cooperated in creating the postwar ideal of the veteran-turned-consumer-civilian. This vision was gendered and included marriage, prosperity, and "congenial employment" for men, and heterosexuality, marriage, and the running of a modern household for women. It submerged race and class into the middle-class consumer ideal. Men were to be Protectors and Providers in a smooth transition to postwar prosperity. Many manufacturers marketed the transition as a presentation of self from soldier to professional. The right clothes would make it all possible. Surgeons who had learned the skills of reconstructing soldiers' wounded faces now touted "plastic surgery" as a way for men to look their best when applying for jobs and to make their way up the corporate ladder.[57] In the postwar recession, women were not the only ones who felt the pressure to make the postwar world safe and right. The weight on men to work and provide was tremendous. Returning veterans were asked to maintain their role as Protectors, making the transition from protecting the nation and all its homes in wartime to standing as Protector and Provider for one wife and home.

Women-at-Arms and the Rhetoric of Postwar Gun Control

The woman-at-arms who claimed the right to defend the nation and to defend herself had no place in this new civic definition of the civilian-consumer. During the war women-at-arms had faced a powerful backlash in the deni-

Advertisement for Ben Selling Clothier, *Portland Oregonian*, January 10, 1919, 5.

gration of the woman soldier. The female soldier was characterized as active in her sexuality—whether homosexual or heterosexual—and therefore someone who "deserved" violence to put her back in her place. This backlash continued as the consumer-civilian model gained power and reinstated men as Protectors and women as passively protected wives. Another aspect to this backlash occurred after the war, as women with guns were "shot down" in the rhetoric of the postwar gun-control movement.

As we have seen, Frederick Hoffman, the consulting statistician for the insurance industry, published a yearly homicide report for the nation and advocated reform of homicide statistics and reporting. Hoffman also became one of the nation's leading voices for gun control. As he reported on the death-from-homicide rates in the decades leading up to the war and then in its aftermath, Hoffman sounded the alarm about the rising tide of murder and the increasing epidemic of firearms that killed. He backed up his warnings with statistical proof. In the period 1910–12, for example, firearms accounted for 62 percent of male deaths by homicide and 52.8 percent of female homicide deaths, and 61 percent of homicides overall in 1915. "The predominating method in the American murder cases is by firearms," he wrote in 1915, a fact he presented in virtually all of his reports from 1911 through 1925. Hoffman opposed the death penalty as a solution. From a political and statistical perspective he saw it as useless as a deterrent to crime. He also spoke out against lynching and racism. "Murder is murder whether the life destroyed is a white person or a person of color, or whether of a native born or a foreigner." For Hoffman, the solution to the homicide problem was clear. "The problem of murder in its final analysis is to a considerable extent a question of the effective regulation of the sale and possession of dangerous weapons."[58]

Hoffman applauded the legislation already in place in a few states and advocated national gun regulation. Before the world war, Texas passed a tax in 1907 assessing retailers 50 percent of gross receipts from the sale of firearms. Oregon began requiring a license for anyone who purchased a handgun in 1913. But New York's Sullivan Law was the model upon which Hoffman and other gun-control supporters wished national legislation were based. Passed in 1911 after New York's Mayor Sullivan was shot in the neck and amid reports of the growing use of guns in New York crime, the Sullivan Law regulated the sale, possession, and carrying of firearms.[59] During the world war many states continued to regulate firearms. While the United States was fighting abroad, California, Connecticut, Indiana, Maine, Massachusetts, Missouri, New Hampshire, New Jersey, Ohio, Oregon, and Washington all considered such legislation.[60]

The debate about the regulation of firearms cast women who used guns in a particularly negative role. The gun-control movement in this period based its constitutional foundation on an interpretation of the Second Amendment right to bear arms published in the *Harvard Law Review* in March 1915. Lucilius Emory wrote that the new class of "gunmen" who used "small firearms easily carried upon the person" was "pressing home the question of the reason, scope, and limitation of the constitutional guaranty of a right to keep and bear arms." He demonstrated that there was no basis in common law for the idea that the right to keep and bear arms was a fundamental right in England. He discussed American legislation and constitutional history to demonstrate that "the single individual or the unorganized crowd, in carrying weapons, is not spoken of or thought of as 'bearing arms.'" The concept, he said, was of a military nature only and stemmed from colonial fears of a standing army. As such, certain classes of weapons—like brass knuckles—could be prohibited. Certain persons could also be prevented from carrying weapons in accord with the Constitution, including "women, young boys, the blind, tramps, persons *non compos mentis,* or [those] dissolute in habits."[61] He gave no justification for the inclusion of women in this list of the "disabled." Perhaps they were there because they could not serve as soldiers in the military.

Homicide statistician Frederick Hoffman asserted that "the evidence is quite conclusive that to an increasing extent women, who consider themselves injured in their marital or sex relations, take the law into their own hands with serious results." The doctrine of self-defense, he wrote, "does not justify one person killing another if by retreating he can reasonably expect to escape death or serious harm." Hoffman understood the concerns people had with the rising crime rate, but "anyone familiar with present day dangers to innocent parties knows full well that unless a person is trained to shoot to kill on sight, possession of firearms only increases the danger."[62]

William McAdoo, Wilson's secretary of the treasury until 1918, Democratic presidential candidate in 1920 and 1924, and chief magistrate of New York after 1918, was also a strong and vocal supporter of gun control. In a variety of publications and on the lecture circuit McAdoo, like Hoffman, voiced his concerns about "crime in the streets" and also the lethal effects of guns at home. "Look at the tragedies in the morning newspapers," he wrote, "where husband shoots wife, man shoots mistress, one child shoots the other, frenzied head of family kills the whole family and then himself."[63] Yet in his chapter "The Curse of the Pistol" in *When the Court Takes a Recess* (1924), McAdoo devoted many strong words of ridicule to women who defended themselves from domestic violence. "Formerly, the pistol was associated with the male sex," he wrote, "but of late years, with political and other equalities, the ladies apparently have determined that a nicely enameled revolver is as much a necessity and ornament as a gold-mesh handbag." Now, one reads in the paper almost daily that "the jilted, disappointed, outraged, jealous, malicious, or angry female has relieved her feelings by shooting the man in question" and then "calmly announced the fact to the police, coupled with a tale which she intends shall appeal at least to the hearts of other ladies." After hearing such a case, McAdoo reported, a New Jersey Supreme Court justice suggested that "the trousseau of a bride would not be complete until she approached the altar with a big revolver strapped to her waist." What was the nation coming to? McAdoo asked his readers. "All over the country the readers of the daily newspapers note the trial of some frenzied woman righting her imagined or real wrong with the revolver." He then reprinted six unattributed news stories of women who had killed their partners. McAdoo concluded that a "rather good-looking woman with a pitiful story on the witness stand" with evidence "that the slain man was not all that he ought to be" could count on an acquittal in a U.S. court.[64]

McAdoo turned to the question of women defending themselves from violence outside their homes. "Then, too," he wrote, "we have the revengeful man with the loaded pistol who seems ready to shoot the woman who tells him she no longer loves him or who resents his persistent wooing. Maybe if this sort of shooting goes on, the Ladies Firearms Union may begin taking pot shots at mashers, those despicable creatures who in public places and under favorable circumstances persist in obtruding themselves and insulting unprotected women." But, he cautioned, "this would involve the risk of the woman's using a gun by mistake on the wrong man or of proving herself a bad shot."[65]

Such concerns that women might "use a gun by mistake on the wrong man" seem to reach to a deeper fear that all men would be vulnerable if women took protection into their own hands. This threat of social disorder was a strong current in the postwar gun-control debate that ridiculed women who used guns to repel the sexual advances of strangers or who resisted domestic violence through shooting their partners. This reflected directly on the claims for safety made by women-at-arms. It also underscores the difference in the definitions of the "cause" and "cure" for male violence put forth by some women during the war and by the construction of male violence by policy makers after the war. Whereas the wartime definition of violence allowed some space for women in defense groups who spoke of protecting their homes and the homeland from enemy invasion during the war, individual women who claimed the right to protect themselves from individual men had no such support. This coupled with the denigration of the "wrong sort" of female solder cast women's self-defense against violence in strongly negative terms indeed.

* * *

The new role of the consumer-civilian addressed both women's claims for civic equality and women's concerns with male violence. Policy makers identified a pervasive threat of male violence that would endanger the home front in the form of domestic violence and "domestic disturbance" in the violence of labor agitation and political revolution. If women wanted to be able to exercise their civic rights without fear of violence, they insisted, they would need to reaffirm the gender conventions of the Protector and the Protected in a consumer-driven society. If not, women could anticipate the very conditions that many had fought against during wartime: violence against women, lack of resources, and impoverishment. When combined with the specific barriers I have identified, including the ridicule and management of the female soldier and resistance to officer status and rank in the military for women, this co-optation was a powerful reframing of women's wartime civic and antiviolence claims.

Conclusion

Historian Linda Kerber observes that "it is in citizenship that the personal and political come together, because citizenship is about how individuals make and remake the state."[1] The claims of the women-at-arms, some women nurses, and some women physicians for more complete female citizenship in the era of the First World War were intensely personal at the same time that they were intensely political. Their activism stemmed from the depths of personal and group experiences and identities and hopes for a possible future of equality and opportunity. It also came from a heightened consciousness of violence against women and a belief that their actions could create conditions of safety on the home front, in the workplace, and in the wake of war's violent impact on women. They saw the wartime state as a responsive institution that they could reshape for the better by undertaking the obligations of citizenship and acting to address important issues such as violence in their arenas of work and action. Their experiences allow us to draw significant conclusions about the relationship of the First World War and these women's claims for equal civic, professional, economic, and social citizenship. Their experiences and activities in the midst of wartime violence also serve as important case studies in the history of antiviolence activism.

Women in all three groups believed that the war represented the convergence of two vital currents. The first of these encompassed the collective accomplishments of women in suffrage, community reform, and workplace and professional advancement. These achievements engendered a strengthened civic identity for women and created a civic platform upon which they could mount their further claims to full female citizenship and equality during the war. The second current was the wartime context that enhanced the meaning and potential of citizens' loyalty and service to the state. They argued that they could fulfill their obligations of citizenship more completely in the context of wartime needs, and in so doing they could claim postwar equality and advancement. In their view, the mobilization of woman power during the war would take women "over the top" to a new postwar world of opportunity.

The women in this study were not alone in their hopes for postwar gains. A cover of the National American Woman Suffrage Association's *Woman Citizen* in late 1918 reflected the perspective of many women who had taken part in the "mobilization of woman-power" during the war. Confronting a member of the Senate opposed to suffrage, a woman points to a board containing a list of women's wartime services to the nation, including fund-raising, the Woman's Committee of National Defense, women's YWCA work, women's work in munitions factories, the Women's Land Army, the Women's Oversea Hospitals, motor corps, and nursing work. These accomplishments constituted women's "right to democracy" and suffrage. Although some suf-fragists, most notably members of Alice Paul's National Woman's Party, did not support the war and focused solely on gaining the vote, many women saw the wartime mobilization of women and their accomplishments as a reason for Congress to finally hear and act on their claims for a national suffrage amendment. The House passed the woman suffrage amendment in January 1918, the Senate in June 1919, and Tennessee became the thirty-sixth state to ratify the amendment into the Constitution in August 1920. In the seventy-two-year journey from Seneca Falls to the Nineteenth Amendment, many suffragists believed that it was women's wartime service that finally took them "over the top" to victory.

During the war women nurses, physicians, and women-at-arms also envi-sioned female citizenship against the backdrop of their evolving definitions of violence in wartime on the home and war fronts. When women marched in the streets of Washington, D.C., for the right to vote in March 1913, they en-countered violent resistance, and this opposition caused them to see violence in a new way. Their claims for the rights of citizenship that emerged from this experience included the rights of safety for all women and the rights of women in public to be protected. They "rediscovered" and "redefined" vio-lence, to employ the terms of Shani D'Cruz, and then built this new definition into their claims for women's civic identity.[2] Their opponents spoke and acted from an alternative definition. They accused women marchers of engaging in violence and therefore argued that they forfeited any sort of protection from men and indeed "deserved" men's violence to put them back in their "proper place" once again. These same patterns showed themselves in the wartime and postwar definitions of and solutions to violence. Women physicians

"Our Right to Democracy," *Woman Citizen* (December 28, 1918).

identified rape and violence against women in the wake of war and created all-female medical units to provide relief at the same time that they offered a critique of war's violent consequences. Women nurses identified a hostile wartime workplace and sought military rank as an institutional solution. Women-at-arms highlighted the dysfunctional nature of the gendered roles of Protector and Protected and claimed the right of home and self-defense. Their opponents responded by blaming women themselves, demonizing the female soldier, denying women an institutional place and protections, and reinstituting patriarchal family roles in the period of demobilization with the consumer-civilian ideal.

Each group, then, pursued wartime activism in a matrix of ideas concerning gender, citizenship, violence, militarism, and women's place in the institutions of the nation. Their visions, strategies, and actions help us to understand women's impact on war and wartime institutions, the role of women's wartime activism in the movement for woman suffrage and citizenship, and women's antiviolence activism.

Women Physicians

Because of their elite status, their extensive professional education and training, and the strong wartime need for doctors, women physicians had some important advantages in their quest for civic and professional equality with male colleagues. When the Medical Women's National Association asked all of the approximately six thousand women physicians in the nation to register their preferences for wartime service in the *Census of Women Physicians,* they were petitioning·Washington and the War Department for the right to become officers. They were professionally prepared citizens who were willing to use their skills to help the wounded and ill in time of war. Mary Elizabeth Bates and the members of the test case for the Committee on Recognition of Medical Women, the Oregon women who applied as a group for positions as officers in the medical corps, and the many individual women physicians who applied all shared this hope in fuller female citizenship. The women who agreed to be part of Bates's test cases, the Portland women physicians, and many of the others who applied for service in the medical corps as officers already had the right of suffrage granted by the states in which they resided. They had achieved one of the key components of citizenship as a foundation for their claims to equal civic service in the medical corps and used it as a basis for their argument for inclusion. Being an officer in the army medical corps therefore had a civic as well as a professional dimension in the minds of women who sought such service. They were ready to fulfill the obligations of wartime civic service, and in return they sought the same status and footing that their male colleagues possessed.

Because women physicians were asking for an equal institutional place within the military, they were able to draw on decades of collective experience in knocking on the doors of colleges and universities, medical schools, residency and scholarship committees, hospital boards, and public health organizations. Many saw the process of entering the institution of the military as equivalent to opening these other doors. Accordingly, they studied and analyzed military regulations and decisions from the Office of the Judge Advocate General. They prepared careful, "airtight" applications and test cases. They used their networks among women and women's organizations and male supporters in government, medicine, and communities to garner public and professional support and action on their behalf. But the military was, for most policy makers, participants, and other Americans, a quintessentially masculine institution. It established the context and experiences for boys to become men and for all men to develop the qualities of honor and valor. Further, many Americans believed that masculinity was in "crisis" in the years surrounding the war, underscoring the role of the military as a "manmaker" and reinforcing the male role as Protector. When women physicians sought entrance into this bastion of maleness, they were contending with these additional challenges. Women physicians were asking to have officer status that signified a permanent and accepted place in military medicine and the army itself. Officer status would also grant them power over men, the power to command as well as to heal. These issues were significant barriers that ultimately prevented the women physicians who wanted officer status from reaching this civic and professional goal in the First World War.

But precisely because of their educational and professional stature and their ability to gain supporters and contributors, women physicians were successful in their determination to respond to the needs of women and children in the wake of wartime violence. Measured by Estelle Freedman's three characteristics of antiviolence movements, which include naming the violence, providing support for survivors, and fighting back with institutional action, women physicians won a significant victory in their ability to shape medical responses to the war. In their efforts to name the violence against women in wartime France, including rape, women physicians discussed the importance of gynecological and obstetrical care and the need to address the physical and emotional scars of wartime violence. They also provided routine medical care and public health and preventative measures to respond to the many ways that wartime dislocation, poverty, and malnutrition were also a part of wartime violence against women. For many women physicians, the creation of all-female medical units and provisions for civilian medical care were specific strategies to provide care for women who suffered from rape and the violence of invasion, occupation, and refugee experiences. Esther Pohl Lovejoy indicted rape and violence against women in *The House of the Good Neighbor* at the same time that she praised women's efforts to support and heal survivors. The continuing postwar work of women physicians in the American Women's Hospitals units across Europe was a lasting legacy of these medical priorities. And the organization and activities of the Medical

Women's International Association strengthened women physicians' global ties and enabled them to provide cooperative services for refugees and survivors of other conflicts.

Yet in many ways, women physicians' work to address wartime violence against women was "safe." It was certainly less threatening than the challenges made by women nurses to address a hostile working environment and the claims of self-defense made by women-at-arms. Women physicians were acting on behalf of other women, the women of "devastated France," as they created their all-female units and supported work among refugees. These survivors were women who had the sympathy of the Allies and the public, women whose experiences with violence were defined as coming from the German enemy. This work of women physicians therefore did not overtly challenge mainstream interpretations of the war or the roles of men or women. They were nurturing other women who had been victimized by the enemy; they were not challenging Allied men directly. Their military roles were as healers, not soldiers. Thus, in their antiviolence activism they did not face the same backlash that women-at-arms faced as they made a direct critique of American men as Protectors. Additionally, women physicians were generally in accord about the importance of providing medical services for women civilians. The leaders of the WOH chose to divide their military and civilian-care facilities but remained committed to both. And the staff of the AWH, with its *hôpital mixte,* did not have to address the problem of such divisions. There were no major conflicts among women physicians or their organizations about providing services to European women who were survivors of violence.

Military Nurses

Military nurses who sought officer rank also had some important advantages in their quest for civic and professional equality during the war years. Nursing leaders were able to draw support from outside the nursing profession and outside the military, including members of suffrage and other women's organizations. They also gained endorsements from leaders and those prominent in military, medical, and civic life. It was also important that there were so many nurses serving in the military. Such large numbers of women needed by the military and serving so many wounded and sick soldiers resulted in significant publicity and backing. Leaders in the campaign for rank for military nurses drew on the same kinds of institutional support and used the same strategies that the women physicians had used. But outside of the military, nurses needed less education than women physicians did, and they commanded far less status in the medical profession as a "feminized" profession among white-collar workers.

Nurses were not asking to be soldiers, but they still had to contend with the power of the masculine institution of the military when they asked for the right to officer status to command men. Nurses who advocated rank as a way to resolve a hostile military workplace were directly challenging the structure of power and authority within the U.S. military. Unlike women physicians whose work was on behalf of other women for whom there was strong sympathy, making the work therefore "safe," nurses were acting on their own behalf. They were naming hostile workplace environments and targeting male military men as those responsible. The compromise position of leaders for "relative rank" did remove the threat of women being in command of male officers, thus easing the way for its passage in 1920. But rank, even relative rank, indicated that women had achieved a place in this most masculine of institutions. In Cynthia Enloe's terms, they had begun to unsettle the masculinized military.

The campaign was also significant because nurses defined and exposed hostile work environments in the military workplace as part of their call for military rank. Although the achievement of relative rank did not resolve this problem, their campaign was a noteworthy milestone in women's claims for a safe workplace. Their actions fulfill Freedman's three characteristics of antiviolence movements. Military nurses named their experience of hostile work-environment harassment by using words such as *indignities, annoyances,* and *humiliations* to describe the behavior of officers who misused their power when nurses "rejected their social attentions" and talked of officers sexualizing the base-hospital workplace "like a Coney Island dance hall." They were demoted, classified as "ill," their authority and competence undermined. Their descriptions echo Vicki Schultz's categories of gender-based hostility in the workplace. Supporters of rank sought a structural, institutional solution by advocating a recognized and authoritative place in the military hierarchy with officer rank and status so that other women would not have to experience what they had during the war. Their voices and actions are an important part of the history of activism against hostile work environments.

It is also significant that the nurses felt most free to tell their stories after they left military service. Their temporary work with the military for the duration of the war made this possible. Yet they continued to be a part of the nursing profession, and this link was an important reason they wished to see the structure and institution of military nursing reformed. They did so to secure the safety of those women who were still in the institution and those who would follow. Their actions emphasize the importance of

networks among women to strengthen the call for change and underscore
the difficulties women face in addressing a hostile workplace environment
while still working within it. These women could speak, but they help us
understand why it is often so costly for women to speak from within a hostile
workplace.

It is also instructive to observe the ways that class divided nurses in their
opinions about the efficacy of rank for addressing the issues of a hostile workplace. Although nurses agreed about the hostile wartime work environment,
they disagreed as to whether rank was the proper remedy. This disagreement
was not a simple division between elite nurses who opposed rank in favor
of class-based respectability and rank-and-file nurses who supported it as
a structural protection. Most elite nursing leaders and many rank-and-file
nurses supported military rank as an important institutional protection at
war's end. Yet Julia Stimson, an elite opponent of rank, continued to believe that class-based codes of ladylike respectability and genteel behavior
were the keys to a safe work environment for nurses in the military. Some
rank-and-file opponents believed that military rank would do nothing to
curb officers' behavior. Further, they feared that it would create additional
barriers between them and the enlisted men with whom they wished to associate. Although these divisions diminished the strength with which nurses
could campaign for a safer military workplace through the achievement of
rank, they highlight the importance of class divisions among women in the
military workplace. Those rank-and-file nurses who joined Julia Stimson in
skepticism about military rank differed with her about the reasons for that
mistrust. Stimson's elite vision held that if women nurses lived the code of
respectability, then the male officers with whom they associated would be
lifted to a higher plane of behavior. Rank-and-file nurses had no such trust
in male officers across the gender and class divide.

Women-at-Arms

Women who took up arms so as not to "endure the fate" of Belgian women
and who offered themselves as citizen soldiers ready for military service
challenged the very core assumptions and power relations of the traditional
gender conventions of the Protector and the Protected. Theirs were perhaps
the most radical and the most threatening claims made by women for full
female citizenship and against violence during the war. By taking up arms,
women asserted either that men had failed as wartime Protectors or that
women had the civic responsibility to share in the work of protecting the
nation, communities, and the home. At the same time that they made their

claims for civic defense, they also argued that they were capable of self-defense in time of war and, by implication, in time of peace. In so doing, they exposed and challenged the role of violence at the heart of the conventions of the Protector and the Protected. They challenged the historic male prerogative of physical force as the last resort for maintaining the racial and gender order and domestic control. Women-at-arms did not have the kind of institutional support or structures that women physicians and women nurses had as a foundation for their claims. They found some supporters among suffragists and other leaders, but women's armed defense did not resonate with most women in the nation, particularly those whose goals were to end war and to resist militarism. Perhaps the staunchest supporters of women-at-arms were the gun companies that saw an important marketing opportunity and profits in the female use of guns at rifle ranges and "cellar clubs." The vigorous popular efforts to "tame" the female soldiers of the Russian Women's Battalion of Death, to challenge and denigrate the sexuality of female soldiers, and the ridicule of women who might seek to protect themselves from intimate violence with guns were powerful deterrents. At a time when the use of guns was more and more associated with members of the military as a legitimate use of force, and at a time when "uncontrolled violence" was seen as the ultimate threat to the nation in the form of labor and radical challenges to the state, members of a women's army who empowered themselves to resist external or domestic violence and to challenge the traditions of the Protector and Protected were absolute threats to military, political, corporate, community, and familial power.

The Postwar Consumer-Civilian

It is important to place the activities of women-at-arms, women physicians, and military nurses in the context of the wartime and postwar campaigns to limit civil liberties and the Red Scare fears about male violence. The "safe" role created by policy makers and the popular press for returning veterans in the consumer-civilian was an antidote for the new construction of veterans as threatening the peace of postwar communities and homes with the violent habits of wartime. A congenial job and marriage would mean that potentially violent returning soldiers would be managed and tamed, and their roles of Protector ensured and reinvigorated. These traditional gendered conventions would be reinforced and the topsy-turvy world of wartime "women on top" reversed. The message to women was that they would need to exchange wartime gains for protection from violence in the postwar world. And the popular press, civic leaders, and policy makers structured their calls in the rhetoric of patriotic civic service. Men were civilians but still civic actors in the postwar world. The state might call on male soldiers to fight abroad or to quell "domestic disturbances" at home, but veterans would be the Protectors of home and hearth for the safety of the home front. Women, by reinstating men in their role as Protectors and accepting their own role as the Protected, marrying and fulfilling the duties of the consumer housewife, were told that this station was the height of female citizenship and civic duty in the postwar years. Washington would employ soldiers to quell labor radicalism and "domestic disturbances," and individual men would exercise their civic duty at home. As historian Michael Sherry notes, "Though obviously expressed in the 'production of violence,' militarization may have sources and outlets far removed from violence and military power."[3] The consumer-civilian and the wife who supported him are important examples of this form of militarization. This civic role was, ironically, called into being to avoid violence. But it was a role that policy makers associated with controlling returning military men and women who had gained from military and home-front participation. As such, these roles may be seen as an important prelude to an American century of militarization.

* * *

The women of this study addressed the problems of wartime violence against women and called for fuller female citizenship from the places where they stood, worked, and observed the world. These were important first steps, but they were limited in their scope. The women's activism took place in isolation rather than in a strong, unified movement across class, racial, and professional lines, thus limiting its effectiveness and power. Although they identified specific aspects of violence against women in wartime, they did not construct a theoretical whole from these individual parts. And these women were also linking their claims for more complete female citizenship to the institution of the military. Militarization also has costs, often hidden costs, in other aspects of women's lives. Women-at-arms, women physicians, and military nurses negotiated a paradoxical relationship with the military as they tried to work within it and also sought to transform it as an institution. The subsequent history of women's efforts to combat violence against women in the military, including recent events such as Tailhook and the Air Force Academy sexual harassment and rape cases, suggests the difficulty in achieving long-term institutional and social change. Alternatively, the continuing efforts of groups such as the American Women's Hospitals and Doctors without Borders suggest the strategic importance of extrainstitutional action in dealing with violence and in responding to military action.

This study also highlights the links between the roles of male Protector and female Protected in the ways that violence against women has been encoded into law and cultural practices. Members of each of these groups of women challenged men's roles as Protectors—by seeking service with the military, by providing services for women who had been raped and victimized by the violence of men at war, by calling for military rank to challenge male power in creating a hostile wartime work environment, and by claiming the right to self-defense as well as national defense. And like the women of the Washington, D.C., suffrage parade of 1913, to the extent that they challenged men's roles as Protectors and challenged violence against women, they encountered men who believed that they "deserved" violence in reprisal. As rape laws and international law regarding crimes against women in war focused on the "honor" of men and communities and focused on women as agents of the violence they received, these women faced deep cultural responses to women and violence.

All told, the actions of First World War–era women physicians, nurses, and women-at-arms offer important case studies in the history of the quest for full citizenship rights and are important chapters in the history of the global movement to combat violence against women. Their successes and challenges, the nature of the opposition they faced, and the impact they had on the way that the nation waged war provide important lessons for continuing responses to the issues they confronted and those that we confront today.

Notes

Preface: "Mobilizing Woman Power" in the First World War

1. See Natalie Davis's classic analysis of ritual gender reversal, "Women on Top," in *Society and Culture in Early Modern France*, 124–51.

2. Willard Waller, *War and the Family*, 33.

3. The phrase "over the top" comes from trench warfare, as soldiers go "over the top" to victory. In popular wartime parlance, going "over the top" meant achieving success. Harriot Stanton Blatch titled the sixth chapter of *Mobilizing Woman-Power* "Women over the Top in America."

4. See Cynthia Enloe, *Maneuvers: The International Politics of Militarizing Women's Lives. Maneuvers* continues Enloe's important work on the impact of the military on women in her other works, including *Does Khaki Become You? The Militarization of Women's Lives.*

5. For more on these issues, see Margaret Randolph Higgonet, Jane Jenson, Sonya Michel, and Margaret Collins Weitz, eds., *Behind the Lines: Gender and the Two World Wars;* Amy Kesselman, *Fleeting Opportunities: Women Shipyard Workers in Portland and Vancouver during World War II and Reconversion;* Leisa Meyer, *Creating GI Jane: Sexuality and Power in the Women's Army Corps during World War II;* and Susan Zeiger, *In Uncle Sam's Service: Women Workers with the American Expeditionary Force, 1917–1919.*

6. Frances C. Van Gasken, M.D., "Introductory Address, Woman's Medical College of Pennsylvania, Delivered at the Opening of the College Session, September 19, 1917," 3–4.

7. For general information on civil liberties in the war and postwar periods, see John Milton Cooper, *Pivotal Decades: The United States, 1900–1920,* 297–305, 322–30; and Nell Irvin Painter, *Standing at Armageddon: The United States, 1877–1919,* 376–82. For the postwar period, see Kim E. Nielsen, *Un-American Womanhood: Antiradicalism, Antifeminism, and the First Red Scare.*

8. See, for example, Mark Ellis, *Race, War, and Surveillance: African Americans and the*

United States Government during World War I; and Frederick Giffin, *Six Who Protested: Radical Opposition to the First World War.*

9. See Kathleen Kennedy, *Disloyal Mothers and Scurrilous Citizens: Women and Subversion during World War I.*

10. For the foundation discussion, see Judith Hicks Stiehm, "The Protected, the Protector, the Defender."

11. See Kristin L. Hoganson, *Fighting for American Manhood: How Gender Politics Provoked the Spanish-American and Philippine-American Wars.*

12. For Progressivism and citizenship, see Alan Dawley, *Changing the World: American Progressives in War and Revolution.*

13. See Shani D'Cruze, "Unguarded Passions: Violence, History, and the Everyday," introduction to *Everyday Violence in Britain, 1850–1950: Gender and Class,* 1 and the essays in the anthology; and D'Cruze, *Crimes of Outrage: Sex, Violence, and Victorian Working Women.*

14. T. H. Marshall, *Citizenship and Social Class, and Other Essays;* Alice Kessler-Harris, *In Pursuit of Equity: Women, Men, and the Quest for Economic Citizenship in 20th Century America;* Linda K. Kerber, *No Constitutional Right to Be Ladies: Women and the Obligations of Citizenship,* 236–43 (quote on 242).

15. Kerber identifies four arguments about bearing arms and citizenship in the period between the American Civil War and after World War I. The first was that the obligation was not bearing arms but risking one's life for the state, something that childbearing women did do. The second was the fact of women-at-arms and women in military service, usually isolated individuals. The third was to deny the relationship of arms-bearing to voting (citing examples of men past military-service years). And the fourth was to "reject arms-bearing entirely and to juxtapose women's nurture against men's destruction" (*No Constitutional Right,* 244–45; quote on 245).

16. Estelle Freedman, *No Turning Back: The History of Feminism and the Future of Women,* 279, 284. Vicki Schultz suggests that the contemporary dominant paradigm of workplace discrimination as "sexual harassment" in the United States since the 1960s should be replaced with a more inclusive vision of workplace harassment as discrimination based on gender that "has the form and function of denigrating women's competence for the purpose of keeping them away from male-dominated jobs or incorporating them as inferior, less capable workers" ("Reconceptualizing Sexual Harassment," 1755). In my view, this description is a more accurate representation of the goal of nurses who sought military rank to provide workplace safety.

17. These are central arguments in Enloe's work, including far-ranging examples in *Maneuvers* and *Does Khaki Become You?*

Prelude: The Washington, D.C., Suffrage Parade of 1913

1. "Suffragists Take City for Pageant," *Washington Post,* March 2, 1913, 1.

2. See Christine Lunardini, *From Equal Suffrage to Equal Rights: Alice Paul and the National Woman's Party, 1910–1928,* 20–26. For additional background on the comparisons between NAWSA and the Paul and Burns style, see Nancy Cott, *The Grounding of Modern Feminism.*

3. Lunardini, *From Equal Suffrage to Equal Rights,* 25–26.

4. The *Washington Post* printed the entire scheduled line of the march the day before the event. See "Suffrage Parade Will Form in Seven Different Sections," *Washington Post,* March 2, 1913, 6.

5. See "Suffrage Parade"; and Lunardini, *From Equal Suffrage to Equal Rights,* 26–28.

6. Henry Stimson quoted this joint resolution in a letter to the Board of Commissioners that he entered for the record as part of his testimony before the congressional subcommittee hearings convened in the aftermath of the parade. See "Testimony of Hon. Henry L. Stimson, Former Secretary of War," in U.S. Senate, Committee on the District of Columbia, *Suffrage Parade: Hearings before a Subcommittee under S. Res. 499 of March 4, 1913, Directing Said Committee to Investigate the Conduct of the District Police and Police Department of the District of Columbia in Connection with the Woman's Suffrage Parade on March 3, 1913,* 119 (hereafter cited as *Suffrage Parade Hearings*).

7. "Sylvester Shocked at Insults to Women," *New York Times,* March 9, 1913, 4:3. See also Lunardini, *From Equal Suffrage to Equal Rights,* 27–28.

8. "Sylvester Shocked"; "Chief Blames Men," *Washington Post,* March 9, 1913, 1–2.

9. Stimson entered the letters and responses into the subcommittee hearing record ("Testimony of Stimson," in *Suffrage Parade Hearings,* 117–19). Stimson was the uncle of Julia Stimson, who became chief nurse of the American Expeditionary Force during the war and then superintendent of the Army Nurse Corps.

10. SR 164/HR 406 is quoted in "Begin Police Grill," *Washington Post,* March 5, 1913, 3. See also Lunardini, *From Equal Suffrage to Equal Rights,* 28.

11. "Testimony of Stimson," in *Suffrage Parade Hearings,* 118.

12. "Further Testimony of Mrs. Sara T. Moller," in *Suffrage Parade Hearings,* 125; "Suffragists Take City for Pageant."

13. See "Cadets Escort General Jones Because of Insult Story," *Washington Post,* March 4, 1913, 10; "Further Testimony of Moller," in *Suffrage Parade Hearings*; "Suffragists Take City for Pageant"; "Throngs Greet Pilgrim's Entry," *Washington Post,* March 1, 1913, 1, 3, 12; and "Testimony of Stimson," in *Suffrage Parade Hearings,* 119.

14. "Stimson Drills a Troop," *New York Times,* March 2, 1913, 1; "Testimony of Stimson," in *Suffrage Parade Hearings,* 120.

15. Lunardini, *From Equal Suffrage to Equal Rights,* 29.

16. "Parade Protest Arouses Senate," *New York Times,* March 5, 1913, 8.

17. See *Suffrage Parade Hearings*; "Parade Protest Arouses Senate"; "Begin Police Grill"; "8,000 Women March, Beset by Crowds," *New York Times,* March 4, 1913, 5; "Sum Up Day's Work," *Washington Post,* March 4, 1913, 3; "Woman's Beauty, Grace, and Art Bewilder the Capital," *Washington Post,* March 4, 1913, 1, 10; Lunardini, *From Equal Suffrage to Equal Rights,* 29–30; and "100 Are in Hospital," *Washington Post,* March 4, 1913, 10 (quote).

18. "Sum Up Day's Work"; "Testimony of Madame Lydia Mountford," in *Suffrage Parade Hearings,* 360; "Testimony of Mrs. Helena Hill Weed," in ibid., 68; "Testimony of Mr. George F. Bowerman," in ibid., 59.

19. "Testimony of Mrs. Keppel Hall," in *Suffrage Parade Hearings,* 72; "100 Are in Hospital"; "Say They Were Mobbed," *New York Times,* March 5, 1913, 8.

20. "Testimony of Mountford," in *Suffrage Parade Hearings,* 359; "Testimony of Mrs. Cordelia Powell Odenheimer," in ibid., 31.

21. See, for example, "Testimony of Miss Bliss Finley," in ibid., 465; "Testimony of Miss Vernat Hetfield," in ibid., 52; "Testimony of Mrs. Agnes M. Jenks," in ibid., 27; and "Testimony of Dr. Nellie V. Mark," in ibid., 476–78.

22. "Testimony of Mrs. Richard Coke Burleson," in ibid., 496; "Testimony of Miss Sarah Agnes Wallace," in ibid., 470–71; "Testimony of Weed," in ibid., 68.

23. "Testimony of Mark," in ibid., 478–79; "Testimony of Hetfield," in ibid., 52.

24. Anna Howard Shaw, president of NAWSA, gave them special recognition. See "Parade Protest Arouses Senate."

25. "Testimony of Bowerman," in *Suffrage Parade Hearings*, 58; "Testimony of Hall," in ibid., 73.

26. "Testimony of Mark," in ibid., 476; "Testimony of Finley," in ibid., 464; "Testimony of Odenheimer," in ibid., 31.

27. "Parade Protest Arouses Senate"; "Testimony of Mrs. Patricia M. Street," in *Suffrage Parade Hearings*, 69–70; "8,000 Women March."

28. "Parade Protest Arouses Senate"; "Begin Police Grill," 12.

29. See "Begin Police Grill"; and "Crowd Will Be Watched by Large Police Force," *Washington Post*, Inauguration Edition, March 4, 1913, 7.

30. See Lunardini, *From Equal Suffrage to Equal Rights*, 29–31; and Inez Hayes Irwin, *The Story of Alice Paul and the National Woman's Party*, 30–31.

31. "Sum Up Day's Work"; "Parade Protest Arouses Senate"; "The Suffragette Parade," *Washington Post*, March 3, 1913, 6.

32. *Address of Everett P. Wheeler, Public Meeting, Berkeley Lyceum, March 6th, 1913: For the Preservation of the Home*, 2, 4–5, 6.

33. "Suffragists Odious," *New York Times*, March 9, 1913, 5:6.

34. For a thoughtful discussion of the "public woman," see Mary Ryan, *Women in Public: Between Banners and Ballots, 1825–1880*.

Chapter 1: Negotiating Gender and Citizenship: Context for the First World War

Portions of this chapter appeared in a different form in "The 'Open Way of Opportunity': Colorado Women Physicians and World War I." Copyright by the Western History Association. Reprinted by permission.

1. For background on these issues, see John Bodnar, *The Transplanted: A History of Immigrants in Urban America*; Roger Daniels, *Guarding the Golden Door: American Immigration Policy and Immigrants since 1882*; Painter, *Standing at Armageddon*; Peggy Pascoe, "Democracy, Citizenship, and Race: The West in the Twentieth Century"; George J. Sanchez, *Becoming Mexican American: Ethnicity, Culture, and Identity in Chicano Los Angeles, 1900–1945*; and Ronald Takaki, *Strangers from a Different Shore: A History of Asian Americans* and *A Different Mirror: A History of Multicultural America*.

2. See the *Reader's Guide to Periodical Literature*.

3. For background on these issues, see Ruth Bordin, *Woman and Temperance: The Quest for Power and Liberty, 1873–1900*; Cott, *Grounding of Modern Feminism*; Ellen Carol DuBois, *Harriot Stanton Blatch and the Winning of Woman Suffrage* and *Feminism and*

Suffrage: The Emergence of an Independent Women's Movement in America, 1848–1869; Nancy Isenberg, *Sex and Citizenship in Antebellum America;* and Kerber, *No Constitutional Right* and *Women of the Republic: Intellect and Ideology in Revolutionary America.*

4. See Hannah Rosen, "'Not That Sort of Women': Race, Gender, and Sexual Violence during the Memphis Riot of 1866"; Tara Hunter, *To 'Joy My Freedom: Southern Black Women's Lives and Labors after the Civil War;* Stephanie Shaw, *What a Woman Ought to Be and Do: Black Professional Women Workers during the Jim Crow Era;* and Evelyn Brooks Higginbotham, *Righteous Discontent: The Women's Movement in the Black Baptist Church, 1880–1920.*

5. See Candace Lewis Bredbenner, *A Nationality of Her Own: Women, Marriage, and the Law of Citizenship.*

6. See Kimberly Jensen, "The 'Open Way of Opportunity': Colorado Women Physicians, and World War I"; and Regina Morantz-Sanchez, *Sympathy and Science: Women Physicians in American Medicine,* 266–311.

7. For women as citizen-consumers in this period, see Lizabeth Cohen, "Citizens and Consumers in the Century of Mass Consumption." For Cohen's analysis of the post–World War II era, see *A Consumer's Republic: The Politics of Mass Consumption in Postwar America.*

8. See Kessler-Harris, *In Pursuit of Equity.*

9. For more information on these developments, see Alice Kessler-Harris, *Out to Work: A History of Wage-Earning Women in the United States;* Morantz-Sanchez, *Sympathy and Science;* Margaret W. Rossiter, *Women Scientists in America: Struggles and Strategies to 1940;* Barbara Miller Solomon, *In the Company of Educated Women: A History of Women and Higher Education in America;* and Lynn Weiner, *From Working Girl to Working Mother: The Female Labor Force in the United States, 1820–1980.* For an informative overview, see Sara Evans's chapter "Women and Modernity: 1890–1920," in her *Born for Liberty: A History of Women in America.*

10. See Cott, *Grounding of Modern Feminism.*

11. Maureen Weiner Greenwald studies the experiences and contributions of these women workers in *Women, War, and Work: The Impact of World War I on Women Workers in the United States.* See also Carrie Brown, *Rosie's Mom: Forgotten Women Workers of the First World War.*

12. Jean Ebbert and Marie-Beth Hall, *Crossed Currents: Navy Women in a Century of Change,* 3–18.

13. Julia C. Stimson, "The Army Nurse Corps," 290.

14. See Zeiger, *In Uncle Sam's Service;* Dorothy Schneider and Carl J. Schneider, *Into the Breach: American Women Overseas in World War I;* and Lettie Gavin, *American Women in World War I: They Also Served.*

15. Hoganson, *Fighting for American Manhood,* 109, 125.

16. For insightful discussions of these issues in addition to Hoganson's work, see Amy Kaplan, "Black and Blue on San Juan Hill."

17. See Gail Bederman, *Manliness and Civilization: A Cultural History of Gender and Race in the United States, 1880–1917.*

18. See E. Anthony Rotundo, *American Manhood: Transformations in Masculinity from the Revolution to the Modern Era,* 222–46; Michael Kimmel, *Manhood in America: A Cultural History,* 81–188; and Kathleen Dalton, *Theodore Roosevelt: A Strenuous Life.*

19. Carrie Chapman Catt, ed., *The Ballot and the Bullet*, 7–8. Suffrage supporters continued this line of reasoning in speeches compiled in 1912 in another anthology, titled *Twenty-five Answers to Antis: Five Minute Speeches on Votes for Women by Eminent Suffragists*.

20. Hoganson, *Fighting for American Manhood*, 127; see also 125–27. For additional information on women's service, see Mercedes H. Graf, "Women Nurses in the Spanish-American War"; and Anita Newcombe McGee, M.D., "Women Nurses in the American Army."

21. See A. S. B. [Alice Stone Blackwell], *Woman's Journal* 29 (June 18, 1898): 193, quoted in Hoganson, *Fighting for American Manhood*, 130.

22. Hoganson, *Fighting for American Manhood*, 130.

23. Kristin Hoganson, "'As Badly Off as the Filipinos': U.S. Women Suffragists and the Imperial Issue at the Turn of the Twentieth Century," 14, 20, 21–22.

24. The *Woman's Journal* and the *Woman Citizen*, for example, had specific sections for this information.

25. "Women and War" (1914), 2; "Another Phantom Laid," 162. For other examples, see "Russian Women and the Ballot," 1; "'Women Cannot Fight!'" 2; and "Women in the War," 2.

26. "Warrior Women," 1460; "Women as Warriors," 265; for example, G. Kay Spencer, "Women in the War," *Tulsa Morning News*, October 22, 1917, 8; "A Female Paul Revere," *Baltimore Sun*, March 20, 1916, 2; "Do Women Believe in War?" 3; "The Battalion of Death," 3. The attitude of Willsie and the *Delineator* was not entirely supportive of all of the implications of this change, however, as I discuss in the next chapter.

27. Alice Foley, "In the Subway," 439.

28. For more on these women, see Jane Addams, *Peace and Bread in Time of War*; Frances H. Early, "Feminism, Peace, and Civil Liberties: Women's Role in the Origins of the World War I Civil Liberties Movement" and *A World without War: How U.S. Feminists and Pacifists Resisted World War I*; Candace Falk, *Love, Anarchy, and Emma Goldman*; Emma Goldman, *Living My Life*; Erika A. Kuhlman, *Petticoats and White Feathers: Gender Conformity, Race, the Progressive Peace Movement, and the Debate over War, 1895–1919*; Edward Marshall, "War's Debasement of Women: Jane Addams Calls It the Greatest Threat against Family, Reducing Women to Tribal Stage of Childbearing to Fill Ranks," *New York Times Magazine*, May 2, 1915, 3–4; Leila Rupp, *Worlds of Women: The Making of an International Women's Movement*; and Barbara J. Steinson, "'The Mother Half of Humanity': American Women in the Peace and Preparedness Movements in World War I," 262.

29. See Kennedy, *Disloyal Mothers*; and Barbara J. Steinson, *American Women's Activism in World War I*.

30. Kennedy, *Disloyal Mothers*, 9; Dalton, *Theodore Roosevelt*, 459. As we have seen, Addams and other pacifist women believed that the way to address the violence against women in wartime was to work to end war.

31. See Kennedy, *Disloyal Mothers*.

32. John J. Vertrees was an attorney for the secretary of the interior during the Ballinger-Pinchot affair. See John J. Vertrees, *Investigations of the Department of the Interior Resulting from the Glavis Charges; or, The Ballinger-Pinchot Controversy* (Washington, D.C.: Government Printing Office, 1910). He also wrote *The Negro Problem* in 1905.

33. Vertrees, *An Address to the Men of Tennessee on Female Suffrage*, 5, 6–7; emphasis in original. The online *Dictionary of Slang* suggests nineteenth-century origins of the phrase "to shoot blanks" as a reference to male impotence (http://www.peevish.co.uk/slang/s.htm, s.v. "shoot blanks"). It is possible that Vertrees had this phrase in mind when he used "'blank-cartridge' ballot." In any case, a blank cartridge would refer to an ineffectual bullet.

34. "The Supreme Struggle," 4; "The Woman Patriot," 4 (emphasis in original).

Chapter 2: Gender and Violence: Context and Experience in the Era of the World War

1. Leslie K. Dunlap, "The Reform of Rape Law and the Problem of White Men: Age-of-Consent Campaigns in the South, 1885–1910"; Elizabeth Pleck, *Domestic Tyranny: The Making of Social Policy against Family Violence from Colonial Times to the Present*; Linda Gordon, *Heroes of Their Own Lives: The Politics and History of Family Violence*; Cynthia Enloe, "Whom Do You Take Seriously?" in *The Curious Feminist: Searching for Women in a New Age of Empire*, 74.

2. Karen Dubinsky, *Improper Advances: Rape and Heterosexual Conflict in Ontario, 1880–1929*; Mary Odem, *Delinquent Daughters: Protecting and Policing Adolescent Female Sexuality in the United States, 1885–1920*; Susan Estrich, "Rape." For more on the legal status of rape in American history, see Merril D. Smith, ed., *Sex without Consent: Rape and Sexual Coercion in America*.

3. Mary Odem, "Cultural Representations and Social Contexts of Rape in the Early Twentieth Century," 362.

4. Frederick Hoffman, *The Homicide Problem*, 26, 46. The homicide rate is imprecise for the period before 1930 because no standardized homicide statistics were available on a national scale. Hoffman, a statistical consultant for the insurance industry, was a committed compiler of statistics and an activist on behalf of modernization and standardization of homicide statistics. He was also a tireless crusader for gun control. Hoffman is considered the standard source for statistics on homicide during this period. For a discussion of the difficulties in statistics and a study of homicide rates for the period, see Margaret Zahn, "Homicide in the Twentieth Century United States." Zahn confirms the steady increase in crime rates for the period.

5. These figures come from my analysis of entries in the *New York Times Index*, s.v. "murder," compiled in three-month increments from July–September 1914 to January–March 1917. There may have been additional murders reported, but these figures from the index reflect the news stories on murder cataloged as such by the editors. Thirty women, 7 percent, were the murderers in the reported cases.

6. "Seven Women's Bodies in Bluebeard's Home," *New York Times*, May 11, 1916, 3.

7. "Slain by 'Bluebeard,'" *Washington Post*, May 12, 1916, 1.

8. "Lured American Women," *New York Times*, May 13, 1916, 5. See also "Bluebeard's List Long," *Portland Oregonian*, May 13, 1916, 2. Magnus Hirschfeld refers to the case in *The Sexual History of the World War*, 293–94.

9. "Little Girl Found Murdered in Hall," *New York Times*, March 20, 1915, 1; "Boy Murdered by East Side Ripper," *New York Times*, May 4, 1915, 1, 10; "Chases Girls with Knife," *New York Times*, May 4, 1915, 10.

10. *New York Times*, May 7, 1915, 6.

11. *New York Times*, May 10, 1915, 9.

12. *New York Times*, May 12, 1915, 7.

13. Christopher Frayling, "The House That Jack Built: Some Stereotypes of the Rapist in the History of Popular Culture," 178.

14. See Hoffman, "Homicide Record for 1915," in *The Homicide Problem*, 33–38. His discussion headed "Deaths from 'Ripper Murders'" is on p. 35.

15. Elizabeth Cerabino-Hess, "On Nation and Violation: Representations of Rape in Popular Theater and Film of the Progressive Era," 1. Cerabino-Hess provides chapter-length discussions on each of these topics but does not give the total number of productions for the period in her analysis.

16. See Higginbotham, *Righteous Discontent*, 185–229.

17. Patricia Hill Collins, *Black Feminist Thought: Knowledge, Consciousness, and the Politics of Empowerment*, 147; Glenda Elizabeth Gilmore, *Gender and Jim Crow: Women and the Politics of White Supremacy in North Carolina, 1896–1920*, 144; Darlene Clark Hine, "Rape and the Inner Lives of Black Women in the Middle West," 914. Hine also notes that African American women developed a culture of dissemblance to protect themselves. See also Higginbotham, *Righteous Discontent*.

18. See Rosalyn Terborg-Penn, "African American Women's Networks in the Anti-Lynching Crusade."

19. National Association for the Advancement of Colored People, *Thirty Years of Lynching in the United States, 1889–1918*, table 2, 30.

20. Rosalyn Terborg-Penn, *African American Women in the Struggle for the Vote, 1850–1920*, 96.

21. John D'Emilio and Estelle Freedman, *Intimate Matters: A History of Sexuality in America*, 217.

22. See, for example, Mary Bularzik, "Sexual Harassment at the Workplace: Historical Notes"; and Kerry Segrave, *The Sexual Harassment of Women in the Workplace, 1600–1993*, 1–69.

23. Segrave, *Sexual Harassment of Women*, 130. See also Sarah Eisenstein, *Give Us Bread but Give Us Roses: Working Women's Consciousness in the United States, 1890 to the First World War*, 28, 100–101.

24. Susan Reverby, *Ordered to Care: The Dilemma of American Nursing, 1850–1945*, 96–97; Barbara Melosh, *"The Physician's Hand": Work Culture and Conflict in American Nursing*. Melosh's collection of fiction about nurses, *American Nurses in Fiction: An Anthology of Short Stories*, is also illustrative.

25. Annelise Orleck, *Common Sense and a Little Fire: Women and Working Class Politics in the United States, 1900–1965*, 72.

26. Pauline Newman to Rose Schneiderman, July 11, 1912, quoted in Orleck, *Common Sense and a Little Fire*, 73; Rose Pastor Stokes quoted in Daniel Bender, "Too Much of Distasteful Masculinity: Historicizing Sexual Harassment in the Garment Sweatshop and Factory," 103; Dolores Janiewski, "Southern Honor, Southern Dishonor: Managerial Ideology and the Construction of Gender, Race, and Class Relations in Southern Industry," 86.

27. V. Schultz, "Reconceptualizing Sexual Harassment," 1750.

28. See Emily Dunning Barringer, *Bowery to Bellevue: The Story of New York's First Woman Ambulance Surgeon*.

29. "Report of the National American Convention of 1910," in *History of Woman Suffrage*, edited by Elizabeth Cady Stanton, Susan B. Anthony, and Matilda Joslyn Gage, 295. *Harper's Bazaar* reprinted the letter from "S.H." with others in "The Girl Who Comes to the City: A Symposium," 693. See also Bularzik, "Sexual Harassment," 124.

30. Quoted in Jacqueline Jones, *Labor of Love, Labor of Sorrow: Black Women, Work, and the Family from Slavery to the Present*, 150.

31. Orleck, *Common Sense and a Little Fire*, 59 (quote), 61–62, 77.

32. For an insightful study of these issues, see Stephen H. Norwood, *Strikebreaking and Intimidation: Mercenaries and Masculinity in Twentieth-Century America*.

33. See Christopher Capozzola, "The Only Badge Needed Is Your Patriotic Service: Vigilance, Coercion, and the Law in World War I America."

34. The penalties were a fine of up to ten thousand dollars or two years' imprisonment or both. Alexander DeConde, *Gun Violence in America: The Struggle for Control*, 111 (quote).

35. Ibid., 117.

36. Ibid., 113.

37. U.S. Army, Office of the Judge Advocate General, *Federal Aid in Domestic Disturbances, 1903–1922*, 312.

38. David Montgomery, *The Fall of the House of Labor: The Workplace, the State, and American Labor Activism, 1865–1925*, 346–47. According to Montgomery, from September 1913 to April 1914, "18 strikers, 10 guards, 19 scabs, 2 militiamen, 3 noncombatants, 2 women and 12 children" were killed, a total of 66 (347).

39. U.S. Army, Office of the Judge Advocate General, *Federal Aid in Domestic Disturbances*, 314.

40. See *New York Times*, September 1, 1914, 2; September 2, 1914, 2; September 12, 1914, 3. See also, for example, "The Case of Belgium," 239–40; and Major Louis Livingston Seaman, "Where Hundreds of Thousands Are Suffering," 18.

41. See Belgian Delegates to the United States, *The Case of Belgium in the Present War: An Account of the Violation of the Neutrality of Belgium and of the Laws of War on Belgian Territory*; and France, Ministère des Affaires Étrangères, *Germany's Violations of the Laws of War, 1914–1915*.

42. See, for example, "Women in War Time," 2. I located the accounts quoted by the editors of the *Suffragist* on pp. 41–43 of Belgian Delegates to the United States, *Case of Belgium*.

43. See Paul Fussel, "Myth, Ritual, and Romance," in *The Great War and Modern Memory*, 114–54; and John Dower's excellent study of propaganda in the Pacific theater of World War II, *War without Mercy: Race and Power in the Pacific War*.

44. See Cynthia Enloe's insightful and far-ranging analysis in *Maneuvers*, particularly her chapter titled "When Soldiers Rape," 108–52; Indai Lourdes Sajor, ed., *Common Grounds: Violence against Women in Armed Conflict Situations*; Astrid Aafjes, *Gender Violence: The Hidden War Crime*; Alexandra Stiglmayer, ed., *Mass Rape: The War against Women in Bosnia-Herzegovina*; and Susan Brownmiller's chapter on rape and war in *Against Our Will: Men, Women, and Rape*, 40–48. For a powerful representation of violence against women in Pakistan at the time of the 1947 partition, see the work of visual artist Nilima Sheikh, particularly her *Parmat Stories, 2001* (see Vishakha N. Desai, *Conversations with Traditions: Nilima Sheikh and Shahzia Sikander*).

45. Catharine A. MacKinnon, "Rape, Genocide, and Women's Human Rights," 188; emphasis in original. The "analytically useful task," Cynthia Enloe asserts, is to "look for the decisions and the policy makers behind these acts of rape" (*Maneuvers,* 127). Enloe warns that "the sheer variety of wartime rape sites may lure us into reducing the cause of wartime rape to raw primal misogyny." The danger that "mere maleness will be accepted as sufficient cause for wartime rape" would mean that "the operation of particular military hierarchies will be deemed not worth examining," and individuals will "decide that they can do nothing to call individual rapists and their superiors to account or even, perhaps, to prevent rape in the next war" (134). Enloe's view reflects the approach of most scholars of women, war, and rape and represents an alternative to some of Susan Brownmiller's assumptions in *Against Our Will.* For a thoughtful overview of theoretical challenges to Brownmiller and the importance of the historical context for studying rape, see Dubinsky, *Improper Advances,* 31–34.

46. See Ruth Harris, "The 'Child of the Barbarian': Rape, Race, and Nationalism in France during the First World War"; and the extensive study by John Horne and Alan Kramer, *German Atrocities, 1914: A History of Denial.*

47. Aafjes, *Gender Violence,* 5.

48. See Enloe, *Maneuvers,* 134; and the report of the United Nations Special Rapporteur on Violence against Women in 1977 quoted in Aafjes, *Gender Violence,* 1–3.

49. See "The Hague Convention Regulations Respecting the Law and Customs of War on Land," October 8, 1907, quoted in Aafjes, *Gender Violence,* 2–3.

50. See Ruth Seifert, "War and Rape: A Preliminary Analysis."

51. Margaret H. Darrow, *French Women and the First World War: War Stories of the Home Front,* 121–22.

52. As Margaret H. Darrow demonstrates, French journalists discussed the topic of the "unwanted little ones" frequently in early 1915 in both mainstream and Catholic newspapers. French feminists and physicians debated the issue in their journals, and members of the French cabinet debated the issue in the spring of 1915. The children conceived as the result of the rape of French women by German soldiers also inspired a number of novels and plays in 1915 and 1916. See ibid., 115; Harris, "'Child of the Barbarian'"; Nancy Sloan Goldberg, *"Woman, Your Hour Is Sounding": Continuity and Change in French Women's Great War Fiction, 1914–1919,* 23–30; and Susan Grayzel, *Women's Identities at War: Gender, Motherhood, and Politics in Britain and France during the First World War,* 86–120.

53. For the American press, see, for example, "War Babies Soon a British Problem," *New York Times,* April 25, 1915, 2:6; "Europe's 'War Baby' Problem," *New York Times Magazine,* May 23, 1915, 5–6; "War Morality and the Rights of War-Mothers and War-Babies," 44–45; and "Women and War" (1915), 2. Further evidence of widespread American sympathy for the women of Belgium is contained in a popular account of relief efforts in that nation, Charlotte Kellogg's *Women of Belgium: Turning Tragedy to Triumph,* which went through four editions in 1917, the year the United States entered the war. For the term *Boche babies,* see "France Will Adopt Her 'Boche Babies,'" *New York Times,* October 28, 1917, 3:12.

54. "War Babies," *New York Times,* April 28, 1915, 12. The editors of the *New York Times Magazine* devoted a lengthy feature article to the topic in May 1915 that drew on reports from the European press, formal announcements by European governments, and other interviews ("Europe's 'War Baby' Problem").

55. Marshall, "War's Debasement of Women," 3–4. See also Leila J. Rupp, "Solidarity and Wartime Violence against Women" and *Worlds of Women*, 86–87.

56. Ellen Newbold La Motte, *The Backwash of War: The Human Wreckage of the Battlefield as Witnessed by an American Hospital Nurse*, v–vi. La Motte was a Johns Hopkins–trained nurse who served as the superintendent of the Tuberculosis Division of the Baltimore Health Department from 1910 to 1913. Members of the medical profession respected her pathbreaking textbook on tuberculosis nursing, published in 1915. La Motte had lived in Paris for a few years before joining the Red Cross effort in Belgium. The *New York Times Book Review* reviewed *Backwash of War* on October 15, 1916 (432). La Motte visited Gertrude Stein and Alice B. Toklas in Paris before nursing in Belgium (Stein, *The Autobiography of Alice B. Toklas*, 158–59, 169–70). La Motte wrote several books and articles exposing the opium trade in the 1920s. See *American Nursing: A Biographical Dictionary*, s.v. "La Motte, Ellen Newbold"; and her obituary in the *New York Times*, March 4, 1961. See also Yvonne M. Klein, ed. *Beyond the Home Front: Women's Autobiographical Writing of the Two World Wars*, 34n1.

57. La Motte, *Backwash of War*, 29–30.

58. Ibid., 98–99, 102–3.

59. Ibid., 107–8.

Chapter 3: "Whether We Vote or Not—We Are Going to Shoot": Women and Armed Defense on the Home Front

1. Harris, "'Child of the Barbarian,'" 186, 197.

2. See Elaine Showalter, "Male Hysteria," in *The Female Malady: Women, Madness, and English Culture, 1830–1980*, 170.

3. See Kimmel, *Manhood in America*, 134–35.

4. Paul Fussell discusses the British focus on masculinity and war in *The Great War and Modern Memory*. In her study of the slaveholding South, Drew Gilpin Faust concludes that "in failing to protect women or to exert control over insolent and even rebellious slaves, Confederate men undermined not only the foundations of the South's peculiar institution, but the legitimacy of their power as white males, as masters of families of white women and black slaves" (*Mothers of Invention: Women of the Slaveholding South in the American Civil War*, 79).

5. Kimmel, *Manhood in America*, 119–20 and chaps. 3–5; Sandra M. Gilbert, "Soldier's Heart: Literary Men, Literary Women, and the Great War."

6. Theodore Roosevelt, *America and the World War*, 136, 146. Kathleen Dalton emphasizes that TR also saw preparedness as universal service that would foster Americanism and citizenship (*Theodore Roosevelt*, 447–49).

7. For information on General Leonard Wood's career, see John Garry Clifford, *The Citizen Soldiers: The Plattsburg Training Camp Movement, 1913–1920*, 1–29; John G. Holme, *The Life of Leonard Wood*; and Jack C. Lane, *Armed Progressive: General Leonard Wood*.

8. Leonard Wood, "Rifle Practice for Public Schools," 16. See also Clifford, *Citizen Soldiers*, 9–11.

9. Clifford, *Citizen Soldiers*, 10. See also Lane, *Armed Progressive*, for Wood's views. For background on the debate concerning citizen soldiers versus a professional army, see

Lawrence Delbert Cress, *Citizens in Arms: The Army and the Militia in American Society to the War of 1812.*

10. See L. E. Eubanks, "Gun Practice a Man-Maker," 485; and "Effeminacy and the Rifle Range," 468.

11. Erman J. Ridgway, "Militant Pacifism," a special column on the regular editorial page titled "You, Us, and Company."

12. See "You, Us, and Company," for both the April 1915 and the June 1915 issues of the *Delineator,* both on p. 1.

13. "Women in a Defense Club," *New York Times,* February 17, 1916, 5; Lurana Sheldon Ferris, "The Women's Defense Club," letter to the editor, *New York Times,* March 31, 1916, 10; Ferris, "Plans of Woman's Defense Club," letter to the editor, *New York Times,* February 18, 1917, 7:4.

14. Quoted in both "Plans Range for Women: Rifle Range for Women," *New York Times,* December 25, 1916, 9; and *Arms and the Man* (January 1917): 293; "Women Form Rifle Corps," *New York Times,* February 10, 1917, 8. See also "Hotel Roof for Women's Rifle Club," *New York Times,* April 8, 1917, 1:2; and *Arms and the Man* (April 28, 1917): 93, for a detailed description of her studio range.

15. "Women Are to Arm and Learn to Drill," *New York Times,* March 10, 1916, 7.

16. See "200 Women Soldiers Give a Public Drill," *New York Times,* March 10, 1916, 8; and "Women Are Bored by Military Drill," *New York Times,* April 2, 1916, 1:24.

17. "Women Scout in the Rain," *New York Times,* May 15, 1916, 9.

18. See "The *Delineator's* Women's Preparedness Bureau: Going in for Military Training and How to Set Up a Camp," 31; and "The *Delineator's* Women's Preparedness Bureau: What Can I Do to Help?" 50.

19. See "Fifty Society Girls to Study War's Art," *New York Times,* June 1, 1916, 14; "Lone Dog Guards Girls' Plattsburg," *New York Times,* June 2, 1916, 5; and "Parents See Girl Campers," *New York Times,* June 5, 1916, 8. Barbara Stenson also discusses women and the preparedness movement in *American Women's Activism in World War I.*

20. "American Battalion of Death," 372; "Women May Fight for Democracy Abroad," 3.

21. "Eleven Thousand Beginners Shoot," 517. For an example of one "Beginners' Day Shoot" in Delaware, see *Arms and the Man* (June 29, 1916): 277; and "Twenty-seven Beginners at Greenhill," 337.

22. See "Feminine Trap Shots Real Sportswomen," 77; "Chicago's Lady Trap Shooters," 437; *Arms and the Man* (August 24, 1916), 437; and for tournaments, "Scattering Shot," 37–38. For other examples of this trend, see "Livermore Women Becoming Shots," 492; a report on activities in Birmingham in *Arms and the Man* (February 11, 1915): 397; and the continuing reports throughout these years for the Nemours Ladies Trapshooting Club of Wilmington, Delaware, in *Arms and the Man.*

23. See *Arms and the Man* (August 4, 1917): 378; "Trapshooting Attracts Both Sexes," 458; "About Women Shots," 338; and Peter B. Carney, "Target Smashing Stimulated by Entrance of U.S. in War," 237.

24. Mrs. Adolph Topperwein, "Why I Took Up Trapshooting," 297. Accounts of her tournament wins and other aspects of her shooting career may be found throughout *Arms and the Man* for the period. See, for example, "Nemours [Ladies] Trapshooting Club," 197; *Arms and the Man* (July 27, 1916): 358; and "The Woman Who Broke 1952 Out of 2,000 Clays," 217.

25. Harriet D. Hammond, "Why I Like Trapshooting," 98. Hammond was a member of the Nemours Ladies Trapshooting Club.

26. See DeConde, *Gun Violence in America,* 116.

27. A. L. McCabe, "How to Construct an Indoor or Cellar Range," 313.

28. See "Chicago's Lady Trap Shooters"; and "Livermore Women Becoming Shots."

29. "What One Woman Does," 38; "Trapshooting Attracts Both Sexes."

30. See "Inquiries of General Interest," 316.

31. See Topperwein, "Why I Took Up Trapshooting." I am grateful to Barbara Handy-Marchello for alerting me to the ways in which women who use rifles can be discouraged by improper fit, and how it is often an unrecognized reason for claims that women do not like to shoot or cannot do it well.

32. Henry Sharp, "Guns for Sportswomen," 398.

33. See "Help for Rifle Clubs," *New York Times,* August 23, 1915, 4; "Civilian Rifle Clubs," 66; and "The N.R.A. on the Job," 228.

34. Section 113 of the Defense Act of June 3, 1916, is quoted in its entirety in *Arms and the Man* (January 19, 1918): 332–33.

35. See, for example, "Universal Military Training Urged," 287; and "The National Rifle Association Meeting," 323–26.

36. The limitations for regular military service for men were the ages of eighteen to forty-five. This regulation follows those limits and allows young men of sixteen and seventeen, "potential soldiers," to participate. See Section 113 of the Defense Act of June 3, 1916, pts. 1 and 2.

37. "Decorations for Women," 494.

38. See "Navy Leases Wakefield Range," 453; and "An Open Letter from Wakefield," 68.

39. The photographer is also present in this photograph: his shadow is cast across the female line.

40. "To Have a Ladies' Auxiliary," 73.

41. "Sergeant Miss—Yes, That's Right," 7; *Arms and the Man* (March 22, 1917): 517; "Girls Form Rifle Club," 93.

42. *Arms and the Man* (April 21, 1917): 78; *Arms and the Man* (August 11, 1917): 393–94; *Arms and the Man* (April 6, 1918): 32.

43. *Arms and the Man* (November 16, 1916): 158.

44. See Claude R. Flory, "Annie Oakley in the South," 336. For background on Oakley's life and career, see Glenda Riley, *The Life and Legacy of Annie Oakley.*

45. "Annie Oakley Visits Camps," 215; Flory, "Annie Oakley in the South," 337.

46. These rates were established in an act of May 11, 1908 (35 Stat., 110) (*Laws Relating to the Navy, Annotated: Including the Constitution of the United States, the Revised Statutes of the United States, and the United States Statutes at Large, in Force March 4, 1921,* 947). In 1918 the commandant of the U.S. Marine Corps recommended that since there were no specific regulations for the pay and other benefits of marine reservists (F), the term *enlisted men* in the appropriate statues for "pay, allowances, gratuities, and other benefits granted by law" should be made applicable to women reservists as well (*Annual Report of the Secretary of the Navy for the Fiscal Year 1918,* 1602).

47. See "Women Yeoman Shoot," 455.

48. The U.S. Marine Corps employed women marine reservists (F) outside of Washing-

ton, D.C., in cities such as Denver, San Francisco, and Portland, where recruiting offices were in need of clerical workers.

49. This episode is taken from an interview with Elizabeth Bertram, part of a series of interviews conducted in 1971 and 1972 with women who had served as marine reservists (F) during the First World War. Part of the Bertram interview is reprinted in Linda L. Hewitt, *Women Marines in World War I*, 28–29.

50. "The *Delineator's* Women's Preparedness Bureau: Let Us Help You toward Greater Self-Dependence in War or Peace," 22.

51. *Woman Citizen* 1 (July 14, 1917): 111; *Arms and the Man* (November 9, 1916): 137.

Chapter 4: "The Fighting, Biting, and Scratching Kind": Good Girls, Bad Girls, and Women's Soldiering

1. Bessie Beatty, *The Red Heart of Russia*, 91. Beatty's chapter on the Battalion of Death follows her reports sent to the *San Francisco Bulletin*. For more on Beatty's activities, see Zena Beth McGlashan, "Women Witness the Russian Revolution: Analyzing Ways of Seeing."

2. See Julie Wheelwright, *Amazons and Military Maids: Women Who Dressed as Men in Pursuit of Life, Liberty, and Happiness.*

3. For T. Hall, see Mary Beth Norton, *Founding Mothers and Fathers: Gendered Power and the Forming of American Society,* 183–97. For an overview, see Sharon Block and Kathleen Brown, "Clio in Search of Eros: Redefining Sexualities in Early America." For Sampson, see Linda Kerber and Jane de Hart, eds., *Women's America: Refocusing the Past,* 116.

4. See Sarah Rosetta Wakeman, *An Uncommon Soldier: The Civil War Letters of Sarah Rosetta Wakeman, Alias Private Lyons Wakeman, 153rd Regiment, New York State Volunteers;* Elizabeth Leonard, *Yankee Women: Gender Battles in the Civil War;* and Sara Emma Edmonds, *Memoirs of a Soldier, Nurse, and Spy: A Woman's Adventures in the Union Army.*

5. Hirschfield devotes an entire chapter to the subject, "Women Soldiers and Female Battalions," in *Sexual History of the World War,* 110–24 (quotes on 119–20); "Draft Evader Is a Woman," *Portland Oregonian,* January 6, 1919, 1. For a thoughtful discussion of the early experiences of transsexuals, see Joanne Meyerowitz, *How Sex Changed: A History of Transsexuality in the United States,* chap. 1. For a general study, see Anne Fausto Sterling, *Sexing the Body: Gender Politics and the Construction of Sexuality.* And for a thoughtful discussion of the importance of transgender analysis, see Peter Boag, "Go West Young Man, Go East Young Woman: Searching for the Trans in Western Gender History."

6. Beatty, *Red Heart of Russia,* 91.

7. See ibid., 112. For general information on Russian women soldiers and the Battalion of Death, see Maria Botchkareva, *Yashka: My Life as Peasant, Officer and Exile;* Anne Eliot Griesse and Richard Stites, "Russia: Revolution and War"; Richard Stites, *The Women's Liberation Movement in Russia,* 295–300; Wheelwright, *Amazons and Military Maids;* as well as the numerous newspaper and magazine articles discussed below.

8. Charles Edward Russell, "Russia's Women Warriors," 170; Caroline Kettle, "The Legion of Death," 435. See also Botchkareva, *Yashka.*

9. William G. Shepherd, "The Soul That Stirs in 'Battalions of Death,'" 6; "Russian Women Warriors Denounce Men: Bid Slackers Beware of 'Tigress Mothers,'" *New York Times,* June 25, 1917, 1; Russell, "Russia's Women Warriors," 173; Beatty, *Red Heart of Russia,* 94–97; "Root Lauds Russian Women," *New York Times,* August 8, 1917, 2. Root was no friend of suffragists in the United States. He publicly opposed woman suffrage at the New York Constitutional Convention in 1894 by stating that political life was a battle and that women were not strong enough to wage any kind of warfare, "illustrating his argument from his experience of weak women in the persons of his own family, 'whose hands were too feeble and nerveless to grasp the ballot,' or any weapon." See Mary Winsor, "Catching Up with Russia," 8; and "Mr. Root, It's You We Quote," 207.

10. "Flag of Women Blessed: Female Warriors Then Parade Through Petrograd Streets," *New York Times,* July 6, 1917, 1; Martha Banta, *Imaging American Women: Idea and Ideals in Cultural History,* 572–77 (quote on 572).

11. "Those Russian Women," 51; Shepherd, "The Soul That Stirs."

12. See, for example, "Russia's Women Soldiers," 20.

13. "Warrior Women," 1460; "Russia's Women Soldiers"; Russell, "Russia's Women Warriors," 166.

14. See "New Artistic Ties with France," 1476–77; and "Jeanne d'Arc," 885–86.

15. C. M. Stevens, *The Wonderful Story of Joan of Arc and the Meaning of Her Life for Americans,* 344, 341; *New York Evening Post* quoted in "New Artistic Ties with France," 1476; "The New Vision," 3.

16. "Jeanne d'Arc"; G. A. Conkling, "The Return of Jeanne D'Arc," 621–23; "Joan of Arc They Are Calling You," words by Alfred Bryan and Willie Weston, music by Jack Wells (New York: Waterson, Berlin, and Snyder, 1917). I am grateful to Sharon Wood for this latter source. Thomas Walsh's comments may be found in "The American Army and Joan of Arc," 209–12.

17. *Address of Everett P. Wheeler,* 3–4.

18. See, for example, "Those Russian Women," 53; and Beatty, *Red Heart of Russia,* 90–94.

19. See especially Shepherd, "The Soul That Stirs"; and "Girls Shave Heads, Train Hard to Fight," *New York Times,* June 22, 1917, 4.

20. See Botchkareva, *Yashka.*

21. "Mere Man to the Rescue," *Tulsa Daily World,* September 22, 1917, 3; "Russian Girl Troops Mob Commander," *New York Times,* September 22, 1917; "Wife of Kerensky in Women's Regiment," *New York Times,* June 11, 1917, 4.

22. Shepherd, "The Soul That Stirs."

23. Ibid. This is the last sentence in the article.

24. Ibid.

25. Dr. George Beard quoted in D'Emilio and Freedman, *Intimate Matters,* 226; Dr. William Lee Howard quoted in George Chauncey, *Gay New York: Gender, Urban Cultures, and the Making of the Gay Male World, 1890–1940,* 122. See also George Chauncey, "From Sexual Inversion to Homosexuality: The Changing Medical Conceptualization of Female 'Deviance'"; and Carroll Smith-Rosenberg, "The New Woman as Androgyne: Social Disorder and Gender Crisis, 1870–1936," in *Disorderly Conduct: Visions of Gender in Victorian America,* 245–96.

26. Lynda Hart, *Fatal Women: Lesbian Sexuality and the Mark of Aggression,* x, xiii; Lisa Duggan, *Sapphic Slashers: Sex, Violence, and American Modernity,* 154–55.

27. See William Blake Tyrrell, *Amazons: A Study in Athenian Mythmaking,* xiv, 113.

28. See McGlashan, "Women Witness the Russian Revolution."

29. Vertrees, *Address to the Men of Tennessee,* 6, 5, 7–8.

30. *Address of Everett P. Wheeler,* 6–7; George McAdam, "When Women Fight," *New York Times Magazine,* September 2, 1917, 3, 14. Hammond was the son of William A. Hammond, surgeon general during the Civil War. See *Dictionary of American Biography,* vol. 8 (New York: Charles Scribner's Sons, 1932), s.v. "Hammond, William Alexander."

Chapter 5: Uncle Sam's Loyal Nieces: Women Physicians, Citizenship, and Wartime Military Service

Portions of this chapter appeared in a different form in "Uncle Sam's Loyal Nieces: American Medical Women, Citizenship, and War Service in the First World War" (© The Johns Hopkins University Press. Reprinted with permission of the Johns Hopkins University Press); "The 'Open Way of Opportunity': Colorado Physicians and World War I" (Copyright by the Western History Association. Reprinted by permission); and "Physicians and Citizens: U.S. Medical Women and Military Service in the First World War" (Copyright by Sutton Publishers. Reprinted by permission).

1. For background on these issues, see Morantz-Sanchez, *Sympathy and Science;* Ellen S. More, *Restoring the Balance: Women Physicians and the Profession of Medicine, 1850–1995;* Steven J. Peitzman, *A New and Untried Course: Woman's Medical College and Medical College of Pennsylvania, 1850–1998;* and Mary Roth Walsh, *Doctors Wanted, No Women Need Apply: Sexual Barriers in the Medical Profession, 1835–1975.*

2. See Mary Sutton Macy, M.D., "The Field for Women of Today in Medicine."

3. See Rossiter, *Women Scientists in America.*

4. For information on the origins of the MWNA and the AWH, see Esther Pohl Lovejoy, *Women Physicians and Surgeons: National and International Organizations. Book One: The American Medical Women's Association, the Medical Women's International Association. Book Two: Twenty Years with the American Women's Hospitals;* Morantz-Sanchez, *Sympathy and Science,* 274–79; More, *Restoring the Balance,* 122–47; "National Association of Medical Women," 14–15; Bertha Van Hoosen's autobiography, *Petticoat Surgeon,* 200–203; and Walsh, *Doctors Wanted,* 216–18.

5. Mary Sutton Macy, M.D., "American Medical Women and the World War," 322–28; Van Gasken, "Introductory Address," 3–5; quote on 3–4.

6. See "The Evolution of the Medical Department," in *The Surgeon General's Office,* by Charles H. Lynch, Frank Watkins Weed, and Loy McAfee; and Franklin Martin, *Fifty Years of Medicine and Surgery: An Autobiographical Sketch,* 379–82. Medical journals contained vigorous editorial commentary during the campaign. See, for example, "Giving the Medical Officer the Rank to Which He Is Entitled"; "Increased Rank and More Authority for Medical Officers"; and "Medical Rank and Army Health."

7. Lynch, Weed, and McAfee, *The Surgeon General's Office,* 138.

8. Dr. C. V. Roman, "The War—What Does It Mean? What Should We Do?" 42. See

also "President's Annual Address" by G. Jarvis Bowens, M.D., in Norfolk, Virginia, April 12, 1917, reprinted in *Journal of the National Medical Association* 9 (July–September 1917): 127.

9. "The World War—What Does It Mean? How Does It Apply to the Afro-American?" 197. See also "News of the Training Camps: Colored Medical Officers' Training Camp at Fort Des Moines."

10. For an insightful analysis of the changing status of the medical profession, see Paul Starr, *The Social Transformation of American Medicine.* Starr quotes the two occupational studies on p. 143. The studies were George S. Counts, "The Social Status of Occupations: A Problem of Vocational Guidance," *School Review* 33 (January 1925): 16–27; and George W. Hartmann, "The Prestige of Occupations: A Comparison of Educational Occupations and Others," *Personnel Journal* 12 (October 1934): 144–52. For other important studies of the rise of medical men in U.S. society and within the scientific community, see Charles E. Rosenberg, *The Care of Strangers: The Rise of America's Hospital System* and *No Other Gods: On Science and American Social Thought.*

11. For information on Elsie Inglis and the Scottish Women's Hospitals, see Susan Kingsley Kent, *Making Peace: The Reconstruction of Gender in Interwar Britain,* 59–60; and Esther Pohl Lovejoy, *Women Doctors of the World,* 282–91. Inglis died while in service and became a symbol of unselfish devotion for women physicians. See "Saved 8,000 Serbs but Died in Effort: Heroic Work of Dr. Elsie Ingles [*sic*] Told by Women Just Here from the Front," *New York Times,* February 11, 1918, 9.

12. For an account of her experiences, see Rosalie Slaughter Morton, *A Woman Surgeon: The Life and Work of Rosalie Slaughter Morton,* 214–68; quote on 270. See also More, *Restoring the Balance,* chap. 5.

13. "American Women's Hospitals, Organized by War Service Committee of the Medical Women's National Association," Box 1, Folder 1, pp. 1–2, AWH Records. I am grateful to Janet Miller, Margaret Jerrido, and Ida Wilson, all on staff at the Archives on Women in Medicine and Homeopathy, Drexel University College of Medicine, Philadelphia, during my first fellowship stay, and to Joanne Grossman and her staff on subsequent visits, for assisting me with these records.

14. See ibid. For praise of Kathleen Burke and her fund-raising success, see letter from [Belle Thomas, M.D.], chairman Organization Committee, New York, to Dr. Kate C. Mead, Middletown, Connecticut, May 31, 1918, a copy of which is found in the Minutes of the American Women's Hospitals Executive Committee and Council Meetings, 1917–1918, Box 30, Folder 292, AWH Records.

15. See Morton, *Woman Surgeon,* 270; and "Origin of the American Women's Hospitals," Box 1, Folder 1, p. 3, AWH Records.

16. In this resolution the California women stressed the large number of women physicians who were prepared for service "not only as anesthetists, radiographers, and hospital laboratory directors, but also as surgeons," and called for equal opportunities for medical women and the "same rank, title and pay given to men holding equivalent positions." See "Origin of the American Women's Hospitals," 1–2; "Secretary Baker Urged to Use Women for the Medical Service," 150; and "California Women Urge Federal Recognition," 227–28. More, in *Restoring the Balance,* 128–34, gives information on this meeting.

17. Morton, *Woman Surgeon,* 270. For the organization of the War Service Commit-

tee, see "Origin of the American Women's Hospitals," 3; "American Women's Hospitals, Organized by War Service Committee," 1–4; Van Hoosen, *Petticoat Surgeon,* 202; Esther Pohl Lovejoy's history of the American Women's Hospitals, *Certain Samaritans,* 7–8; and Lovejoy, *Women Physicians and Surgeons.*

18. See Morton, *Woman Surgeon,* 272. Over the course of the war women suggested that the American Women's Hospitals change its rather awkward name, but it did not change and still continues today.

19. A graduate of Cornell Medical School in 1901, Emily Dunning Barringer had gained fame as the first woman to win a position as an intern in a nonwomen's medical institution in New York. She served on the house staff of Gouverneur Hospital, associated with Bellevue, and was celebrated in the New York press as the first woman ambulance surgeon. In 1917 she was attending surgeon at the New York Infirmary for Women and Children. See Barringer, *Bowery to Bellevue,* particularly for rich information on her early years and education. See also several references in Morantz-Sanchez, *Sympathy and Science.*

20. Following her graduation from Cornell Medical School in 1907, Mary Merritt Crawford served an internship at Williamsburg Hospital in Brooklyn. By 1917 she held the post of assistant surgeon in the Department of Gynecology at Williamsburg, the only woman on the staff. An active suffragist, Crawford was a member of the Political Equality League, Women's Political Union, and Woman's Suffrage Party of New York. See *Woman's Who's Who of America: A Biographical Dictionary of Contemporary Women of the United States and Canada, 1914–1915,* s.v. "Crawford, Mary Merritt."

21. Frances Cohen was a graduate of Vassar and a 1900 graduate of Cornell Medical School. Belle Thomas was a 1907 Cornell graduate. Sue Racliffe was an 1894 graduate of the Woman's Medical College of Baltimore. See ibid., s.v. "Cohen, Frances"; and *Census of Women Physicians,* 71, 79, 81.

22. Minutes of the Executive Committee and Council of the American Women's Hospitals, November 8, 1917, Box 30, Folder 292, AWH Records.

23. See *AWH Report, June 6th to October 6th, 1917,* Box 1, Folder 2, p. 13, AWH Records; Morton, *Woman Surgeon,* 279–80; and "Committee of Women Physicians to Serve on Medical Board of Council of Defense Has Been Appointed," 186.

24. Information concerning this war service registration may be found in various reports, especially in Box 30, Folders 292 and 293, AWH Records.

25. The information that follows is from my analysis of the *Census of Women Physicians.*

26. Morton, *Woman Surgeon,* 281, 283. For more on the protest, see Emma Wheat Gilmore, "Report of the Committee, Women Physicians, General Medical Board, Committee of National Defense," 136–47.

27. The *Census of Women Physicians* contains data on graduation year and institution, state of residence, professional affiliation, and other information about medical activities. Neither age, state of residence, nor the medical institution from which women graduated seems to have affected wartime registration. The *Census of Women Physicians* does not give the year of birth for the medical women, but most entries list the date of graduation from medical school. We cannot, of course, strictly determine age by graduation year, but it does give us some indication of age groupings. The average graduation year for all of the women included was 1899, and the average graduation year for those women who

registered for war service was also 1899. Women just completing their medical school course work may not have been as inclined to register, especially when they had internships following graduation, and older women may not have considered themselves as fit for service as middle-aged or younger women colleagues.

28. By 1918 new members of the Medical Women's National Association were required to also be members of the American Medical Association, but the original constitution did not have this requirement. Therefore, in the 1918 *Census of Women Physicians* there are women who list MWNA membership without being members of the AMA. AMA members constituted 19 percent of the total, MWNA members 8 percent.

29. The sixth edition of the *American Medical Directory* contains the names of 159,444 physicians. I subtracted 5,991, the number of women physicians in the *Census of Women Physicians,* from this figure for a total of 153,453 male physicians in 1918.

30. See *History of Medicine and Surgery and Physicians and Surgeons of Chicago.*

31. See Van Hoosen, *Petticoat Surgeon,* 202.

32. Lynch, Weed, and McAfee, *The Surgeon General's Office,* 42. The term *curiosity* is Lynch's.

33. Ibid., 151; Colonel Joseph H. Ford, M.C., *Administration, American Expeditionary Force,* 102; *History of Medicine and Surgery,* s.v. "Bassoe, Peter."

34. Caroline M. Purnell, M.D., "The Work of the American Women's Hospitals in Foreign Service," 97; Martha Whelpton to Rosalie Slaughter Morton, New York City, November 26, 1917, Box 2, Folder 14, AWH Records; *Bulletin of the Medical Women's Club of Chicago* 6 (September 1917): 5.

35. U.S. Judge Advocate General's Department (Army), *Opinions of the Judge Advocate General of the Army,* 126; Blanton Winship, acting judge advocate general, to the surgeon general of the United States, August 13, 1917, quoted in Anita Newcombe McGee, M.D., "Can Women Physicians Serve in the Army?" 26–28.

36. See my discussion of these interpretations in the text.

37. Here even the limited authority the medical men had achieved was considerable when compared to contract service.

38. Purnell, "Work of the American Women's Hospitals," 97; "Women in the Medical Reserve Corps," 5.

39. Lovejoy, *Women Doctors of the World,* 303.

40. Lovejoy discusses Gilmore's role and other aspects of contract service in ibid., 302–4. I have gathered information for this profile of women contract surgeons from a five-page typewritten list dated November 13, 1919, titled "Women Contract Surgeons, U.S. Army, Who Served during the War with Germany," Box 17f, Folder 142, AWH Records. At the end of the list is this typewritten notation: "CHAIRMAN OF COMMITTEE OF WOMEN PHYSICIANS, Emma Wheat Gilmore, M.D." I have also used information from the *Census of Women Physicians* and individual sources listed below to augment the information in the 1919 list for this profile.

41. See "Haines, Frances Edith, Memoirs of War Service"; Elizabeth Van Cortlandt Hocker, M.D., "The Personal Experience of a Contract Surgeon in the United States Army," 9–11; Ford, *Administration, American Expeditionary Force,* 102; "Contract Surgeon: Dolores Mercedes Pinero, M.D.," 310, 324; and Lovejoy, *Women Doctors of the World,* 275, 303.

42. The overseas women are listed in *Woman's Medical Journal* 28 (November 1918):

247. The figures come from the information on these women in my *Census of Women Physicians* database.

43. Information on Mary Brown may be found in *Crisis* 16 (May 1918): 36. Sara Brown reports on Harriet Rice's achievements in "Colored Women Physicians," 583.

44. Jessie W. Fisher to "Dear Lady," Paris, May 12, 1918, copy of letter with "Kate Campbell Mead, M.D." written by hand across the top in "Minutes, Executives Committee Meeting, 1918–1919," AWH Records.

45. When most women talked about military service they referred to service with the Medical Reserve Corps—in other words, service for the duration of the war and not career service with the regular Medical Corps of the army. This was the type of service of most male physicians in the war. Sometimes women used the terms interchangeably or referred to their right to service in both organizations. For the specific requirements, see "Article I: The Medical Department, Its Organization and Personnel," in *Manual for the Medical Department,* reprinted in *The Surgeon General's Office,* by Lynch, Weed, and McAfee, 762–67; and my specific discussion of these regulations below.

46. See Ellen Carol DuBois, "Taking the Law into Our Own Hands: *Bradwell, Minor,* and Suffrage Militance in the 1870s." A number of cases of such direct action in relation to voting under a Fourteenth Amendment claim may be found in Elizabeth Cady Stanton, Susan B. Anthony, and Matilda Joslyn Gage, eds., *History of Woman Suffrage,* 2:586–755. This work includes transcripts of the trials of Susan B. Anthony and Virginia Minor and the Supreme Court decision in *Minor v. Happersett* (1875).

47. Stanton, Anthony, and Gage, *History of Woman Suffrage,* 2:630–31.

48. Chief Justice Morrison R. Waite delivered the unanimous opinion. See the transcript of the *Minor* case in ibid.

49. "Women Doctors Find Opportunity Does Not Knock," *Oregon Journal,* May 5, 1918, sec. 1, pp. 1, 10. The editors of the *Woman's Medical Journal* reprinted parts of the story in *Woman's Medical Journal* 28 (July 1918): 155–56.

50. This appears in the biographical entry on Manion in the *Medical Woman's Journal* coinciding with her election to the presidency of the Medical Women's National Association in 1924. See "Katherine C. Manion, M.D.," 179.

51. See "A Most Interesting Report of Work of Colorado Medical Women's War Service League," 39–40; quote on 39. For more on Mary Elizabeth Bates and Colorado medical women's activism, see Jensen, "Open Way of Opportunity."

52. McGee, "Can Women Physicians Serve in the Army?" 26.

53. *Manual for the Medical Department,* reprinted in *The Surgeon General's Office,* by Lynch, Weed, and McAfee, 763, 766. These regulations also illustrate the extent to which the professionalization of medicine had been encoded in the army.

54. "A Most Interesting Report of Work," 39.

55. The case in question for justice of the peace is 107 Mass. 604 (1871) and for notaries 165 Mass. 599 (1896). Quoted in U.S. Judge Advocate General's Department (Army), *Opinions of the Judge Advocate General,* 126–27.

56. Ibid., 127. There were several statutes that used the word *male.* The *Revised Statutes,* sec. 1116, detailing general qualifications for enlistment, specified "effective and able bodied men," and the Draft Act of May 18, 1917, included the term *enlistmen.* See U.S. Judge Advocate General's Department (Army), *Opinions of the Judge Advocate General,* 223.

57. "A Most Interesting Report of Work," 39; "Briefs for Suffrage," 821. The sixty-three-

year-old John Franklin Shafroth had practiced law in Missouri before coming to Denver in 1879. He practiced law, became active in Democratic politics, and served as governor of Colorado for two terms, from 1909 to 1913. He was senator from 1913 to 1919 and died in 1922. See *Who Was Who in America*, vol. 1, *1897–1942* (Chicago: Marquis Who's Who, 1968), s.v. "Shafroth, John Franklin."

58. I have augmented the information on these women given by Mary Bates in "A Most Interesting Report of Work" with information from the *Census of Women Physicians*. There, Marion H. Rea-Lucks's name is given as Marion Reil Lucke.

59. The group included Senator McNary of Oregon, Senator Calder of New York, Senator Jones of Washington, Senator Phelan of California, Senator Knox of Pennsylvania, Senator Smith of Georgia, Representative Nolan of California, and Representatives Keating, Taylor, and Timberlake of Colorado, led by Senator Shafroth of Colorado. See "A Most Interesting Report of Work," 39.

60. McGee, "Can Women Physicians Serve in the Army?" 28.

61. "A Most Interesting Report of Work," 39; McGee, "Can Women Physicians Serve in the Army?" 28.

62. Quoted in ibid., 28.

63. Ibid.; "A Most Interesting Report of Work," 40; "Will the War Department Recognize Medical Women and Give Them Equal Rank?" 41.

64. The influence and hard work of the Colorado and California medical women are evident here. "Proceedings of the Chicago Session: Minutes of the Sixty-ninth Annual Session of the American Medical Association, Held at Chicago, June 10–14, 1918" contains an account of the resolutions and the action taken (1855, 1858). See also "Resolutions Pertaining to Women Physicians as Recommended to the AMA by Legislative Committee," 138–39. For Wetherill, see *Who Was Who in America*, vol. 4, *1961–1968* (Chicago: Marquis Who's Who, 1968), s.v. "Wethcrill, Horace Greeley." For Kress, see *Who Was Who in America*, vol. 3, *1951–1960* (Chicago: Marquis Who's Who, 1960), s.v. "Kress, George Henry"; and for Smith, see *Who Was Who in America*, vol. 1, *1879–1942* (Chicago: Marquis Who's Who, 1942), s.v. "Smith, E. Otis."

65. Aileen Kraditor, *The Ideas of the Woman Suffrage Movement, 1890–1920*. The resolutions may be found in "Proceedings of the Chicago Session," 1858.

66. This was part of the Smith resolution.

67. "Report of Reference Committee on Legislation and Political Action," in "Proceedings of the Chicago Session," 1858.

68. Historians of workers in World War II provide us with similar case studies concerning the question of equal pay for equal work. As Ruth Milkman has shown in her study of the relationship between male and female workers in the auto and electrical industries during World War II, *Gender at Work: The Dynamics of Job Segregation by Sex during World War II*, male union members supported female workers' claims for equal pay during wartime. In her analysis, such support for women's "equality" by male workers was directly linked to their own self-interest in promoting standards and pay for jobs that they believed would return to the hands of men following the war. Carrie Brown notes this same pattern for railroad work in World War I (*Rosie's Mom*, 161). For a broad analysis of women's quest to be defined as workers worthy of equal economic citizenship, see Kessler-Harris, *In Pursuit of Equity*.

69. Purnell, "Work of the American Women's Hospitals," 98.

70. The *Medical Woman's Journal* for 1941 and 1942 is full of reminiscences and biographies of women who served as contract surgeons and with medical units in France during the First World War. For the editors, these histories were an important part of the Second World War campaign for officer rank and status for women physicians. Emily Dunning Barringer used her experience as American Women's Hospitals executive committee member in the First World War to help lead the successful campaign in the 1940s. See Dunning Barringer, *Bowery to Bellevue*, 241–42; and More, *Restoring the Balance*, 182–86.

Chapter 6: Helping Women Who Pay the "Rapacious Price" of War: Women's Medical Units in France

1. I am grateful to archivists Sara Piasecki and Karen Peterson of the Oregon Health & Science University Historical Collections & Archives in Portland for their assistance with the Esther Pohl Lovejoy Collection. See also More, *Restoring the Balance*, 131–34.

2. Lovejoy, *Women Physicians and Surgeons*, 33–34. See also "Dr. Lovejoy Learns Opportunity in War for Women Is Large," *Oregon Journal*, June 27, 1917, 7.

3. Ida Clyde Clarke, *American Women and the World War*, 38. Dr. Eliza Mosher was also in attendance representing the MWNA.

4. Lovejoy, *Women Physicians and Surgeons*, 34–35; Lovejoy, *Women Doctors of the World*, 304. For the Red Cross's "official statement" regarding her overseas work with the organization, see J. A. L. Sayer, chief clerk, American Red Cross, New York City, to Esther Lovejoy, chairman, American Women's Hospitals, New York City, March 14, 1930, Box 3, Folder 17, Lovejoy Collection.

5. Macmillan published the first edition of *The House of the Good Neighbor* in November 1919 and a second edition, with a foreword by Herbert Hoover, in 1920.

6. Ibid., 14 (quote), 138–39.

7. Ibid., 167, 172, 173.

8. Ibid., 179–81.

9. W. I. Eyres, hull inspector, Wilson Shipbuilding, Astoria, Oregon, to C. W. Tebault, chief of National Service Section, District no. 11, Emergency Fleet Corporation, Portland, August 22, 1918; Tebault, Oregon representative, National Service Section, to Lovejoy, Portland, August 27, 1918, both in Box 3, Folder 17, Lovejoy Collection.

10. Lovejoy, *Women Physicians and Surgeons*, 34–35.

11. "France Accepts Hospital Unit," 334; "Women's Oversea Hospitals of the U.S.A.," 197.

12. Lovejoy, *Women Doctors of the World*, 302.

13. The editors of the *Woman Citizen* gave continuing coverage of the WOH, primarily by reprinting letters from medical women and other women personnel of the group. See "First Words from the Hospital Unit," 354; "Hospital in Active Service," 395; and "With the Women's Oversea Hospitals," 449, 453.

14. "With the Women's Oversea Hospitals," 449.

15. Ibid. Anna Sholly's report is on pp. 449 and 453. See also "With the Suffrage Hospitals in the French War Zone," 128.

16. "Finishing Up in France," 820–21.

17. Minutes of the Meeting of the Executive Committee and General Association of the American Women's Hospitals, July 19, 1917, Box 30, Folder 293, p. 4, AWH Records.

18. Morton, *Woman Surgeon,* 273.

19. For details of the meeting, see Lovejoy, *Certain Samaritans,* 8–9; and Clarke, *American Women and the World War,* 37–38.

20. See "Some Interesting Data Regarding the Physicians of the Historic First Hospital Sent to France by the American Women's Hospitals," 142–44; and "Hospital no. 1 of the American Women's Hospitals, Qualifications of Unit—1918," Box 2, Folder 10, AWH Records. See also More, *Restoring the Balance,* 122–47, for information on the unit.

21. See "American Women's Hospital no. 1 in the Advanced Area," 5–6; and Minutes of the Meeting of the Executive Committee of the American Women's Hospitals, December 9, 1918, Box 30, Folder 295, p. 4, AWH Records.

22. See discussion in Minutes of the Executive Committee of the American Women's Hospitals, November 11, 1918, Box 30, Folder 295, AWH Records.

23. See "American Women's Hospital no. 1 in the Advanced Area," 5–6.

24. "Report of American Women's Hospitals no. 1 from August 1, 1918, to March 1, 1919," 10.

25. "Dispensaries of American Women's Hospitals no. 1," 7.

26. See Lovejoy, *Certain Samaritans,* 24, 18, 15.

27. Ibid., 21, 16.

28. "Report from August 1, 1918, to March 1, 1919," 11, 14; "The Maire's Address," 10.

29. For Mary Breckinridge's experiences in France, see her *Wide Neighborhoods: A Story of the Frontier Nursing Service,* 75–106; quote on 83.

30. See "American Women's Hospital no. 1 at Luzancy Co-operating with the American Committee for Devastated France," 7.

31. Editorial in *Woman's Medical Journal* 28 (December 1918): 263; M. Louise Hurrell, Luzancy, France, to Executive Committee, AWH, February 22, 1919, Box 8, Folder 59, AWH Records. For an overview of this postwar work through the 1920s, see Lovejoy, *Certain Samaritans.*

32. Lovejoy, *Women Doctors of the World,* 309–10.

33. Lovejoy outlines these nine clinics in detail in *Certain Samaritans.* See also More, *Restoring the Balance,* 147; and More, "The American Medical Women's Association and the Role of the Woman Physician, 1915–1990," 165–80.

34. Lovejoy, *Women Physicians and Surgeons,* provides details of these collaborative arrangements.

35. Ibid., 225, 224.

Chapter 7: A Base Hospital Is Not a Coney Island Dance Hall: Nurses, Citizenship, Hostile Work Environment, and Military Rank

Portions of this chapter appeared in a different form in "A Base Hospital Is Not a Coney Island Dance Hall: American Women Nurses, Hostile Work Environment, and Miliary Rank in the First World War." © University of Nebraska Press. Reprinted by permission.

1. See Barton C. Hacker, "Women and Military Institutions in Early Modern Europe: A Reconnaissance"; Kerber, *Women of the Republic,* 58–60; Julia C. Stimson, "Earliest Known Connection of Nurses with Army Hospitals in the United States," 18; and Julia C. Stimson, Sayres L. Millikin, and Ethel C. S. Thompson, "The Forerunners of the American Army Nurse," 133–41. For an overview of military nurses and nursing, see Enloe, "Nursing the Military," in *Maneuvers,* 198–234; Jeanne Holm, *Women in the Military: An Unfinished Revolution;* and U.S. Army, Office of Medical History, Office of the Surgeon General, Army Nurse Corps History. http://history.amedd.army.mil/ANCWebsite/anchhome.html.

2. Kerber, *Women of the Republic,* 60, 57; Jane E. Schultz, *Women at the Front: Hospital Workers in Civil War America.* The consequences of this hierarchy based on race and class reached into the late nineteenth century as women sought pensions for their work in the Civil War. For studies of nurses who were members of religious sisterhoods in this period, see Mary Denis Maher, *To Bind Up the Wounds: Catholic Sister Nurses in the U.S. Civil War;* and Sioban Nelson, *Say Little, Do Much: Nurses, Nuns, and Hospitals in the Nineteenth Century.*

3. For an overview of nurses in the Spanish-American War, see Graf, "Women Nurses in the Spanish American War."

4. See *Notable American Women: A Biographical Dictionary,* s.v. "McGee, Anita Newcombe." For an example of the resistance of military authorities to women's services in the Spanish-American War, see Ellis Meredith, "Dr. Rose Kidd Beere, First Colorado Nurse in the Philippines." Beere had to keep quiet about her Red Cross assignment to Manila after winning it through testimonial letters of her skill as a medical doctor and community leader and behind-the-scenes maneuvering that included flattery of military officials and promises of a "scoop" to an influential editor.

5. J. Stimson, "The Army Nurse Corps," 287.

6. See Reverby, *Ordered to Care,* 42; see also 39–59. Kristie Ross's excellent article on the tensions between middle-class women nurses and Civil War surgeons, "Arranging a Doll's House: Refined Women as Union Nurses," outlines this poor treatment. See also Jane Schultz's study of Clara Barton, "Between Scylla and Charybdis: Clara Barton's Wartime Odyssey," and *Women at the Front.*

7. See Reverby, *Ordered to Care.* Many women who did not finish the two or three years of course work at nursing schools or who had other vocational training also claimed a "trained" status. The 1910 census lists 76,468 women in the category of "trained nurses." Seventy-five percent of these women were native born and white, 22 percent were immigrant white women, 3 percent were African American, and only 33 were Asian, American Indian, or other women of color. See U.S. Bureau of the Census, *Thirteenth Census of the United States Taken in the Year 1910,* 428–29. The figures for these groups of women are: native-born white, 57,544; immigrant white, 16,733; African American, 2,158; and other women of color, 33. By contrast, 110,912 women were categorized as untrained nurses, 16 percent of whom were African American. See U.S. Bureau of the Census, *Thirteenth Census,* 431. The figures for untrained female nurses are: native-born white, 68,554; immigrant white, 24,442; African American, 17,874; and other women of color, 62.

8. See Melosh, *American Nurses in Fiction.* See also M. Patricia Donahue, *Nursing, the Finest Art: An Illustrated History.*

9. For a thoughtful discussion of these "controlling images," see Collins, *Black Feminist*

Thought. For a discussion of the origins of the Jezebel stereotype and its consequences in the antebellum period, see Deborah Gray White, *Ar'n't I a Woman? Female Slaves in the Plantation South*, 27–46.

10. Mary Mahoney was the first black woman to receive a professional degree, granted in 1879 from the New England Hospital for Women and Children in Boston. The 1915 figures are from table 1 in the appendix of Darlene Clark Hine, *Black Women in White: Racial Conflict and Cooperation in the Nursing Profession, 1890–1950*, 197; see also 4–9.

11. For more on this campaign, see Darlene Clark Hine, "The Call That Never Came: Black Women Nurses and World War I, an Historical Note," and *Black Women in White*; Kimberly Jensen, "Minerva on the Field of Mars: American Women, Citizenship, and Military Service in the First World War," 316–44; and Adah B. Thoms, *Pathfinders: A History of the Progress of Colored Graduate Nurses*.

12. See Zeiger, *In Uncle Sam's Service*, 104–36; Mary Sarnecky, *A History of the U.S. Army Nurse Corps*; and J. Stimson, "The Army Nurse Corps," 290, 351.

13. Harriot Stanton Blatch borrowed this term, which realistically describes the anomalous position of military nurses, from a military nurse. See Blatch, *Mobilizing Woman-Power*, 132; and her letter to the editor, "Military Rank for Nurses," *New York Times*, March 9, 1918, 14.

14. This can certainly be seen as part of the larger pattern and the dilemma of nursing that Susan Reverby has identified as being "ordered to care." See her book of that title.

15. "The Nurse as a Citizen," 673; Isabel M. Stewart, "Testing the Nursing Spirit," 707–11; quote on 709.

16. Sandra Beth Lewenson, *Taking Charge: Nursing, Suffrage, and Feminism in America, 1873–1920*, 210. See particularly her chapter "The Expanding Years: Nursing Supports Suffrage."

17. More information may be found throughout the files on rank for nurses in the History of Nursing Microfiche Collection: The Adelaide Nutting Historical Nursing Collection and the Archives of the Department of Nursing Education of Teachers College, Columbia University; and the *American Journal of Nursing*. See Franklin H. Martin, *Digest of the Proceedings of the Council of National Defense during the World War*, for example, 387–88, 462. Martin says the General Medical Board approved of rank for military nurses "in principle" (462). See also Philip A. Kalisch, "How Army Nurses Became Officers"; and Zeiger, "'Compassionate Sympathizers and Active Combatants': Army Nurses in France," in *In Uncle Sam's Service*, 104–36.

18. See "Resolutions Adopted at the Annual Convention of the National American Woman Suffrage Association," 949.

19. See, for example, "Proposed Rank for Army Nurses," 4; "Why They Need Military Rank," 6; "Concerning Nurses' Rank," 528; "Neither Rank nor Honor," 1079.

20. Helen Hoy Greeley's role is well documented in her various letters and reports for the committee. See, for example, the typescript copy of "Report of Secretary and Counsel to the National Committee to Secure Rank for Nurses of Work Done October 22, 1918, to January 18, 1919," Fiche 292, History of Nursing Microfiche Collection.

21. In addition to chairing the New York Committee to Secure Rank for Nurses, Blatch's wartime activities included suffrage work for the Women's Political Union, which merged with Alice Paul's Congressional Union in 1917; directing women's wartime agricultural

labor in the Woman's Land Army; and heading the Speaker's Bureau of the Food Administration to instill popular support for food conservation and gardening, especially among women. For information on Blatch's activities, see DuBois, *Harriot Stanton Blatch*. For Blatch's wartime views, see her work *Mobilizing Woman-Power* and letter to the editor, "Military Rank for Nurses," *New York Times,* March 9, 1918, 14.

22. See "Military Rank for Nurses."

23. See *Hearing before the Committee on Military Affairs, House of Representatives, Sixty-fifth Congress, Second Session, on Suggested Changes in Medical Reserve Corps, Nurse Corps, and Other Matters Relating to the Medical Department, April 16, 20, and June 7, 1918,* 36.

24. The committee used this expert testimony in its literature, in hearings before Congress, and in speeches and addresses. Some examples are the pamphlet *The World War and the Army Nurse;* and "Rank for Nurses—What Some Doctors Say about It," 302–6.

25. "Rank and Title Their Due," *New York Times,* March 12, 1918, 12. For other letters to the editor in favor of military rank for nurses, see William Montague Geer, "Rank for Army Nurses," *New York Times,* March 13, 1918, 10; and George Gordon Battle, "Military Rank for Nurses," *New York Times,* March 26, 1918, 10.

26. "Young Man's War? Ask Mr. Schwab, Help-Us-Win Club Membership Not Even Confined to Males," 5.

27. See, for example, Bularzik, "Sexual Harassment"; and Segrave, *Sexual Harassment of Women,* 1–69. For specifics on nurses, see Melosh, *"The Physician's Hand";* and Reverby, *Ordered to Care,* 96–97.

28. V. Schultz, "Reconceptualizing Sexual Harassment," 1687, 1766.

29. Stewart, "Nursing Spirit," 710.

30. Martin quotes Crile in his autobiography, *Fifty Years of Medicine and Surgery,* 372. See also Harry D. Piercy, M.D., *History of the Lakeside Unit of World War I;* and Lavinia L. Dock et al., *History of American Red Cross Nursing,* 327–42.

31. See J. Stimson, "The Army Nurse Corps," 317–23; and Dock et al., *American Red Cross Nursing,* 425–505 and the appendix, which provides a complete listing of all of the base hospitals and other hospital units of the war.

32. For two detailed examples of this organization, see information on the formation on Base Hospital no. 12 in Piercy, *Lakeside Unit;* and for Base Hospital no. 21, see *Base Hospital 21, France, May 1917–April 1919* (n.p., 1919), copy in Julia C. Stimson Papers; and Julia C. Stimson, *Finding Themselves: The Letters of an American Army Chief Nurse in a British Hospital in France.*

33. Piercy, *Lakeside Unit,* 4.

34. See J. Stimson, "The Army Nurse Corps," 299–300.

35. Dora E. Thompson to Edna Breyer, December 1, 1917, Box 3, Folder "Letters, etc., 1899–1944," Entry 103, Army Nurse Corps Historical Data File, 1898–1917.

36. Ford, *Administration, American Expeditionary Force,* 242.

37. This is evident in the letters to the editors of nursing journals discussed below and in the case of Daisy Urch. See also specific histories of units such as the Lakeside Unit and Julia Stimson's *Finding Themselves.*

38. For Urch, see *American Nursing: A Biographical Dictionary,* s.v. "Urch, Daisy"; and *Dictionary of American Nursing Biography,* s.v. "Urch, Daisy." For the unit, see Grace Fay

Schryver, *A History of the Illinois Training School for Nurses, 1880–1929*, 122–23; and Dock et al., *American Red Cross Nursing,* 469.

39. At forty-eight Besley was well established in a successful surgical career. In addition to organizing a base hospital unit for overseas service, he served on the Committee of Physicians of the General Medical Board of the Council of National Defense under the direction of his colleague Franklin Martin. See *National Cyclopaedia of American Biography* (Ann Arbor: University Microfilms, 1967), s.v. "Besley, Frederick"; *Who Was Who in America*, vol. 2, *1943–1950* (Chicago: Marquis Who's Who, 1950), s.v. "Besley, Frederick"; and numerous references in Martin, *Fifty Years of Medicine and Surgery.*

40. Urch's letter is summarized in Dock et al., *American Red Cross Nursing,* 471–72.

41. See Urch to Miss Robinson, October 27, 1917, reprinted in Schryver, *Illinois Training School for Nurses,* 125; and Dock et al., *American Red Cross Nursing,* 470–72.

42. Collins later used this rule, paragraph 61 of the *Manual of the Medical Department,* to remove Urch from her position.

43. See the signed "Statement of Major Frederick A. Besley, M.R.C., U.S.A.," Decimal File 211.29, Box 4957, Folder 36, Entry 2065, Chief Nurse, American Expeditionary Force File, Record Group 120, National Archives, Washington, D.C. (hereafter referred to as Chief Nurse, American Expeditionary Force File, Folder 36). Collins's testimony is contained in the signed "Statement of Colonel C. C. Collins, Medical Corps, U.S. Army," in ibid.

44. E. M. Welles Jr. to Commanding Officer, Base Hospital no. 12, regarding Nurse, Miss Daisy D. Urch, June 20, 1918, in ibid.

45. Urch to J. Stimson, June 3, 1919, Box 3, Folder "Letters, etc., 1899–1944," Entry 103, Army Nurse Corps Historical Date File.

46. Notes by secretary for Julia Stimson on the fourth page of Ransom's official complaint. See Jane Ransom to chief surgeon, AEF, February 11, 1919, Chief Nurse, American Expeditionary Force File, Folder 36.

47. Ibid., 1.

48. P. J. H. Farrell to chief surgeon, AEF, December 29, 1918, ibid.

49. See notes on p. 4 of Ransom to chief surgeon. Urch to J. Stimson, March 12, 1919, ibid.

50. Ransom to J. Stimson, March 1, 1919, 1–2, ibid. See also Ransom to chief surgeon, AEF, March 1, 1919, 1–2, ibid.

51. The petition, dated September 24, 1918, is located in ibid. Two women added their names to the original seventy-nine after the petition was sent.

52. The nurses of Base Hospital no. 69 to the chief surgeon, AEF, April 22, 1919, ibid.; Emma H. Byrne to J. Stimson, n.d., ibid.

53. Urch, letter to the editor, *American Journal of Nursing* 20, no. 3 (December 1919): 246–48.

54. Ibid.

55. Sarnecky, *Army Nurse Corps,* 135, 136.

56. See Sara E. Parsons, "Impressions and Conclusions Based on Experience Abroad by Overseas Nurses," paper presented at the convention of the National League of Nursing Education, Chicago, June 26, 1919, reprinted in *American Journal of Nursing* 19, no. 11 (August 1919): 829–34; quote on 830.

57. "Discussion on Rank," 851–53 (quote on 851); "An Old Army Nurse," letter to the editor, 63–64; "Discussion on Rank," 851.

58. M. A. Nutting, letter to the editor, *American Journal of Nursing* 19, no. 10 (July 1919): 799–800; M. M. Riddle, letter to the editor, *American Journal of Nursing* 19, no. 10 (July 1919): 800; "An Old Army Nurse"; "A Navy Nurse," letter to the editor, 64–65.

59. R. Inde Albaugh, letter to the editor, *American Journal of Nursing* 19, no. 10 (July 1919): 798.

60. For more on working-class patterns of sexuality, see Kathy Peiss, *Cheap Amusements: Working Women and Leisure in Turn-of-the-Century New York*; and D'Emilio and Freedman, *Intimate Matters*.

61. M. M. M., letter to the editor, *American Journal of Nursing* 20, no. 3 (December 1919): 242–43.

62. "A Regular Army Nurse," letter to the editor, 416; "A New England Nurse," 252.

63. The papers of Julia Catherine Stimson are located at the New York Weill Cornell Medical Center Archives. For other biographical information on Stimson, see *Notable American Women,* s.v. "Stimon, Julia Catherine"; and Mary T. Weber Sarnecky, "A Woman for All Seasons: A Biography of Julia Catherine Stimson, 1881–1948."

64. Henry A. Stimson, *The Right Life and How to Live It,* 172.

65. J. Stimson, *Finding Themselves,* v.

66. J. Stimson to family, July 18, 1918, Box 4, Folder 3, p. 3; October 23, 1918, Box 4, Folder 3, pp. 2–3; April 15, 1919, Box 4, Folder 4, p. 2, all in J. Stimson Papers.

67. J. Stimson to Isabelle Carson, February 25, 1919, Box 3, Folder "Letters, etc., 1899–1944," Entry 103, Army Nurse Corps Historical Date File; J. Stimson, "The Army Nurse Corps," 300, 299; J. Stimson to All Chief Nurses, December 23, 1918, Box 3, Folder "Letters, etc., 1899–1944," Entry 102, Army Nurse Corps Historical Date File.

68. J. Stimson, *Finding Themselves,* 62; J. Stimson to family, December 2, 1918, Box 4, Folder 3, p. 2, J. Stimson Papers.

69. Julia C. Stimson, "Nursing Overseas," 24–30; quote on 29. Stimson may also have been defensive because she was the person responsible for fielding nurses' complaints and was also the administrator for the European theater.

70. "Some Quotations from the Hearings before the Sub-Committee of the Committee on Military Affairs, United States Senate," 30–34.

71. B. B., letter to the editor, *American Journal of Nursing* 20, no. 3 (December 1919): 245–46.

72. Urch, letter to the editor; Vroom quoted in *American Journal of Nursing* 20, no. 3 (December 1919): 244.

73. See "Rank for Nurses Achieved," 867–68; J. Stimson, "Rank," 997; Sarnecky, *Army Nurse Corps;* Zeiger, *In Uncle Sam's Service;* and Kalisch, "How Army Nurses Became Officers."

74. Julia C. Stimson, "Rank for Nurses: What Have Five Years of Rank Done for the Army Nurse Corps?" 271–74; quotes on 271–73.

75. Ibid., 273–74.

76. Ibid., 274.

77. Sarnecky, *Army Nurse Corps,* 269.

78. Janann Sherman, "'They Either Need These Women or They Do Not': Margaret

Chase Smith and the Fight for Regular Status for Women in the Military"; Sarnecky, *Army Nurse Corps,* 290–92.

79. Enloe, *Maneuvers,* 226.

Chapter 8: "Danger Ahead for the Country": Civic Roles and Safety for the Consumer-Civilian in Postwar America

1. See Mary Louise Roberts, *Civilization without Sexes: Reconstructing Gender in Postwar France, 1917–1927.*

2. Grayzel, *Women's Identities at War,* 226–42; Kent, *Making Peace,* 141; L. Cohen, *Consumer's Republic;* Erica Carter, *How German Is She? Postwar West German Reconstruction and the Consuming Woman.*

3. Waller uses this as the second section of his classic work *The Veteran Comes Back.*

4. Jonathan Shay, *Odysseus in America: Combat Trauma and the Trials of Homecoming.* See also, for example, Deborah Cohen, *The War Come Home: Disabled Veterans in Britain and Germany, 1914–1939;* Eric T. Dean, *Shook over Hell: Post-traumatic Stress, Vietnam, and the Civil War;* Jennifer D. Keene, *Doughboys, the Great War, and the Remaking of America;* Showalter, "Male Hysteria," in *Female Malady,* 167–94; and Zahava Solomon, *Combat Stress Reaction: The Enduring Toll of War.*

5. "America's Murder Record," 355.

6. Quoted in Edith Abbott, "Crime and the War," 33, 34–35, 39. For additional statistics, see "Crime Decreases in England," *New York Times,* July 16, 1917, 4; and "Shows Decrease in Crime," *New York Times,* January 13, 1918, sec. 1, p. 6.

7. Letter from J. K. Codding quoted in University of Kansas sociologist F. W. Blackmar, "Does War Increase Crime?" 123; William Healy, "Delinquency and Crime," 424.

8. Abbott, "Crime and the War," 40. Abbott and others were also concerned about the postwar years and called for thoughtful and humane policies to deal with these issues after the war was over.

9. "Ex-Soldier Hurls Bomb Into Crowd," *New York Times,* September 11, 1916, 2; "Increasing Crime Is Alarming Germany: 300 Burglar Claims Daily on One Firm," *New York Times,* March 13, 1918, 1; "Wave of Crime in Germany," *New York Times,* January 2, 1918, 6; "Belief in Victory Unites Germans," *New York Times,* April 18, 1918, 6; Kent, *Making Peace,* 96–100.

10. Dr. W. F. Lorenz and Dr. W. S. Middleton, both veterans, undertook the study. See Fred Holmes, "Ex-soldier Crimes Following the War," 434; and Holmes, "Making Criminals Out of Soldiers," 114–16.

11. Holmes, "Making Criminals Out of Soldiers," 115–16; Waller, *The Veteran Comes Back,* 126.

12. Keene, *Doughboys,* 51; Waller, *The Veteran Comes Back,* 234–40; Stanley Frost, "What's a Sick Veteran between Friends," 106–9; Frost, "Grab-Bag Training for Veterans," "Agencies Which Aided War-Crippled," *New York Times,* August 24, 1919, sec. 4, p. 6.

13. Stoddard Dewey, "War's Second Nature," 12–13; "Preparing to Care for Shell-Shocked Men," *New York Times Magazine,* June 16, 1918, 8; M. Allen Starr, M.D., "The Occupation Cure for Shell Shock," 3; Dr. H. R. Humphries, "Home Treatment of Shell Shock: 'Taking Care of Your Boy,'" 110; Mary C. Jarrett, "War Neuroses after the War: Extra-Institutional

Preparation," 558, 559; Jarrett, "Home Treatment of Shell Shock: The Need of Wisdom and Sympathy to Help Recovery," 510–11. In the latter article, Jarrett indicates that of the 156 state hospitals in existence, most were overcrowded, and "for observation and treatment of early cases of mental disease and cases of neuroses not suitable for admission to state hospitals there are six psychopathic hospitals and eleven psychopathic wards in the country" (512).

14. "Wounded and Disabled Soldiers: Informal Discussion," 68, 71; James H. Tufts, "Wartime Gains for the American Family," 331–32. The Russell Sage Foundation also published Tufts's article as a pamphlet, *Wartime Gains for the American Family, by James H. Tufts: Address before the Division on the Family of the National Conference of Social Work, June 2, 1919* (New York: Russell Sage Foundation, 1919).

15. Keene, *Doughboys,* 132, 134, 140–41. See also articles such as "'The Mill' Awaits Each Doughboy Homeward Bound," 106–7.

16. "Soldiers' Grievances Heard in Congress," *New York Times,* February 16, 1919, sec. 4, p. 11. Keene quotes the last part of this article in *Doughboys,* 141.

17. Cooper, *Pivotal Decades,* 321–22; Montgomery, *Fall of the House of Labor,* 388–89. For more on the strike, see Robert L. Friedheim, "The Seattle General Strike of 1919"; and Painter, *Standing at Armageddon,* 346–47.

18. Montgomery, *Fall of the House of Labor,* 392–93.

19. "Americans Chafe under Restraint," *Portland Oregonian,* January 10, 1919, 1, 5; Walton H. Hamilton, "The Impending Industrial Crisis," 496–500 (quote on 500). For the Tacoma council, see Keene, *Doughboys,* 168–69; and "Tacoma Strikers Organize: Soldiers', Sailors', and Workmen's Council is Formed," *Portland Oregonian,* January 23, 1919, 16. For Portland, see "Bolshevik Doctrine Spread in Portland: Workmen and Soldiers Council Organized at Meeting," *Portland Oregonian,* January 10, 1919, 10.

20. "Bolshevik Doctrine Spread in Portland." See also Dennis E. Hoffman and Vincent J. Webb, "Police Response to Labor Radicalism in Portland and Seattle, 1913–19," 361; Philip S. Foner, *History of the Labor Movement in the United States,* 72–73; Robert L. Friedheim, *The Seattle General Strike,* 125–26; and *The Seattle General Strike: An Account of What Happened in Seattle, and Especially in the Seattle Labor Movement during the General Strike, February 6 to 11, 1919, Issued by the History Committee of the General Strike Committee,* 50.

21. "Rioters Damage Yale Buildings," *New York Times,* May 28, 1919, 1; "Militia on Guard at Yale Campus," *New York Times,* May 29, 1919, 3. See also Capozzola, "Only Badge Needed," 19. Some Yale students served as strikebreakers during this period. See Norwood, *Strikebreaking and Intimidation,* 20–33.

22. Frank Tannenbaum, "The Moral Devastation of War," 335–36.

23. See Roderick Phillips, *Putting Asunder: A History of Divorce in Western Society,* 517. Phillips's figures come from Paul H. Jacobson and Pauline F. Jacobson, *American Marriage and Divorce,* 90. The term *watershed* is from Phillips, *Putting Asunder,* 89.

24. Glenda Riley, *Divorce: An American Tradition,* 133.

25. See Elaine Tyler May, *Great Expectations: Marriage and Divorce in Post-Victorian America.*

26. See J. Herbie DiFonzo, *Beneath the Fault Line: The Popular and Legal Culture of Divorce in Twentieth-Century America.*

27. Phillips, *Putting Asunder,* 519, 522.

28. There are a number of cases of dissolution of marriage for 1918 in the records of the Multnomah County Courthouse (Portland, Oregon) that indicate postponement because of soldiers' immunity from civil prosecution until their return. See "Moratorium Will Be Urged to Protect Our Soldiers and Sailors Absent at War," *New York Times,* September 18, 1917, 1; "Move to Enact Bill to Protect Fighters," *New York Times,* October 2, 1917, 4; "Civil Rights Bill Passed by House," *New York Times,* October 5, 1917, 2; "Signs Soldiers' Moratorium Bill," *New York Times,* March 9, 1918, 19; and "How the American Moratorium Protects Those in Service Overseas," *New York Times,* April 27, 1918, 16. Women in service, such as nurses in the nurse corps, were also covered. Some states also passed similar legislation. See Fred Holmes, *Wisconsin's War Record,* 94–95.

29. See, for example, "Cupid Hit Hard by Portland Divorces," *Portland Oregonian,* November 3, 1919, 15.

30. U.S. Bureau of the Census, *Marriage and Divorce, 1916.* See also "Divorce Follows Ninth of Marriages," *New York Times,* March 21, 1919, 11.

31. "Lawyers Lift Fees to Curb Divorce Evil," *Portland Oregonian,* August 27, 1919, 7.

32. Anna Steese Richardson, "Now That They're Back: An Open Letter to the Readers of the 'Soldiers All' Department," 24. Richardson, *Companion* editors announced, would continue to contribute to the magazine now that this department was closing after the end of the war. Her next article was to be titled "The Woman Who Couldn't Manage."

33. A. Evelyn Newman, "Old Husbands for New!" 59–60.

34. Richardson, "Now That They're Back," 24.

35. Laura Spencer Porter, "He Is So Changed," 26, 87; quote on 87.

36. Corra Harris, "Marrying Off the American Army," 260–61.

37. See particularly the chapters "Reconstruction and Political Misjudgement, 1918–1919" and "Postwar Reckoning," in *Labor Market Politics and the Great War: The Department of Labor, the States, and the First U.S. Employment Service, 1907–1933,* by William Breen, 133–59.

38. Breen uses a USES report for these figures. See ibid., 149.

39. E. Alexander Powell, "Training the Soldier for Peace," 621.

40. Katherine Mayo, "While Our Boys Are Marking Time," 8.

41. Powell, "Training the Soldier for Peace," 629.

42. These and subsequent figures are from my analysis of the state-by-state reports listed in U.S. Council of National Defense, Reconstruction Research Division, *Readjustment and Reconstruction Information.*

43. Plans were made across the country to provide additional employment opportunities in agricultural and forest work. See U.S. Department of Labor, *Employment and Natural Resources: Possibilities of Making New Opportunities for Employment through the Settlement and Development of Agricultural and Forest Lands and Other Resources.* For more on land policies, see Franklin K. Lane, *Memorandum for the Press: [Relating to Plans for Providing Opportunity for American Soldiers Returning from the War].*

44. U.S. Council of National Defense, Reconstruction Research Division, *Readjustment and Reconstruction Information,* 269.

45. World War Veterans' State Aid Commission of Oregon, *Biennial Report, 1922,* 41.

46. See Anna Steese Richardson, "When Johnny Comes Marching Home Again," 24, 43; and Carey Edmunds, "The Social Hut instead of the Saloon," 65.

47. "Plans Outlined to Care for Soldiers," *Portland Oregonian*, January 12, 1919, 22.

48. "Veterans to Get Preference," *Portland Oregonian*, January 14, 1919, 1; "Soldiers' Relief Bill Passes Both Houses," *Portland Oregonian*, January 23, 1919, 1.

49. Kessler-Harris, *In Pursuit of Equity*, 31–32.

50. See also Cott, *Grounding of Modern Feminism*, 117–42.

51. American Federation of Labor, Committee on Reconstruction, *American Federation of Labor Reconstruction Program*.

52. See Greenwald, *Women, War, and Work*; and Kessler-Harris, *Out to Work*, 217–29.

53. Kessler-Harris, *Out to Work*, 224; Greenwald, *Women, War, and Work*, 243.

54. Evans, *Born for Liberty*, 182.

55. Kessler-Harris, *In Pursuit of Equity*, 34–45; quote on 39.

56. Again I draw this concept of the construction of violence from Shani D'Cruze. See her "Unguarded Passions," introduction to *Everyday Violence in Britain*.

57. Elizabeth Haiken, "The Making of the Modern Face: Cosmetic Surgery," 82–98.

58. F. Hoffman, *The Homicide Problem*, 24, 28, 29, 70, 74. Hoffman reprinted his yearly reports in this volume.

59. For an excellent discussion of these specifics, see Lee Kennett and James LaVerne Anderson, *The Gun in America: The Origins of a National Dilemma*, 165–86. And for more on "Big Tim" Sullivan, see Daniel Czitrom, "Underworlds and Underdogs: Big Tim Sullivan and Metropolitan Politics in New York, 1889–1913," 536–58.

60. The United States Rifle Association reported on them in detail because they were so opposed to the action. See the report of the association's annual meeting in January 1918 in Kendrick Scofield, "U.S.R.A. Names New Officers," 345–46.

61. Lucilius Emery, "The Constitutional Right to Keep and Bear Arms," 473–77.

62. F. Hoffman, *The Homicide Problem*, 5.

63. Quoted in Kennett and Anderson, *Gun in America*, 191.

64. William McAdoo, *When the Court Takes a Recess*, 95, 129–30.

65. Ibid., 131.

Conclusion

1. Linda K. Kerber, "The Meanings of Citizenship," 854.

2. See D'Cruze, "Unguarded Passions," introduction to *Everyday Violence in Britain*, 1.

3. Michael Sherry, *In the Shadow of War: The United States since the 1930s*, xi.

Bibliography

Contemporary Newspapers and Periodicals

American Journal of Nursing
American Medicine
American Women's Hospitals Bulletin
Arms and the Man
Bookman
Bulletin of the Medical Women's Club of Chicago
Bulletin of the Woman's Medical College of Pennsylvania
Colorado Medicine
Crisis
Current Opinion
Delineator
Good Housekeeping
Independent
Journal of the American Medical Association
Journal of the National Medical Association
Ladies' Home Journal
Literary Digest
Medical Woman's Journal
Nation
New York Times
New York Times Magazine
Outlook
Portland Oregonian
Stars and Stripes
Suffragist
Touchstone
Trained Nurse and Hospital Review

Washington Post
Woman Citizen
Woman Patriot
Woman's Home Companion
Woman's Medical Journal

Government Documents

Annual Report of the Secretary of the Navy for the Fiscal Year 1918. Washington, D.C.: Government Printing Office, 1918.

Hearing before the Committee on Military Affairs, House of Representatives, Sixty-fifth Congress, Second Session, on Suggested Changes in Medical Reserve Corps, Nurse Corps, and Other Matters Relating to the Medical Department, April 16, 20, and June 7, 1918. Washington, D.C.: Government Printing Office, 1918.

Lane, Franklin K. *Memorandum for the Press: [Relating to Plans for Providing Opportunity for American Soldiers Returning from the War].* Washington, D.C.: U.S. Department of the Interior, 1918.

Laws Relating to the Navy, Annotated, Including the Constitution of the United States, the Revised Statutes of the United States, and the United States Statutes at Large, in Force March 4, 1921. Compiled by George Melling. Washington, D.C.: Government Printing Office, 1922.

U.S. Army, Office of the Judge Advocate General. *Federal Aid in Domestic Disturbances, 1903–1922.* 67th Cong., 2d sess., S. Doc. 263. Washington, D.C.: Government Printing Office, 1922.

U.S. Bureau of the Census. *Marriage and Divorce, 1916.* Washington, D.C.: Government Printing Office, 1919.

———. *Thirteenth Census of the United States Taken in the Year 1910.* Vol. 4, *Population, 1910: Occupation Statistics.* Washington, D.C.: Government Printing Office, 1914.

U.S. Council of National Defense, Reconstruction Research Division. *Readjustment and Reconstruction Information.* Vol. 2, *Readjustment and Reconstruction in the States.* Washington, D.C.: Government Printing Office, 1920.

U.S. Department of Labor. *Employment and Natural Resources: Possibilities of Making New Opportunities for Employment through the Settlement and Development of Agricultural and Forest Lands and Other Resources.* Washington, D.C.: Government Printing Office, 1919.

U.S. Judge Advocate General's Department (Army). *Opinions of the Judge Advocate General of the Army.* Vol. 1, *April 1, 1917, to December 31, 1917.* Washington, D.C.: Government Printing Office, 1919.

U.S. Senate, Committee on the District of Columbia. *Suffrage Parade: Hearings before a Subcommittee under S. Res. 499 of March 4, 1913, Directing Said Committee to Investigate the Conduct of the District Police and Police Department of the District of Columbia in Connection with the Woman's Suffrage Parade on March 3, 1913.* Hearings held March 6–April 17, 1913. Washington, D.C.: Government Printing Office, 1913. Microfilm. New Haven, Connecticut: Research Publications, Inc., 1976. History of Women Collection, Series 1, Reel 86, no. 7084.

World War Veterans' State Aid Commission of Oregon. *Biennial Report, 1922.* Salem: World War Veterans' State Aid Commission, 1922.

Manuscripts and Manuscript Collections

American Women's Hospital Records, 1917–1982. Accession 144, Archives and Special Collections on Women in Medicine and Homeopathy, Drexel University College of Medicine, Philadelphia.

Army Nurse Corps Historical Data File, 1898–1917. Record Group 112, National Archives, Washington, D.C.

Chief Nurse, American Expeditionary Forces File. Record Group 120, National Archives, Washington, D.C.

"Haines, Frances Edith, Memoirs of War Service." Accession 103, Archives and Special Collections on Women in Medicine and Homeopathy, Drexel University College of Medicine, Philadelphia.

History of Nursing Microfiche Collection: The Adelaide Nutting Historical Nursing Collection and the Archives of the Department of Nursing Education of Teachers College, Columbia University. Ann Arbor: University Microfilms International, 1985.

Lovejoy, Esther Pohl, Collection. Accession 2001–011, Oregon Health & Science University Historical Collections & Archives, Portland.

National Archives Photographic Collection. Record Group 165, National Archives, Washington, D.C.

Stimson, Julia C. Papers. New York Weill Cornell Medical Center Archives, New York.

Other Sources

Aafjes, Astrid. *Gender Violence: The Hidden War Crime.* Washington, D.C.: Women, Law, and Development International, 1998.

Abbott, Edith. "Crime and the War." *Journal of the American Institute of Criminal Law and Criminology* 9, no. 1 (May 1918): 32–45.

"About Women Shots." *Arms and the Man* (January 19, 1918).

Addams, Jane. *Peace and Bread in Time of War.* New York: Macmillan, 1922.

Address of Everett P. Wheeler, Public Meeting, Berkeley Lyceum, March 6th, 1913: For the Preservation of the Home. New York: New York State Association Opposed to Woman Suffrage, 1913. Microfilm. New Haven, Conn.: Research Publications, 1976, History of Women Collection, Series 1, Reel 952, no. 9326.

"The American Army and Joan of Arc." *Bookman* 48 (October 1918).

"American Battalion of Death." *Woman Citizen* (October 13, 1917).

American Federation of Labor, Committee on Reconstruction. *American Federation of Labor Reconstruction Program.* Washington, D.C.: American Federation of Labor, 1918.

American Medical Directory. Chicago: American Medical Association, 1918.

American Nursing: A Biographical Dictionary. Edited by Vern L. Bullough, Olga Maranjian Church, and Alice P. Stein. 2 vols. New York: Garland, 1988.

"American Women's Hospital no. 1 at Luzancy Co-operating with the American Committee for Devastated France." *American Women's Hospitals Bulletin* 1, no. 2 (January 1919).

"American Women's Hospital no. 1 in the Advanced Area." *American Women's Hospitals Bulletin* 1, no. 1 (October 1918).

"America's Murder Record." *Outlook* 134 (July 11, 1923).

"Annie Oakley Visits Camps." *Arms and the Man* (June 8, 1918).

"Another Phantom Laid." *Woman Citizen* (August 4, 1917).

Banta, Martha. *Imaging American Women: Idea and Ideals in Cultural History.* New York: Columbia University Press, 1987.

Barringer, Emily Dunning. *Bowery to Bellevue: The Story of New York's First Woman Ambulance Surgeon.* New York: W. W. Norton, 1950.

"The Battalion of Death." *Delineator* 92 (January 1918).

Beatty, Bessie. *The Red Heart of Russia.* New York: Century, 1918.

Bederman, Gail. *Manliness and Civilization: A Cultural History of Gender and Race in the United States, 1880–1917.* Chicago: University of Chicago Press, 1995.

The Belgian Delegates to the United States. *The Case of Belgium in the Present War: An Account of the Violation of the Neutrality of Belgium and of the Laws of War on Belgian Territory.* New York: Macmillan, 1914.

Bender, Daniel. "Too Much of Distasteful Masculinity: Historicizing Sexual Harassment in the Garment Sweatshop and Factory." *Journal of Women's History* 15, no. 4 (Winter 2004): 91–116.

Blackmar, F. W. "Does War Increase Crime?" *Proceedings of the National Conference on Social Work at the Forty-fifth Annual Session Held in Kansas City, Missouri, May 15–22, 1918,* 121–24. Chicago: Rogers and Hall, 1919.

Blatch, Harriot Stanton. *Mobilizing Woman-Power.* New York: Woman's Press, 1918.

Block, Sharon, and Kathleen Brown. "Clio in Search of Eros: Redefining Sexualities in Early America." *William and Mary Quarterly* 60, no. 1 (January 2003): 5–12.

Boag, Peter. "Go West Young Man, Go East Young Woman: Searching for the Trans in Western Gender History." *Western Historical Quarterly* 36, no. 4 (2005): 477–97.

Bodnar, John. *The Transplanted: A History of Immigrants in Urban America.* Bloomington: Indiana University Press, 1995.

Bordin, Ruth. *Woman and Temperance: The Quest for Power and Liberty, 1873–1900.* New Brunswick: Rutgers University Press, 1990.

Botchkareva, Maria. *Yashka: My Life as Peasant, Officer and Exile.* New York: F. A. Stokes, 1919.

Breckinridge, Mary. *Wide Neighborhoods: A Story of the Frontier Nursing Service.* New York: Harper and Brothers, 1952.

Bredbenner, Candace Lewis. *A Nationality of Her Own: Women, Marriage, and the Law of Citizenship.* Berkeley and Los Angeles: University of California Press, 1998.

Breen, William. *Labor Market Politics and the Great War: The Department of Labor, the States, and the First U.S. Employment Service, 1907–1933.* Kent, Ohio: Kent State University Press, 1997.

"Briefs for Suffrage." *Woman Citizen* (March 1, 1919).

Brown, Carrie. *Rosie's Mom: Forgotten Women Workers of the First World War.* Boston: Northeastern Press, 2002.

Brownmiller, Susan. *Against Our Will: Men, Women, and Rape.* New York: Simon and Schuster, 1975.

Bularzik, Mary. "Sexual Harassment at the Workplace: Historical Notes." In *Workers' Struggles Past and Present: A "Radical America" Reader*, edited by James Green, 115–35. Philadelphia: Temple University Press, 1983.

"California Women Urge Federal Recognition." *Woman's Medical Journal* 27 (October 1917).

Capozzola, Christopher. "The Only Badge Needed Is Your Patriotic Service: Vigilance, Coercion, and the Law in World War I America." *Journal of American History* 88, no. 4 (March 2002). Available online at http://www.historycooperative.org/journals/jah/88.4/capozzola.html.

Carney, Peter B. "Target Smashing Stimulated by Entrance of U.S. in War." *Arms and the Man* (December 15, 1917).

Carter, Erica. *How German Is She? Postwar West German Reconstruction and the Consuming Woman*. Ann Arbor: University of Michigan Press, 1997.

"The Case of Belgium." *Outlook* 108 (September 30, 1914).

Catt, Carrie Chapman, ed. *The Ballot and the Bullet*. Philadelphia: Alfred J. Ferris Press, 1897.

Census of Women Physicians. New York: American Women's Hospitals, 1918.

Cerabino-Hess, Elizabeth. "On Nation and Violation: Representations of Rape in Popular Theater and Film of the Progressive Era." Ph.D. diss., New York University, 1997.

Chauncey, George. "From Sexual Inversion to Homosexuality: The Changing Medical Conceptualization of Female 'Deviance.'" In *Passion and Power: Sexuality in History*. Edited by Kathy Peiss and Christina Simmons, 87–117. Philadelphia: Temple University Press, 1989.

———. *Gay New York: Gender, Urban Cultures, and the Making of the Gay Male World, 1890–1940*. New York: Basic Books, 1994.

"Chicago's Lady Trap Shooters." *Arms and the Man* (February 24, 1916).

"Civilian Rifle Clubs." *Arms and the Man* (April 22, 1915).

Clarke, Ida Clyde. *American Women and the World War*. New York: D. Appleton, 1918.

Clifford, John Garry. *The Citizen Soldiers: The Plattsburg Training Camp Movement, 1913–1920*. Lexington: University Press of Kentucky, 1972.

Cohen, Deborah. *The War Come Home: Disabled Veterans in Britain and Germany, 1914–1939*. Berkeley and Los Angeles: University of California Press, 2001.

Cohen, Lizabeth. "Citizens and Consumers in the Century of Mass Consumption." In *Perspectives on Modern America: Making Sense of the Twentieth Century*, edited by Harvard Sitkoff, 145–61. New York: Oxford University Press, 2001.

———. *A Consumer's Republic: The Politics of Mass Consumption in Postwar America*. New York: Alfred A. Knopf, 2003.

Collins, Patricia Hill. *Black Feminist Thought: Knowledge, Consciousness, and the Politics of Empowerment*. 2d ed. New York: Routledge, 2000.

"Colored Women Physicians." *Southern Workman* 52 (1923).

"Committee of Women Physicians to Serve on Medical Board of Council of Defense Has Been Appointed." *Woman's Medical Journal* 27 (August 1917).

"Concerning Nurses' Rank." *Woman Citizen* (November 23, 1918).

Conkling, G. A. "The Return of Jeanne D'Arc." *Bookman* 44 (February 1917).

"Contract Surgeon: Dolores Mercedes Pinero, M.D." *Medical Woman's Journal* 49 (1942).

Cooper, John Milton. *Pivotal Decades: The United States, 1900–1920*. New York: W. W. Norton, 1990.

Cott, Nancy. *The Grounding of Modern Feminism*. New Haven: Yale University Press, 1987.

Cress, Lawrence Delbert. *Citizens in Arms: The Army and the Militia in American Society to the War of 1812*. Chapel Hill: University of North Carolina Press, 1982.

Czitrom, Daniel. "Underworlds and Underdogs: Big Tim Sullivan and Metropolitan Politics in New York, 1889–1913." *Journal of American History* 78, no. 2 (1991): 536–58.

Dalton, Kathleen. *Theodore Roosevelt: A Strenuous Life*. New York: Alfred A. Knopf, 2002.

Daniels, Roger. *Guarding the Golden Door: American Immigration Policy and Immigrants since 1882*. New York: Hill and Wang, 2004.

Darrow, Margaret H. *French Women and the First World War: War Stories of the Home Front*. Oxford, N.Y.: Berg, 2000.

Davis, Natalie. *Society and Culture in Early Modern France*. Stanford: Stanford University Press, 1975.

Dawley, Alan. *Changing the World: American Progressives in War and Revolution*. Princeton: Princeton University Press, 2003.

D'Cruze, Shani. *Crimes of Outrage: Sex, Violence, and Victorian Working Women*. DeKalb: Northern Illinois University Press. 1998.

———, ed. *Everyday Violence in Britain, 1850–1950: Gender and Class*. London: Pearson Education, 2000.

Dean, Eric T. *Shook over Hell: Post-traumatic Stress, Vietnam, and the Civil War*. Cambridge: Harvard University Press, 1997.

DeConde, Alexander. *Gun Violence in America: The Struggle for Control*. Boston: Northeastern University Press, 2001.

"Decorations for Women." *Arms and the Man* (September 14, 1916).

"The *Delineator*'s Women's Preparedness Bureau: Going in for Military Training and How to Set Up a Camp." *Delineator* 91 (August 1917).

"The *Delineator*'s Women's Preparedness Bureau: Let Us Help You toward Greater Self-Dependence in War or Peace." *Delineator* 91 (July 1917).

"The *Delineator*'s Women's Preparedness Bureau: What Can I Do to Help?" *Delineator* 91 (November 1917).

D'Emilio, John, and Estelle Freedman. *Intimate Matters: A History of Sexuality in America*. 2d ed. Chicago: University of Chicago Press, 1997.

Desai, Vishakha N. *Conversations with Traditions: Nilima Sheikh and Shahzia Sikander*. New York: Asia Society, 2001.

Dewey, Stoddard. "War's Second Nature." *Nation* 107 (July 6, 1918).

Dictionary of American Nursing Biography. Edited by Joellen Watson Hawkins, Loretta P. Higgins, and Alice Howell Friedman. Westport, Conn.: Greenwood Press, 1988.

DiFonzo, J. Herbie. *Beneath the Fault Line: The Popular and Legal Culture of Divorce in Twentieth-Century America*. Charlottesville: University Press of Virginia, 1997.

"Discussion on Rank." *American Journal of Nursing* 19 (August 1919).

"Dispensaries of American Women's Hospitals no. 1." *American Women's Hospitals Bulletin* 1, no. 2 (January 1919).

Dock, Lavinia L., et al. *History of American Red Cross Nursing.* New York: Macmillan, 1922.

Donahue, M. Patricia. *Nursing, the Finest Art: An Illustrated History.* St. Louis: Mosby, 1996.

Dower, John. *War without Mercy: Race and Power in the Pacific War.* New York: Pantheon, 1986.

"Do Women Believe in War?" *Delineator* 89 (October 1916).

Dubinsky, Karen. *Improper Advances: Rape and Heterosexual Conflict in Ontario, 1880–1929.* Chicago: University of Chicago Press, 1993.

DuBois, Ellen Carol. *Feminism and Suffrage: The Emergence of an Independent Women's Movement in America, 1848–1869.* Ithaca: Cornell University Press, 1978.

———. *Harriot Stanton Blatch and the Winning of Woman Suffrage.* New Haven: Yale University Press, 1997.

———. "Taking the Law into Our Own Hands: *Bradwell, Minor,* and Suffrage Militance in the 1870s." In *Visible Women: New Essays on American Activism,* edited by Nancy A. Hewitt and Suzanne Lebsock, 19–40. Urbana: University of Illinois Press, 1993.

Duggan, Lisa. *Sapphic Slashers: Sex, Violence, and American Modernity.* Durham: Duke University Press, 2000.

Dunlap, Leslie K. "The Reform of Rape Law and the Problem of White Men: Age-of-Consent Campaigns in the South, 1885–1910." In *Sex, Love, Race: Crossing Boundaries in North America,* edited by Martha Hodes, 352–72. New York: New York University Press, 1999.

Early, Frances H. "Feminism, Peace, and Civil Liberties: Women's Role in the Origins of the World War I Civil Liberties Movement." *Women's Studies* 18, nos. 2–3 (1990): 95–115.

———. *A World without War: How U.S. Feminists and Pacifists Resisted World War I.* Syracuse: Syracuse University Press, 1997.

Ebbert, Jean, and Marie-Beth Hall. *Crossed Currents: Navy Women in a Century of Change.* 3d ed. Washington, D.C.: Brassey's, 1999.

Edmonds, Sara Emma. *Memoirs of a Soldier, Nurse, and Spy: A Woman's Adventures in the Union Army.* Introduction and annotations by Elizabeth D. Leonard. DeKalb: Northern Illinois University Press, 1999.

Edmunds, Carey. "The Social Hut instead of the Saloon." *Ladies' Home Journal* 36 (April 1919).

"Effeminacy and the Rifle Range." *Arms and the Man.* (March 8, 1917).

Eisenstein, Sarah. *Give Us Bread but Give Us Roses: Working Women's Consciousness in the United States, 1890 to the First World War.* Boston: Routledge and Kegan Paul, 1983.

"Eleven Thousand Beginners Shoot." *Arms and the Man* (September 21, 1916).

Ellis, Mark. *Race, War, and Surveillance: African Americans and the United States Government during World War I.* Bloomington: Indiana University Press, 2001.

Emery, Lucilius. "The Constitutional Right to Keep and Bear Arms." *Harvard Law Review* 28 (1915): 473–77.

Enloe, Cynthia. *The Curious Feminist: Searching for Women in a New Age of Empire.* Berkeley and Los Angeles: University of California Press, 2004.

———. *Does Khaki Become You? The Militarization of Women's Lives.* London: Pandora Press, 1988.

————. *Maneuvers: The International Politics of Militarizing Women's Lives.* Berkeley and Los Angeles: University of California Press, 2000.

Estrich, Susan. "Rape." *Yale Law Journal* 95, no. 1087 (1986): 1087–1184.

Eubanks, L. E. "Gun Practice a Man-Maker." *Arms and the Man* (September 14, 1916).

Evans, Sara. *Born for Liberty: A History of Women in America.* New York: Free Press, 1989.

Falk, Candace. *Love, Anarchy, and Emma Goldman.* New York: Holt, Rinehart, and Winston, 1984.

Faust, Drew Gilpin. *Mothers of Invention: Women of the Slaveholding South in the American Civil War.* Chapel Hill: University of North Carolina Press, 1996.

Fausto Sterling, Anne. *Sexing the Body: Gender Politics and the Construction of Sexuality.* New York: Basic Books, 2000.

"Feminine Trap Shots Real Sportswomen." *Arms and the Man* (October 19, 1916).

"Finishing Up in France." *Woman Citizen* (March 1, 1919).

"First Words from the Hospital Unit." *Woman Citizen* (March 30, 1918).

Flory, Claude R. "Annie Oakley in the South." *North Carolina Historical Review* 43 (July 1966): 333–43.

Foley, Alice. "In the Subway." *Woman Citizen* (November 3, 1917).

Foner, Philip S. *History of the Labor Movement in the United States.* Vol. 8, *Postwar Struggles, 1918–1920.* New York: International Publishers, 1988.

Ford, Colonel Joseph H., M.C. *Administration, American Expeditionary Force.* Vol. 2, *The Medical Department of the United States Army in the World War.* Washington, D.C.: Government Printing Office, 1927.

France, Ministère Des Affaires Étrangères. *Germany's Violations of the Laws of War, 1914–1915.* Translated with an introduction by J. O. P. Bland. New York: G. P. Putnam's Sons, 1915.

"France Accepts Hospital Unit." *Woman Citizen* (September 29, 1917).

Frayling, Christopher. "The House That Jack Built: Some Stereotypes of the Rapist in the History of Popular Culture." In *Rape: An Historical and Cultural Enquiry,* edited by Sylvana Tomaselli and Roy Porter, 174–215. New York: Basil Blackwell, 1986.

Freedman, Estelle. *No Turning Back: The History of Feminism and the Future of Women.* New York: Ballantine, 2002.

Friedheim, Robert L. *The Seattle General Strike.* Seattle: University of Washington Press, 1964.

————. "The Seattle General Strike of 1919." *Pacific Northwest Quarterly* 52, no. 3 (Spring 1961): 81–98.

Frost, Stanley. "Grab-Bag Training for Veterans." *Outlook* 135 (September 26, 1923).

————. "What's a Sick Veteran between Friends." *Outlook* 135 (September 19, 1923).

Fussel, Paul. *The Great War and Modern Memory.* New York: Oxford University Press, 1975.

Gavin, Lettie. *American Women in World War I: They Also Served.* Niwot: University Press of Colorado, 1997.

Giffin, Frederick. *Six Who Protested: Radical Opposition to the First World War.* Port Washington, N.Y.: Kennikat Press, 1977.

Gilbert, Sandra M. "Soldier's Heart: Literary Men, Literary Women, and the Great War." In *Behind the Lines: Gender and the Two World Wars,* edited by Margaret Randolph Higonnet, Jane Jenson, Sonya Michel, Margaret Collins Weitz, 197–226. New Haven: Yale University Press, 1987.

Gilman, Charlotte Perkins. *Herland.* Edited by Barbara Solomon. New York: Signet, 1992.

Gilmore, Emma Wheat. "Report of the Committee, Women Physicians, General Medical Board, Committee of National Defense." *Woman's Medical Journal* 29 (1919).

Gilmore, Glenda Elizabeth. *Gender and Jim Crow: Women and the Politics of White Supremacy in North Carolina, 1896–1920.* Chapel Hill: University of North Carolina Press, 1996.

"Girls Form Rifle Club." *Arms and the Man* (April 28, 1917).

"The Girl Who Comes to the City: A Symposium." *Harper's Bazaar* (March 1908).

"Giving the Medical Officer the Rank to Which He Is Entitled." *Journal of the American Medical Association* 69 (1917): 292–94.

Goldberg, Nancy Sloan. *"Woman, Your Hour Is Sounding": Continuity and Change in French Women's Great War Fiction, 1914–1919.* New York: St. Martin's Press, 1999.

Goldman, Emma. *Living My Life.* Vol. 2. New York: Alfred A. Knopf, 1931.

Gordon, Linda. *Heroes of Their Own Lives: The Politics and History of Family Violence.* New York: Penguin Books, 1988.

Graf, Mercedes H. "Women Nurses in the Spanish-American War." *Minerva: Quarterly Report on Women and the Military* 19, no. 1 (2001): 3–38.

Grayzel, Susan. *Women's Identities at War: Gender, Motherhood, and Politics in Britain and France during the First World War.* Chapel Hill: University of North Carolina Press, 1999.

Greenwald, Maureen Weiner. *Women, War, and Work: The Impact of World War I on Women Workers in the United States.* Ithaca: Cornell University Press, 1990.

Griesse, Anne Eliot, and Richard Stites. "Russia: Revolution and War." In *Female Soldiers—Combatants or Noncombatants? Historical and Contemporary Perspectives,* edited by Nancy Loring Goldman, 61–84. Westport, Conn.: Greenwood Press, 1982.

Hacker, Barton C. "Women and Military Institutions in Early Modern Europe: A Reconnaissance." *Signs: Journal of Women in Culture and Society* 6 (1981): 643–71.

Haiken, Elizabeth. "The Making of the Modern Face: Cosmetic Surgery." *Social Research* 67, no. 1 (Spring 2000): 82–98.

Hamilton, Walton H. "The Impending Industrial Crisis." *Dial* 66 (May 17, 1919).

Hammond, Harriet D. "Why I Like Trapshooting." *Arms and the Man* (October 27, 1917).

Harris, Corra. "Marrying Off the American Army." *Independent* 97 (February 22, 1919): 260–61.

Harris, Ruth. "The 'Child of the Barbarian': Rape, Race, and Nationalism in France during the First World War." *Past and Present* 141 (November 1993): 170–206.

Hart, Lynda. *Fatal Women: Lesbian Sexuality and the Mark of Aggression.* Princeton: Princeton University Press, 1994.

Healy, Willliam. "Delinquency and Crime." In *America and the New Era: A Symposium on Social Reconstruction,* edited by Elisha M. Friedman, 415–32. New York: E. P. Dutton, 1920.

Hewitt, Linda L. *Women Marines in World War I.* Washington, D.C.: History and Museums Division, Headquarters, U.S. Marine Corps, 1974.

Higginbotham, Evelyn Brooks. *Righteous Discontent: The Women's Movement in the Black Baptist Church, 1880–1920.* Cambridge: Harvard University Press, 1993.

Higgonet, Margaret Randolph, Jane Jenson, Sonya Michel, and Margaret Collins Weitz, eds. *Behind the Lines: Gender and the Two World Wars.* New Haven: Yale University Press, 1987.

Hine, Darlene Clark. *Black Women in White: Racial Conflict and Cooperation in the Nursing Profession, 1890–1950.* Bloomington: Indiana University Press, 1989.

———. "The Call That Never Came: Black Women Nurses and World War I, an Historical Note." *Indiana Military History Journal* 8 (January 1983): 23–27.

———. "Rape and the Inner Lives of Black Women in the Middle West." *Signs: Journal of Women in Culture and Society* 14, no. 4 (Summer 1989): 912–20.

Hirschfeld, Magnus. *The Sexual History of the World War.* New York: Panurge Press, 1934.

History of Medicine and Surgery and Physicians and Surgeons of Chicago. Chicago: Biographical Publishing, 1922.

Hocker, Elizabeth Van Cortlandt, M.D. "The Personal Experience of a Contract Surgeon in the United States Army." *Medical Woman's Journal* 49 (January 1942),

Hoffman, Dennis E., and Vincent J. Webb. "Police Response to Labor Radicalism in Portland and Seattle, 1913–19." *Oregon Historical Quarterly* 87, no. 4 (Winter 1986): 341–66.

Hoffman, Frederick. *The Homicide Problem.* Newark: Prudential Press, 1925.

Hoganson, Kristin L. "'As Badly Off as the Filipinos': U.S. Women Suffragists and the Imperial Issue at the Turn of the Twentieth Century." *Journal of Women's History* 13, no. 2 (Summer 2001): 9–33.

———. *Fighting for American Manhood: How Gender Politics Provoked the Spanish-American and Philippine-American Wars.* New Haven: Yale University Press, 1998.

Holm, Jeanne. *Women in the Military: An Unfinished Revolution.* Novato, Calif.: Presidio Press, 1992.

Holme, John G. *The Life of Leonard Wood.* New York: Doubleday, Page, 1920.

Holmes, Fred. "Ex-soldier Crimes Following the War." *Outlook* 134 (July 18, 1923).

———. "Making Criminals Out of Soldiers." *Nation* 121 (July 22, 1925).

———. *Wisconsin's War Record.* Madison: Capital Historical Publishing, 1919.

Horne, John, and Alan Kramer. *German Atrocities, 1914: A History of Denial.* New Haven: Yale University Press, 2001.

"Hospital in Active Service." *Woman Citizen* (April 13, 1918).

Humphries, Dr. H. R. "Home Treatment of Shell Shock: 'Taking Care of Your Boy.'" *Touchstone* 4, no. 2 (November 1918).

Hunter, Tara. *To 'Joy My Freedom: Southern Black Women's Lives and Labors after the Civil War.* Cambridge: Harvard University Press, 1997.

"Increased Rank and More Authority for Medical Officers." *Journal of the American Medical Association* 69 (November 10, 1917): 1612–13.

"Inquiries of General Interest." *Arms and the Man* (January 12, 1918).

Irwin, Inez Hayes. *The Story of Alice Paul and the National Woman's Party.* Fairfax, Va.: Denlinger's Publishers, 1977.

Isenberg, Nancy. *Sex and Citizenship in Antebellum America*. Chapel Hill: University of North Carolina Press, 1998.

Jacobson, Paul H., and Pauline F. Jacobson. *American Marriage and Divorce*. New York: Rinehart, 1959.

Janiewski, Dolores. "Southern Honor, Southern Dishonor: Managerial Ideology and the Construction of Gender, Race, and Class Relations in Southern Industry." In *Work Engendered: Toward a New History of American Labor,* edited by Ava Baron 70–91. Ithaca: Cornell University Press, 1991.

Jarrett, Mary C. "Home Treatment of Shell Shock: The Need of Wisdom and Sympathy to Help Recovery." *Touchstone* 4, no. 6 (March 1919).

———. "War Neuroses after the War: Extra-Institutional Preparation." In *Proceedings of the National Conference on Social Work at the Forty-fifth Annual Session Held in Kansas City, Missouri, May 15–22, 1918*. Chicago: Rogers and Hall, 1919.

"Jeanne d'Arc." *Outlook* 111 (December 15, 1915).

Jensen, Kimberly. "A Base Hospital Is Not a Coney Island Dance Hall: American Women Nurses, Hostile Work Environment, and Miliary Rank in the First World War." *Frontiers: A Journal of Women Studies* 26, no. 2 (2005): 206–35.

———. "Minerva on the Field of Mars: American Women, Citizenship, and Military Service in the First World War." Ph.D. diss., University of Iowa, 1992.

———. "The 'Open Way of Opportunity': Colorado Women Physicians and World War I." *Western Historical Quarterly* 27 (1996): 327–48.

———. "Physicians and Citizens: U.S. Medical Women and Military Service in the First World War." In *War, Medicine, and Modernity, 1860–1945,* edited by Roger Cooter et al., 106–24. London: Sutton Publishers, 1998.

———. "Uncle Sam's Loyal Nieces: American Medical Women, Citizenship, and War Service in the First World War." *Bulletin of the History of Medicine,* 67, no. 4 (1993): 760–90.

———. "Uncle Sam's Loyal Nieces: American Medical Women, Citizenship, and War Service in World War I." In *Women and Health in America,* edited by Judith Walzer Leavitt, 540–55. 2d ed. Madison: University of Wisconsin Press, 1999.

———. "Women, Citizenship, and Civic Sacrifice: Engendering Patriotism in the First World War." In *Bonds of Affection: Americans Define Their Patriotism,* edited by John Bodnar, 139–59. Princeton: Princeton University Press, 1996.

Jones, Jacqueline, *Labor of Love, Labor of Sorrow: Black Women, Work, and the Family from Slavery to the Present*. New York: Basic Books, 1985.

Kalisch, Philip A. "How Army Nurses Became Officers." *Nursing Research* 25 (May–June 1976): 164–77.

Kaplan, Amy. "Black and Blue on San Juan Hill." In *Cultures of United States Imperialism,* edited by Amy Kaplan and Donald E. Pease, 219–36. Durham: Duke University Press, 1993.

"Katherine C. Manion, M.D." *Medical Woman's Journal* 31 (June 1924).

Keene, Jennifer D. *Doughboys, the Great War, and the Remaking of America*. Baltimore: Johns Hopkins University Press, 2001.

Kellogg, Charlotte. *Women of Belgium: Turning Tragedy to Triumph*. New York: Funk and Wagnalls, 1917.

Kennedy, Kathleen. *Disloyal Mothers and Scurrilous Citizens: Women and Subversion during World War I*. Bloomington: Indiana University Press, 1999.

Kennett, Lee, and James LaVerne Anderson. *The Gun in America: The Origins of a National Dilemma.* Westport, Conn.: Greenwood Press, 1975.

Kent, Susan Kingsley. *Making Peace: The Reconstruction of Gender in Interwar Britain.* Princeton: Princeton University Press, 1993.

Kerber, Linda K. "The Meanings of Citizenship." *Journal of American History* (December 1997): 833–54.

———. *No Constitutional Right to Be Ladies: Women and the Obligations of Citizenship.* New York: Hill and Wang, 1998.

———. *Women of the Republic: Intellect and Ideology in Revolutionary America.* New York: W. W. Norton, 1986.

Kerber, Linda, and Jane de Hart, eds. *Women's America: Refocusing the Past,* 6th ed. New York: Oxford University Press, 2004.

Kesselman, Amy. *Fleeting Opportunities: Women Shipyard Workers in Portland and Vancouver during World War II and Reconversion.* Albany: State University of New York Press, 1990.

Kessler-Harris, Alice. *In Pursuit of Equity: Women, Men, and the Quest for Economic Citizenship in 20th Century America.* New York: Oxford University Press, 2001.

———. *Out to Work: A History of Wage-Earning Women in the United States.* New York: Oxford University Press, 1982.

Kettle, Caroline. "The Legion of Death." *Woman Citizen* (April 27, 1918).

Kimmel, Michael. *Manhood in America: A Cultural History.* New York: Free Press, 1996.

Klein, Yvonne M., ed. *Beyond the Home Front: Women's Autobiographical Writing of the Two World Wars.* New York: New York University Press, 1997.

Kraditor, Aileen. *The Ideas of the Woman Suffrage Movement, 1890–1920.* New York: Columbia University Press, 1965.

Kuhlman, Erika A. *Petticoats and White Feathers: Gender Conformity, Race, the Progressive Peace Movement, and the Debate over War, 1895–1919.* Westport, Conn.: Greenwood Press, 1997.

La Motte, Ellen Newbold. *The Backwash of War: The Human Wreckage of the Battlefield as Witnessed by an American Hospital Nurse.* New York: G. P. Putnam's Sons, 1916.

Lane, Jack C. *Armed Progressive: General Leonard Wood.* San Rafael, Calif.: Presidio Press, 1978.

Leonard, Elizabeth. *Yankee Women: Gender Battles in the Civil War.* New York: W. W. Norton, 1995.

Lewenson, Sandra Beth. *Taking Charge: Nursing, Suffrage, and Feminism in America, 1873–1920.* New York: National League for Nursing Press, 1996.

"Livermore Women Becoming Shots." *Arms and the Man* (March 16, 1916).

Lovejoy, Esther Pohl. *Certain Samaritans.* New York: Macmillan, 1933.

———. *The House of the Good Neighbor.* New York: Macmillan, 1919.

———. *Women Doctors of the World.* New York: Macmillan, 1957.

———. *Women Physicians and Surgeons: National and International Organizations. Book One: The American Medical Women's Association, the Medical Women's International Association. Book Two: Twenty Years with The American Women's Hospitals.* Livingston, N.Y.: Livingston Press, 1939.

Lunardini, Christine. *From Equal Suffrage to Equal Rights: Alice Paul and the National Woman's Party, 1910–1928.* New York: New York University Press, 1986.

Lynch, Charles H., Frank Watkins Weed, and Loy McAfee. *The Surgeon General's Office.* Vol. 1, *The Medical Department of the United States Army in the World War.* Washington, D.C.: Government Printing Office, 1923.

MacKinnon, Catharine A. "Rape, Genocide, and Women's Human Rights." In *Mass Rape: The War against Women in Bosnia-Herzegovina,* edited by Alexandra Stiglmayer, 183–96. Lincoln: University of Nebraska Press, 1994.

Macy, Mary Sutton, M.D. "American Medical Women and the World War." *American Medicine* 23 (May 1917).

———. "The Field for Women of Today in Medicine." *Woman's Medical Journal* 27 (March 1917): 49–58.

Maher, Mary Denis. *To Bind Up the Wounds: Catholic Sister Nurses in the U.S. Civil War.* New York: Greenwood Press, 1989.

"The Maire's Address." *American Women's Hospitals Bulletin* 1, no. 2 (January 1919).

Marshall, T. H. *Citizenship and Social Class, and Other Essays.* Cambridge: Cambridge University Press, 1950.

Martin, Franklin. *Fifty Years of Medicine and Surgery: An Autobiographical Sketch.* Chicago: Surgical Publishing, 1934.

Martin, Franklin H. *Digest of the Proceedings of the Council of National Defense during the World War.* Washington, D.C.: Government Printing Office, 1934.

May, Elaine Tyler. *Great Expectations: Marriage and Divorce in Post-Victorian America.* Chicago: University of Chicago Press, 1980.

Mayo, Katherine. "While Our Boys Are Marking Time." *Ladies' Home Journal* 36 (January 1919).

McAdoo, William. *When the Court Takes a Recess.* New York: E. P. Dutton, 1924.

McCabe, A. L. "How to Construct an Indoor or Cellar Range." *Arms and the Man* (January 11, 1917).

McGee, Anita Newcombe, M.D. "Can Women Physicians Serve in the Army?" *Woman's Medical Journal* 28 (February 1918).

———. "Women Nurses in the American Army." In *Proceedings of the Eighth Annual Meeting of the Association of Military Surgeons of the United States,* 242–48. Columbus, Ohio: Berlin Printing Company, 1900.

McGlashan, Zena Beth. "Women Witness the Russian Revolution: Analyzing Ways of Seeing." *Journalism History* 12 (Summer 1985): 54–61.

"Medical Rank and Army Health." *Colorado Medicine* 14 (September 1917): 231–32.

Melosh, Barbara. *American Nurses in Fiction: An Anthology of Short Stories.* New York: Garland, 1984.

———. *"The Physician's Hand": Work Culture and Conflict in American Nursing.* Philadelphia: Temple University Press, 1982.

Meredith, Ellis. "Dr. Rose Kidd Beere, First Colorado Nurse in the Philippines." *Colorado Magazine* 26 (July 1949): 161–65.

Meyer, Leisa. *Creating GI Jane: Sexuality and Power in the Women's Army Corps during World War II.* New York: Columbia University Press, 1996.

Meyerowitz, Joanne. *How Sex Changed: A History of Transsexuality in the United States.* Cambridge: Harvard University Press, 2002.

Milkman, Ruth. *Gender at Work: The Dynamics of Job Segregation by Sex during World War II.* Urbana: University of Illinois Press, 1987.

"'The Mill' Awaits Each Doughboy Homeward Bound." *Literary Digest* 60 (February 15, 1919).

Montgomery, David. *The Fall of the House of Labor: The Workplace, the State, and American Labor Activism, 1865–1925*. New York: Cambridge University Press, 1987.

Morantz-Sanchez, Regina. *Sympathy and Science: Women Physicians in American Medicine*. New York: Oxford University Press, 1985.

More, Ellen S. "The American Medical Women's Association and the Role of the Woman Physician, 1915–1990." *Journal of the American Medical Women's Association* 45, no. 5 (1990).

———. *Restoring the Balance: Women Physicians and the Profession of Medicine, 1850–1995*. Cambridge: Harvard University Press, 1999.

Morton, Rosalie Slaughter. *A Woman Surgeon: The Life and Work of Rosalie Slaughter Morton*. New York: Frederick Stokes, 1937.

"A Most Interesting Report of Work of Colorado Medical Women's War Service League." *Woman's Medical Journal* 28 (February 1918): 39–40.

"Mr. Root, It's You We Quote." *Woman Citizen* (August 18, 1917).

National Association for the Advancement of Colored People. *Thirty Years of Lynching in the United States, 1889–1918*. New York: National Association for the Advancement of Colored People, 1919.

"National Association of Medical Women." *Woman's Medical Journal* 26 (January 1916).

"The National Rifle Association Meeting." *Arms and the Man* (January 20, 1917).

"Navy Leases Wakefield Range." *Arms and the Man* (September 1, 1917).

"A Navy Nurse." *American Journal of Nursing* 20 (October 1919).

"Neither Rank nor Honor." *Woman Citizen* (May 10, 1919).

Nelson, Sioban. *Say Little, Do Much: Nurses, Nuns, and Hospitals in the Nineteenth Century*. Philadelphia: University of Pennsylvania Press, 2001.

"Nemours [Ladies] Trapshooting Club." *Arms and the Man* (June 3, 1915).

"New Artistic Ties with France." *Literary Digest* 51 (December 25, 1915).

"A New England Nurse." *Trained Nurse and Hospital Review* 63 (October 1919).

Newman, A. Evelyn. "Old Husbands for New!" *Ladies' Home Journal* 36, no. 12 (December 1919).

"News of the Training Camps: Colored Medical Officers' Training Camp at Fort Des Moines." *Journal of the American Medical Association* 69 (November 10, 1917): 1615–16.

"The New Vision." *Delineator* 88 (March 1916).

New York Times Index. New York: New York Times Company, 1914–1917.

Nielsen, Kim E. *Un-American Womanhood: Antiradicalism, Antifeminism, and the First Red Scare*. Columbus: Ohio State University Press, 2001.

Norton, Mary Beth. *Founding Mothers and Fathers: Gendered Power and the Forming of American Society*. New York: Alfred A. Knopf, 1996.

Norwood, Stephen H. *Strikebreaking and Intimidation: Mercenaries and Masculinity in Twentieth-Century America*. Chapel Hill: University of North Carolina Press, 2002.

Notable American Women: A Biographical Dictionary. Edited by Edward T. James, Janet Wilson James, and Paul S. Boyer. Cambridge: Harvard University Press, Belknap Press, 1971.

"The N.R.A. on the Job." *Arms and the Man* (June 17, 1915).

"The Nurse as a Citizen." *American Journal of Nursing* 17 (May 1917).

Odem, Mary. "Cultural Representations and Social Contexts of Rape in the Early Twentieth Century." In *Lethal Imagination: Violence and Brutality in American History*, edited by Michael A. Bellesiles, 352–70. New York: New York University Press, 1999.

———. *Delinquent Daughters: Protecting and Policing Adolescent Female Sexuality in the United States, 1885–1920*. Chapel Hill: University of North Carolina Press, 1995.

"An Old Army Nurse." *American Journal of Nursing* 20, (October 1919).

"An Open Letter from Wakefield." *Arms and the Man* (April 20, 1918).

Orleck, Annelise. *Common Sense and a Little Fire: Women and Working Class Politics in the United States, 1900–1965*. Chapel Hill: University of North Carolina Press, 1995.

Painter, Nell Irvin. *Standing at Armageddon: The United States, 1877–1919*. New York: W. W. Norton, 1987.

Pascoe, Peggy. "Democracy, Citizenship, and Race: The West in the Twentieth Century." In *Perspectives on Modern America: Making Sense of the Twentieth Century*, edited by Harvard Sitkoff, 227–46. New York: Oxford University Press, 2001.

Peiss, Kathy. *Cheap Amusements: Working Women and Leisure in Turn-of-the-Century New York*. Philadelphia: Temple University Press, 1985.

Peitzman, Steven J. *A New and Untried Course: Woman's Medical College and Medical College of Pennsylvania, 1850–1998*. New Brunswick: Rutgers University Press, 2000.

Phillips, Roderick. *Putting Asunder: A History of Divorce in Western Society*. New York: Cambridge University Press, 1988.

Piercy, Harry D., M.D. *History of the Lakeside Unit of World War I*. Ohio: n.p., 1962.

Pleck, Elizabeth. *Domestic Tyranny: The Making of Social Policy against Family Violence from Colonial Times to the Present*. New York: Oxford University Press, 1987.

Porter, Laura Spencer. "He Is So Changed." *Woman's Home Companion* 46, no. 7 (July 1919).

Powell, E. Alexander. "Training the Soldier for Peace." *Harper's Magazine* 142 (April 1921).

"Proceedings of the Chicago Session: Minutes of the Sixty-ninth Annual Session of the American Medical Association, Held at Chicago, June 10–14, 1918." *Journal of the American Medical Association* 70 (June 16, 1918).

"Proposed Rank for Army Nurses." *Suffragist* (October 26, 1918).

Purnell, Caroline M., M.D. "The Work of the American Women's Hospitals in Foreign Service." In *Transactions of the Forty-third Annual Meeting of the Alumnae Association of the Woman's Medical College of Pennsylvania*. Philadelphia: Alumnae Association of the Women's Medical College of Pennsylvania, 1918.

"Rank for Nurses—What Some Doctors Say about It." *American Journal of Nursing* 20 (January 1920).

"Rank for Nurses Achieved." *American Journal of Nursing* 20 (July 1920).

Reader's Guide to Periodical Literature. Vols. 1–4. Minneapolis: H. W. Wilson, 1905–1919.

"A Regular Army Nurse." *American Journal of Nursing* 20 (February 1920).

"Report of American Women's Hospitals no. 1 from August 1, 1918, to March 1, 1919." *American Women's Hospitals Bulletin* 1, no. 3 (April 1919).

"Resolutions Adopted at the Annual Convention of the National American Woman Suffrage Association." *Woman Citizen* (April 5, 1919).

"Resolutions Pertaining to Women Physicians as Recommended to the AMA by Legislative Committee." *Woman's Medical Journal* 28 (June 1918).

Reverby, Susan. *Ordered to Care: The Dilemma of American Nursing, 1850–1945.* New York: Cambridge University Press, 1987.

Richardson, Anna Steese. "Now That They're Back: An Open Letter to the Readers of the 'Soldiers All' Department." *Woman's Home Companion* 46, no. 4 (April 1919).

———. "When Johnny Comes Marching Home Again." *Woman's Home Companion* 46, no. 3 (March 1919).

Ridgway, Erman J. "Militant Pacifism." *Delineator* 86 (February 1915): 1.

Riley, Glenda. *Divorce: An American Tradition.* New York: Oxford University Press, 1991.

———. *The Life and Legacy of Annie Oakley.* Norman: University of Oklahoma Press, 1994.

Roberts, Mary Louise. *Civilization without Sexes: Reconstructing Gender in Postwar France, 1917–1927.* Chicago: University of Chicago Press, 1994.

Roman, Dr. C. V. "The War—What Does It Mean? What Should We Do?" *Journal of the National Medical Association* 10 (January–March 1918): 41–42.

Roosevelt, Theodore. *America and the World War.* New York: C. Scribner's Sons, 1915.

Rosen, Hannah. "'Not That Sort of Women': Race, Gender, and Sexual Violence during the Memphis Riot of 1866." In *Sex, Love, Race: Crossing Boundaries in North American History,* edited by Martha Hodes, 267–91. New York: New York University Press, 1999.

Rosenberg, Charles E. *The Care of Strangers: The Rise of America's Hospital System.* New York: Basic Books, 1987.

———. *No Other Gods: On Science and American Social Thought.* Baltimore: Johns Hopkins University Press, 1976.

Ross, Kristie. "Arranging a Doll's House: Refined Women as Union Nurses." In *Divided Houses: Gender and the Civil War,* edited by Catherine Clinton and Nina Silber, 97–113. New York: Oxford University Press, 1992.

Rossiter, Margaret W. *Women Scientists in America: Struggles and Strategies to 1940.* Baltimore: Johns Hopkins University Press, 1982.

Rotundo, E. Anthony. *American Manhood: Transformations in Masculinity from the Revolution to the Modern Era.* New York: Basic Books, 1993.

Rupp, Leila J. "Solidarity and Wartime Violence against Women." In *The Women and War Reader,* edited by Lois Ann Lorentzen and Jennifer Turpin, 303–7. New York: New York University Press, 1998.

———. *Worlds of Women: The Making of an International Women's Movement.* Princeton: Princeton University Press, 1997

Russell, Charles Edward. "Russia's Women Warriors." *Good Housekeeping* 65 (October 1917).

"Russian Women and the Ballot." *Suffragist* (February 26, 1915).

"Russia's Women Soldiers." *Literary Digest* 55 (August 25, 1917).

Ryan, Mary. *Women in Public: Between Banners and Ballots, 1825–1880.* Baltimore: Johns Hopkins University Press, 1990.

Sajor, Indai Lourdes, ed. *Common Grounds: Violence against Women in Armed Conflict Situations*. Quezon City, Philippines: Asian Center for Women's Human Rights, 1998.

Sanchez, George J. *Becoming Mexican American: Ethnicity, Culture, and Identity in Chicano Los Angeles, 1900–1945*. New York: Oxford University Press, 1995.

Sarnecky, Mary. *A History of the U.S. Army Nurse Corps*. Philadelphia: University of Pennsylvania Press, 1999.

———. "A Woman for All Seasons: A Biography of Julia Catherine Stimson, 1881–1948." Ph.D. diss., Philip Y. Hahn School of Nursing, University of San Diego, 1990.

"Scattering Shot." *Arms and the Man* (October 5, 1916).

Schneider, Dorothy, and Carl J. Schneider. *Into the Breach: American Women Overseas in World War I*. New York: Viking Press, 1991.

Schryver, Grace Fay. *A History of the Illinois Training School for Nurses, 1880–1929*. Chicago: Board of Directors for the Illinois Training School for Nurses, 1930.

Schultz, Jane E. "Between Scylla and Charybdis: Clara Barton's Wartime Odyssey." *Minerva: Quarterly Report on Women and the Military* 14, nos. 3–4 (1996): 45–68.

———. *Women at the Front: Hospital Workers in Civil War America*. Chapel Hill: University of North Carolina Press, 2004.

Schultz, Vicki. "Reconceptualizing Sexual Harassment." *Yale Law Review* 107 (April 1998): 1683–1805.

Scofield, Kendrick. "U.S.R.A. Names New Officers." *Arms and the Man* (January 26, 1918).

Seaman, Major Louis Livingston. "Where Hundreds of Thousands Are Suffering." *Independent* 80 (October 5, 1914).

The Seattle General Strike: An Account of What Happened in Seattle, and Especially in the Seattle Labor Movement during the General Strike, February 6 to 11, 1919, Issued by the History Committee of the General Strike Committee. Reprint ed. Seattle: Shorey Book Store, 1971.

"Secretary Baker Urged to Use Women for the Medical Service." *Woman Citizen* (July 28, 1917).

Segrave, Kerry. *The Sexual Harassment of Women in the Workplace, 1600–1993*. Jefferson, N.C.: MaFarland, 1994.

Seifert, Ruth. "War and Rape: A Preliminary Analysis." In *Mass Rape: The War against Women in Bosnia-Herzegovina*, edited by Alexandra Stiglmayer, 54–72. Lincoln: University of Nebraska Press, 1994.

"Sergeant Miss—Yes, That's Right." *Stars and Stripes* (May 17, 1918).

Sharp, Henry. "Guns for Sportswomen." *Arms and the Man* (February 8, 1919).

Shaw, Stephanie. *What a Woman Ought to Be and Do: Black Professional Women Workers during the Jim Crow Era*. Chicago: University of Chicago Press, 1996.

Shay, Jonathan. *Odysseus in America: Combat Trauma and the Trials of Homecoming*. New York: Scribner, 2002.

Shepherd, William G. "The Soul That Stirs in 'Battalions of Death.'" *Delineator* 92 (March 1918): 5–7, 56.

Sherman, Janann. "'They Either Need These Women or They Do Not': Margaret Chase Smith and the Fight for Regular Status for Women in the Military." *Journal of Military History* 54, no. 1 (January 1990): 47–78.

Sherry, Michael. *In the Shadow of War: The United States since the 1930s.* New Haven: Yale University Press, 1995.

Showalter, Elaine. *The Female Malady: Women, Madness, and English Culture, 1830–1980.* New York: Penguin, 1985.

Smith, Merril D., ed. *Sex without Consent: Rape and Sexual Coercion in America.* New York: New York University Press, 2001.

Smith-Rosenberg, Carroll. *Disorderly Conduct: Visions of Gender in Victorian America.* New York: Oxford University Press, 1985.

Solomon, Barbara Miller. *In the Company of Educated Women: A History of Women and Higher Education in America.* New Haven: Yale University Press, 1985.

Solomon, Zahava. *Combat Stress Reaction: The Enduring Toll of War.* New York: Plenum Press, 1993.

"Some Interesting Data Regarding the Physicians of the Historic First Hospital Sent to France by the American Women's Hospitals." *Woman's Medical Journal* 28 (June 1918).

"Some Quotations from the Hearings before the Sub-Committee of the Committee on Military Affairs, United States Senate." *American Journal of Nursing* 20, no. 1 (October 1919).

Stanton, Elizabeth Cady, Susan B. Anthony, and Matilda Joslyn Gage. *History of Woman Suffrage.* 6 vols. 1881–1922. Reprint, New York: Arno Press, 1969.

Starr, M. Allen, M.D. "The Occupation Cure for Shell Shock." *Touchstone* 4 (October 1918).

Starr, Paul. *The Social Transformation of American Medicine.* New York: Basic Books, 1982.

Stein, Gertrude. *The Autobiography of Alice B. Toklas.* New York: Vintage, 1933.

Steinson, Barbara J. *American Women's Activism in World War I.* New York: Garland, 1892.

———. "'The Mother Half of Humanity': American Women in the Peace and Preparedness Movements in World War I." In *Women, War, and Revolution,* edited by Carol R. Berkin and Clara M. Lovett, 259–84. New York: Holmes and Meier, 1980.

Stevens, C. M. *The Wonderful Story of Joan of Arc and the Meaning of Her Life for Americans.* New York: Cupples and Leon, 1918.

Stewart, Isabel M. "Testing the Nursing Spirit." *American Journal of Nursing* 17 (May 1917).

Stiehm, Judith Hicks. "The Protected, the Protector, the Defender." *Women's Studies International Forum* 5 (1982): 367–76.

Stiglmayer, Alexandra, ed. *Mass Rape: The War against Women in Bosnia-Herzegovina.* Lincoln: University of Nebraska Press, 1994.

Stimson, Henry A. *The Right Life and How to Live It.* New York: A. S. Barnes, 1905.

Stimson, Julia C. "The Army Nurse Corps." In *The Medical Department of the United States Army in the World War,* pt. 2 of vol. 8. Washington, D.C.: Government Printing Office, 1927.

———. "Earliest Known Connection of Nurses with Army Hospitals in the United States." *American Journal of Nursing* 25 (January 1925).

———. *Finding Themselves: The Letters of an American Army Chief Nurse in a British Hospital in France.* New York: Macmillan, 1918.

———. "Nursing Overseas." *American Journal of Nursing* 20 (October 1919).

———. "Rank." *American Journal of Nursing* 20 (September 1920).

———. "Rank for Nurses: What Have Five Years of Rank Done for the Army Nurse Corps?" *American Journal of Nursing* 26 (April 1926).

Stimson, Julia C., Sayres L. Millikin, and Ethel C. S. Thompson. "The Forerunners of the American Army Nurse." *Military Surgeon* 58 (February 1926).

Stites, Richard. *The Women's Liberation Movement in Russia.* Princeton: Princeton University Press, 1978.

"The Supreme Struggle." *Woman Patriot* 1 (April 27, 1918).

Takaki, Ronald. *A Different Mirror: A History of Multicultural America.* Boston: Little, Brown, 1993.

———. *Strangers from a Different Shore: A History of Asian Americans.* New York: Penguin, 1989.

Tannenbaum, Frank. "The Moral Devastation of War." *Dial* 66 (April 5, 1919): 333–36.

Terborg-Penn, Rosalyn. *African American Women in the Struggle for the Vote, 1850–1920.* Bloomington: Indiana University Press, 1998.

———. "African American Women's Networks in the Anti-lynching Crusade." In *Gender, Class, Race, and Reform in the Progressive Era,* edited by Noralee Frankel and Nancy S. Dye, 148–61. Lexington: University Press of Kentucky, 1991.

Thoms, Adah B. *Pathfinders: A History of the Progress of Colored Graduate Nurses.* 1929. Reprint, New York: Garland, 1985.

"Those Russian Women." *Literary Digest* 55 (September 29, 1917).

"To Have a Ladies' Auxiliary." *Arms and the Man* (October 19, 1916).

Topperwein, Mrs. Adolph. "Why I Took Up Trapshooting." *Arms and the Man* (July 7, 1917).

"Trapshooting Attracts Both Sexes." *Arms and the Man* (March 1, 1917).

Tufts, James H. "Wartime Gains for the American Family." In *Proceedings of the National Conference on Social Work at the Forty-sixth Annual Session Held in Atlantic City, New Jersey, June 1–8, 1919.* Chicago: Rogers and Hall, 1920.

Twenty-five Answers to Antis: Five Minute Speeches on Votes for Women by Eminent Suffragists. New York: National Woman Suffrage Publishing, 1912.

"Twenty-seven Beginners at Greenhill." *Arms and the Man* (July 20, 1916).

Tyrrell, William Blake. *Amazons: A Study in Athenian Mythmaking.* Baltimore: Johns Hopkins University Press, 1984.

"Universal Military Training Urged." *Arms and the Man* (January 6, 1916).

Van Gasken, Frances C., M.D. "Introductory Address, Woman's Medical College of Pennsylvania, Delivered at the Opening of the College Session, September 19, 1917." *Bulletin of the Woman's Medical College of Pennsylvania* 68 (December 1917).

Van Hoosen, Bertha. *Petticoat Surgeon.* Chicago: People's Book Club, 1947.

Vertrees, John J. *An Address to the Men of Tennessee on Female Suffrage.* Nashville: n.p., 1916.

Wakeman, Sarah Rosetta. *An Uncommon Soldier: The Civil War Letters of Sarah Rosetta Wakeman, Alias Private Lyons Wakeman, 153rd Regiment, New York State Volunteers.* Edited by Lauren Cook Burgess. New York: Oxford University Press, 1995.

Waller, Willard. *The Veteran Comes Back.* New York: Dryden Press, 1944.

————. *War and the Family.* New York: Dryden Press, 1940.

Walsh, Mary Roth. *Doctors Wanted, No Women Need Apply: Sexual Barriers in the Medical Profession, 1835–1975.* New Haven: Yale University Press, 1977.

"War Morality and the Rights of War-Mothers and War-Babies." *Current Opinion* 59, no. 1 (July 1915).

"Warrior Women." *Literary Digest* 50 (June 19, 1915).

Weiner, Lynn. *From Working Girl to Working Mother: The Female Labor Force in the United States, 1820–1980.* Chapel Hill: University of North Carolina Press, 1985.

"What One Woman Does." *Arms and the Man* (October 7, 1915).

Wheelwright, Julie. *Amazons and Military Maids: Women Who Dressed as Men in Pursuit of Life, Liberty, and Happiness.* London: Pandora Press, 1989.

White, Deborah Gray. *Ar'n't I a Woman? Female Slaves in the Plantation South.* New York: W. W. Norton, 1985.

"Why They Need Military Rank." *Woman Citizen* (June 1, 1918).

"Will the War Department Recognize Medical Women and Give Them Equal Rank?" *Woman's Medical Journal* 28 (February 1918).

Winsor, Mary. "Catching Up with Russia." *Suffragist* (August 18, 1917).

"With the Suffrage Hospitals in the French War Zone." *Woman Citizen* (July 13, 1918).

"With the Women's Oversea Hospitals." *Woman Citizen* (May 4, 1918).

"The Woman Patriot." *Woman Patriot* 1 (April 27, 1918).

Woman's Who's Who of America: A Biographical Dictionary of Contemporary Women of the United States and Canada, 1914–1915. Edited by John William Leonard. New York, 1914.

"The Woman Who Broke 1952 Out of 2,000 Clays." *Arms and the Man* (December 7, 1916).

"Women and War." *Suffragist* (December 12, 1914).

"Women and War." *Suffragist* (March 6, 1915).

"Women as Warriors." *Arms and the Man* (July 1, 1915).

"'Women Cannot Fight!'" *Suffragist* (September 25, 1915).

"Women in the Medical Reserve Corps." *Bulletin of the Medical Women's Club of Chicago* 6 (September 1917).

"Women in the War." *Suffragist* (June 26, 1915).

"Women in War Time." *Suffragist* (October 3, 1914).

"Women May Fight for Democracy Abroad." *Suffragist* (October 6, 1917).

"Women's Oversea Hospitals of the U.S.A." *Woman Citizen* (February 2, 1918).

"Women Yeoman Shoot." *Arms and the Man* (March 1, 1919).

Wood, Leonard. "Rifle Practice for Public Schools." *Collier's* 46 (December 7, 1910).

"The World War—What Does It Mean? How Does It Apply to the Afro-American?" *Journal of the National Medical Associaton* 9 (October–December 1917).

"Wounded and Disabled Soldiers: Informal Discussion." In *Proceedings of the National Conference on Social Work at the Forty-fourth Annual Session Held in Pittsburgh, Pennsylvania, June 6–13, 1917,* 63–74. Chicago: National Conference of Social Work, 1918.

"Young Man's War? Ask Mr. Schwab, Help-Us-Win Club Membership Not Even Confined to Males." *Stars and Stripes* (May 24, 1918).

Zahn, Margaret. "Homicide in the Twentieth-Century United States." In *History and*

Crime: Implications for Criminal Justice Policy, edited by James A. Inciardi and Charles Faupel, 111–31. Beverly Hills: Sage, 1980.

Zeiger, Susan. *In Uncle Sam's Service: Women Workers with the American Expeditionary Force, 1917–1919.* Ithaca: Cornell University Press, 1999.

Index

KIMBERLY JENSEN is a professor
of history and gender studies
at Western Oregon University.

The University of Illinois Press
is a founding member of the
Association of American University Presses.

———————————————

University of Illinois Press
1325 South Oak Street
Champaign, IL 61820-6903
www.press.uillinois.edu